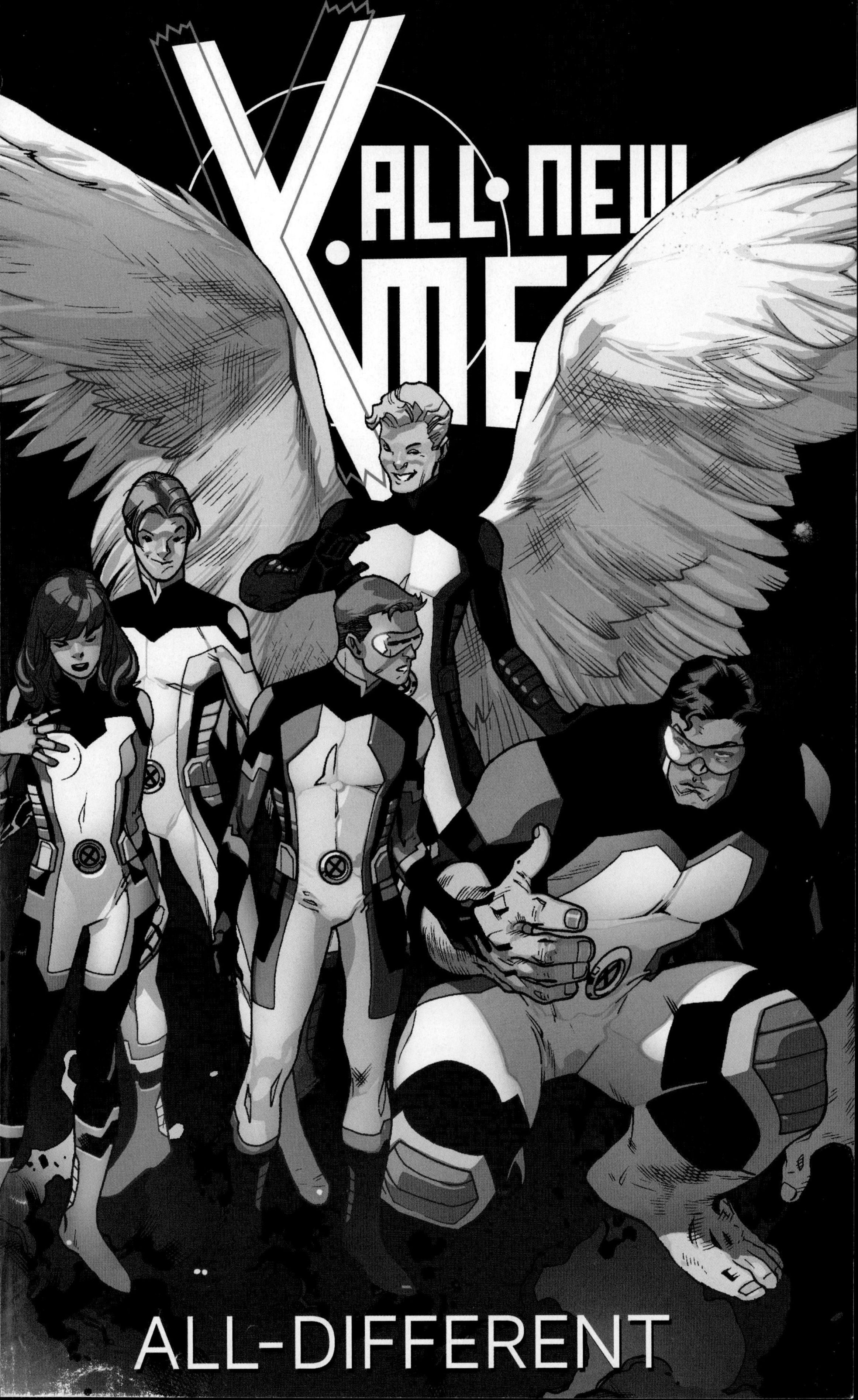
ALL·NEW
ALL-DIFFERENT

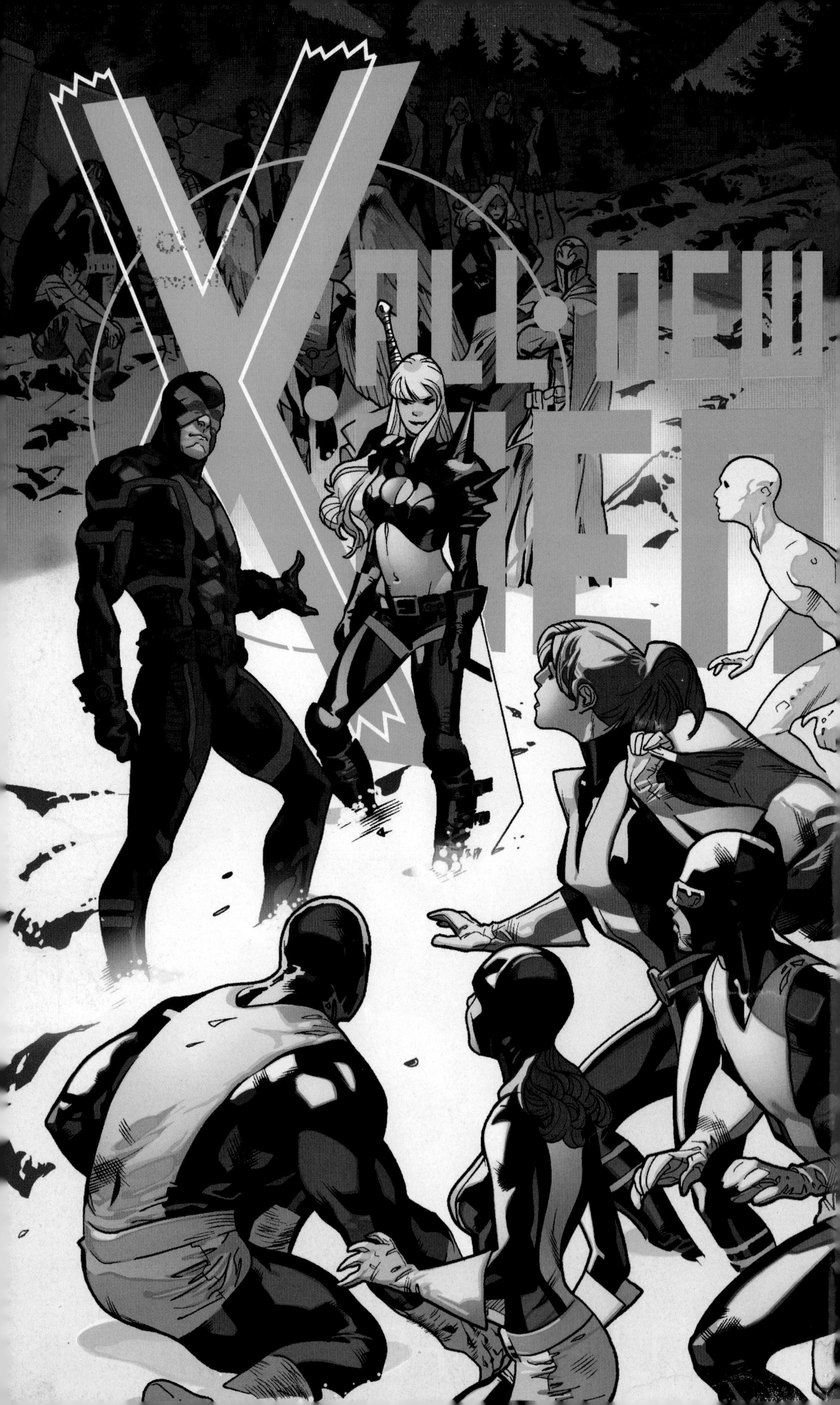
ALL-NEW
X-MEN

BEAST
HANK McCOY

MARVEL GIRL
JEAN GREY

CYCLOPS
SCOTT SUMMERS

ANGEL
WARREN WORTHINGTON III

ICEMAN
BOBBY DRAKE

ALL-DIFFERENT

AN MICHAEL **ENDIS**
WRITER

STUART **IMMONEN**
PENCILER, #18

WADE VON **GRAWBADGER**
INKER, #18

BRANDON **PETERSON**
WITH MAHMUD ASRAR (#20)
ARTISTS, #19-21

MARTE **RACIA**
COLORIST, #18 & #20

ISRAEL **SILVA**
COLORIST, #19-21

VC'S CORY **PETIT**
LETTERER

XANDER **JAROWEY**
ASSISTANT EDITOR

JORDAN D. **WHITE**
ASSOCIATE EDITOR

NICK **LOWE**
EDITOR

COVER ART: **BRANDON PETERSON**

X-MEN: GOLD #1

WRITERS: **CHRIS CLAREMONT, STAN LEE & LOUISE SIMONSON, LEN WEIN** AND **FABIAN NICIEZA**
ARTISTS: **BOB McLEOD, WALTER SIMONSON & BOB WIACEK, JORGE MOLINA** AND **SALVADOR LARROCA**
COLORISTS: **ISRAEL SILVA, ANDRES MOSSA** AND **DAVID OCAMPO**
LETTERER: **TOM ORZECHOWSKI**
COVER ART: **OLIVIER COIPEL**
ASSOCIATE EDITORS: **TOM BRENNAN** & **JORDAN D. WHITE**
EDITOR: **TOM BREVOORT**

COLLECTION EDITOR: **JENNIFER GRÜNWALD** ASSOCIATE MANAGING EDITOR: **ALEX STARBUCK**
EDITOR, SPECIAL PROJECTS: **MARK D. BEAZLEY** SENIOR EDITOR, SPECIAL PROJECTS: **JEFF YOUNGQUIST**
SVP PRINT, SALES & MARKETING: **DAVID GABRIEL** BOOK DESIGNER: **RODOLFO MURAGUCHI**

EDITOR IN CHIEF: **AXEL ALONSO** CHIEF CREATIVE OFFICER: **JOE QUESADA**
PUBLISHER: **DAN BUCKLEY** EXECUTIVE PRODUCER: **ALAN FINE**

ALL-NEW X-MEN VOL. 4: ALL-DIFFERENT. Contains material originally published in magazine form as ALL-NEW X-MEN #18-21 and X-MEN: GOLD #1. First printing 2014. ISBN# 978-0-7851-8860-5. Published by MARVEL WORLDWIDE, INC., a subsidiary of MARVEL ENTERTAINMENT, LLC. OFFICE OF PUBLICATION: 135 West 50th Street, New York, NY 10020. Copyright © 2013 and 2014 Marvel Characters, Inc. All rights reserved. All characters featured in this issue and the distinctive names and likenesses thereof, and all related indicia are trademarks of Marvel Characters, Inc. No similarity between any of the names, characters, persons, and/or institutions in this magazine with those of any living or dead person or institution is intended, and any such similarity which may exist is purely coincidental. **Printed in the U.S.A.** ALAN FINE, EVP - Office of the President, Marvel Worldwide, Inc. and EVP & CMO Marvel Characters B.V.; DAN BUCKLEY, Publisher & President - Print, Animation & Digital Divisions; JOE QUESADA, Chief Creative Officer; TOM BREVOORT, SVP of Publishing; DAVID BOGART, SVP of Operations & Procurement, Publishing; C.B. CEBULSKI, SVP of Creator & Content Development; DAVID GABRIEL, SVP Print, Sales & Marketing; JIM O'KEEFE, VP of Operations & Logistics; DAN CARR, Executive Director of Publishing Technology; SUSAN CRESPI, Editorial Operations Manager; ALEX MORALES, Publishing Operations Manager; STAN LEE, Chairman Emeritus. For information regarding advertising in Marvel Comics or on Marvel.com, please contact Niza Disla, Director of Marvel Partnerships, at ndisla@marvel.com. For Marvel subscription inquiries, please call 800-217-9158. **Manufactured between 2/28/2014 and 4/14/2014 by R.R. DONNELLEY, INC., SALEM, VA, USA.**

10 9 8 7 6 5 4 3 2 1

Born with genetic mutations that gave them abilities beyond those of normal humans, mutants are the next stage in evolution. As such, they are feared and hated by humanity. A group of mutants known as the X-Men fight for peaceful coexistence between mutants and humankind. But not all mutants see peaceful coexistence as a reality.

X ALL·NEW X·MEN

Despite the future Brotherhood of Evil's best efforts, the All-New X-Men cannot return to their original time. Kitty Pryde, the only member of the Jean Grey school who stood up for the All-New X-Men's right to make their own decision about returning to the past, felt betrayed by her teammates and left, deciding to join Cyclops and the Uncanny X-Men at the New Xavier School. Feeling an allegiance to their professor, the All-New X-Men joined her...

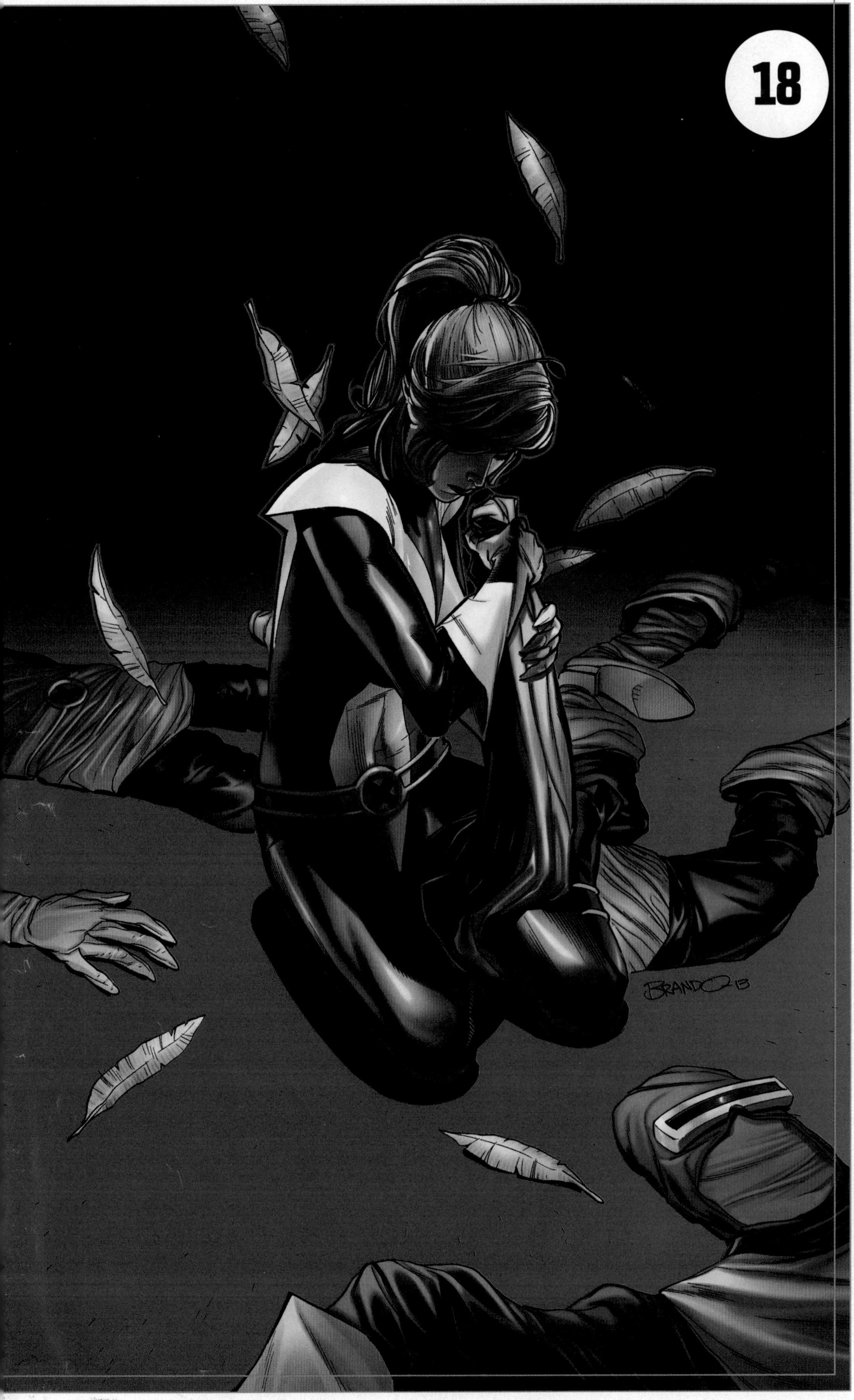
18
BRANDO '13

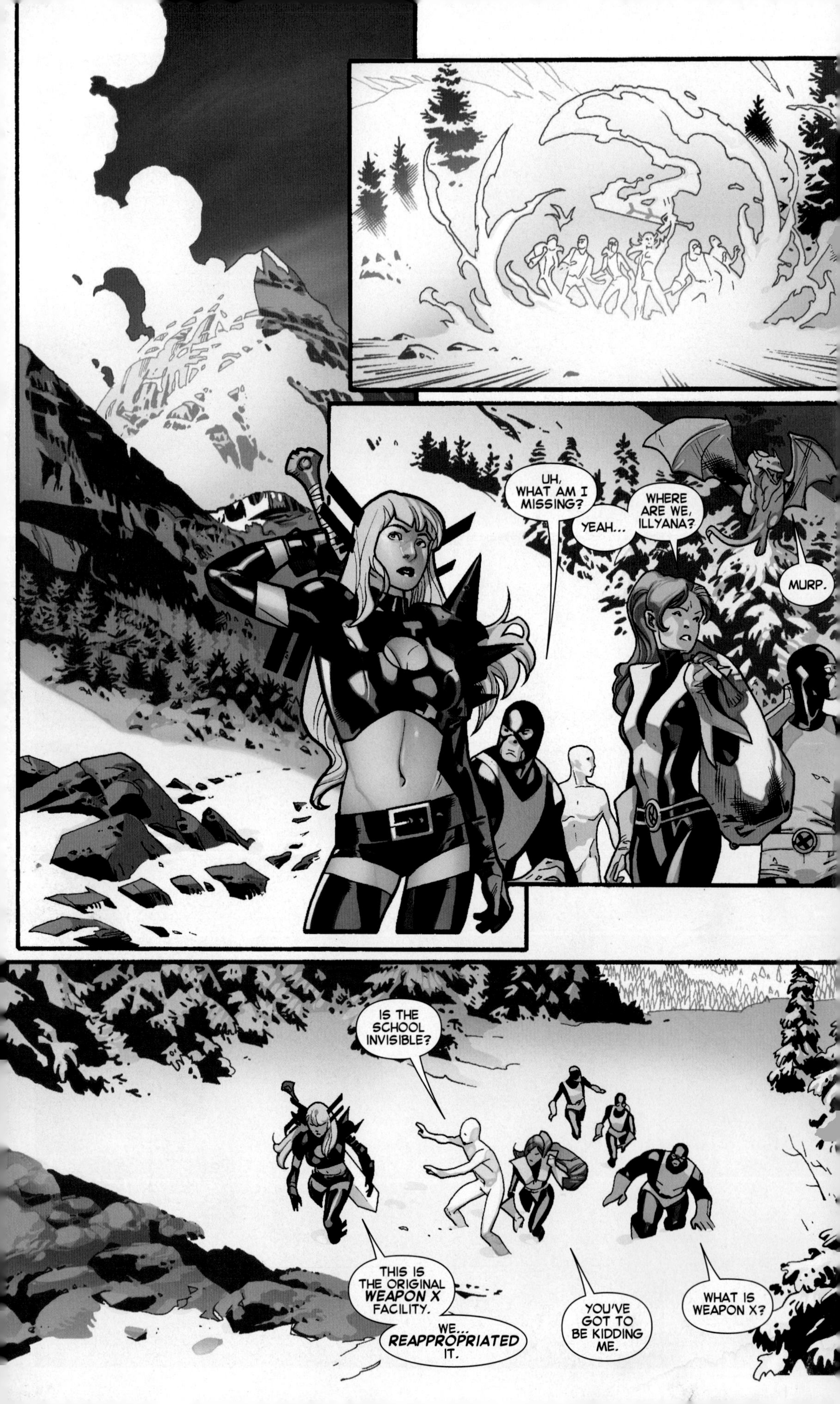

UH, WHAT AM I MISSING?
YEAH...
WHERE ARE WE, ILLYANA?
MURP.
IS THE SCHOOL INVISIBLE?
THIS IS THE ORIGINAL WEAPON X FACILITY.
WE... REAPPROPRIATED IT.
YOU'VE GOT TO BE KIDDING ME.
WHAT IS WEAPON X?

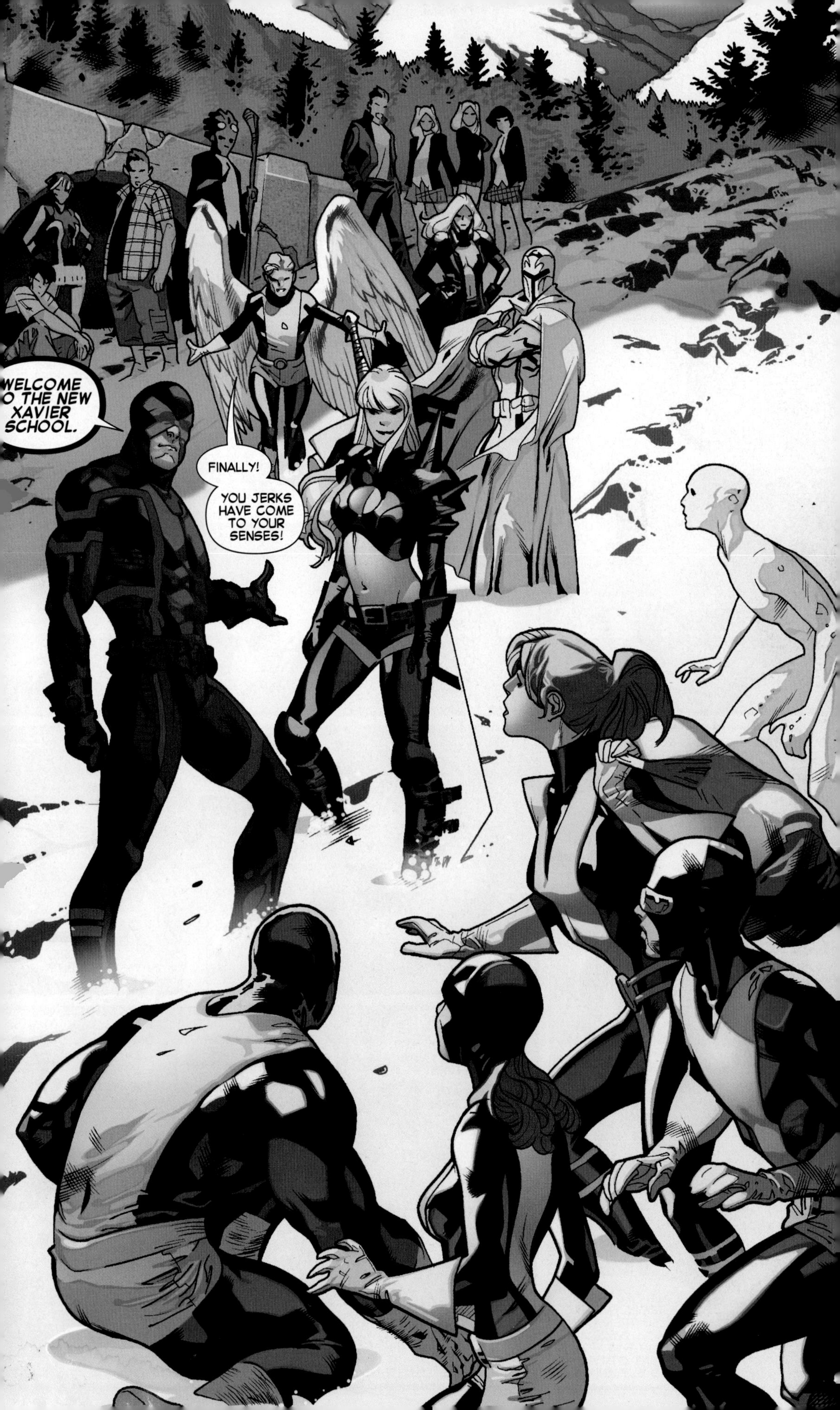
WELCOME TO THE NEW XAVIER SCHOOL.
FINALLY!
YOU JERKS HAVE COME TO YOUR SENSES!

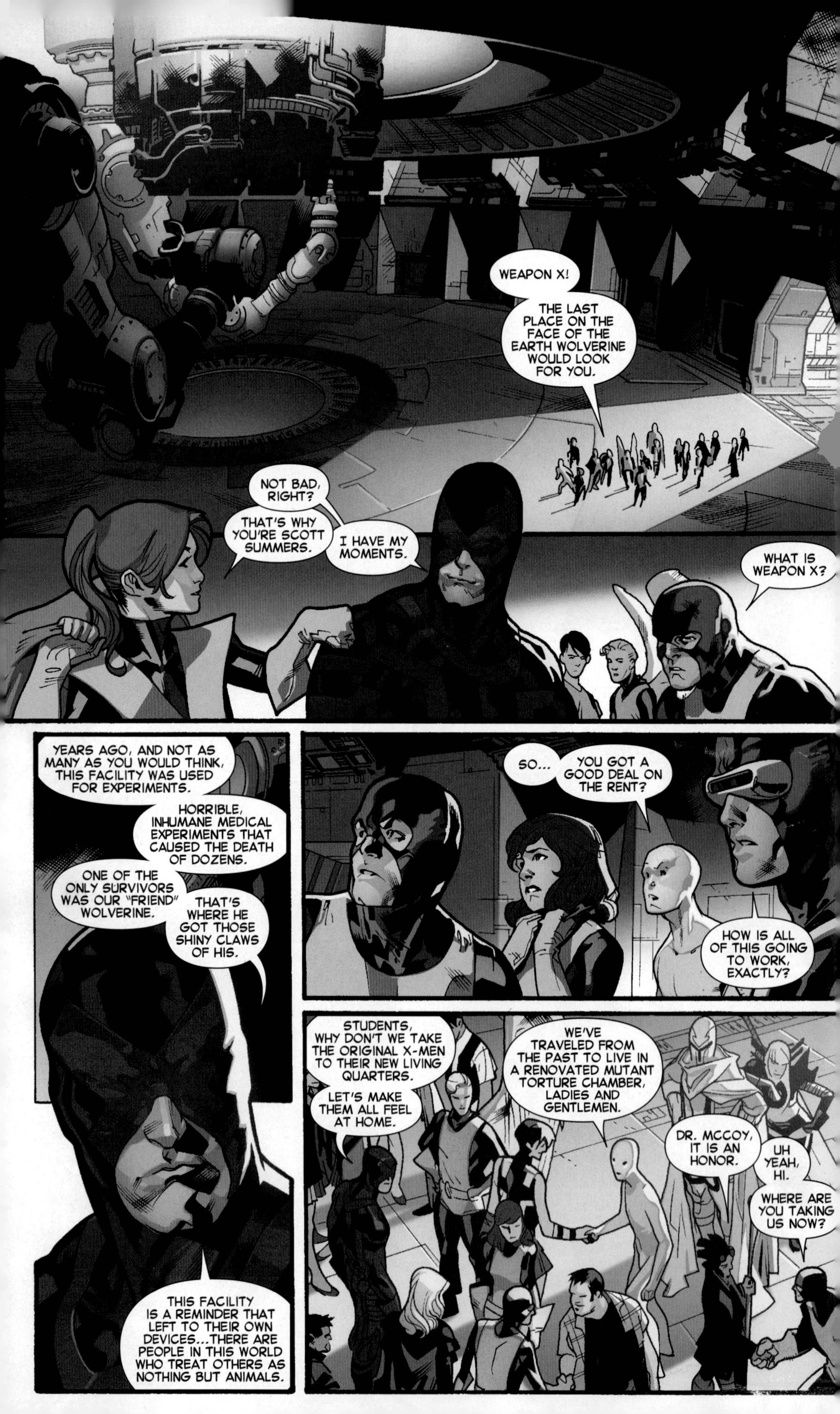
WEAPON X!
THE LAST PLACE ON THE FACE OF THE EARTH WOLVERINE WOULD LOOK FOR YOU.
NOT BAD, RIGHT?
THAT'S WHY YOU'RE SCOTT SUMMERS.
I HAVE MY MOMENTS.
WHAT IS WEAPON X?
YEARS AGO, AND NOT AS MANY AS YOU WOULD THINK, THIS FACILITY WAS USED FOR EXPERIMENTS.
HORRIBLE, INHUMANE MEDICAL EXPERIMENTS THAT CAUSED THE DEATH OF DOZENS.
ONE OF THE ONLY SURVIVORS WAS OUR "FRIEND" WOLVERINE.
THAT'S WHERE HE GOT THOSE SHINY CLAWS OF HIS.
THIS FACILITY IS A REMINDER THAT LEFT TO THEIR OWN DEVICES...THERE ARE PEOPLE IN THIS WORLD WHO TREAT OTHERS AS NOTHING BUT ANIMALS.
SO...
YOU GOT A GOOD DEAL ON THE RENT?
HOW IS ALL OF THIS GOING TO WORK, EXACTLY?
STUDENTS, WHY DON'T WE TAKE THE ORIGINAL X-MEN TO THEIR NEW LIVING QUARTERS.
LET'S MAKE THEM ALL FEEL AT HOME.
WE'VE TRAVELED FROM THE PAST TO LIVE IN A RENOVATED MUTANT TORTURE CHAMBER, LADIES AND GENTLEMEN.
DR. MCCOY, IT IS AN HONOR.
UH YEAH, HI.
WHERE ARE YOU TAKING US NOW?

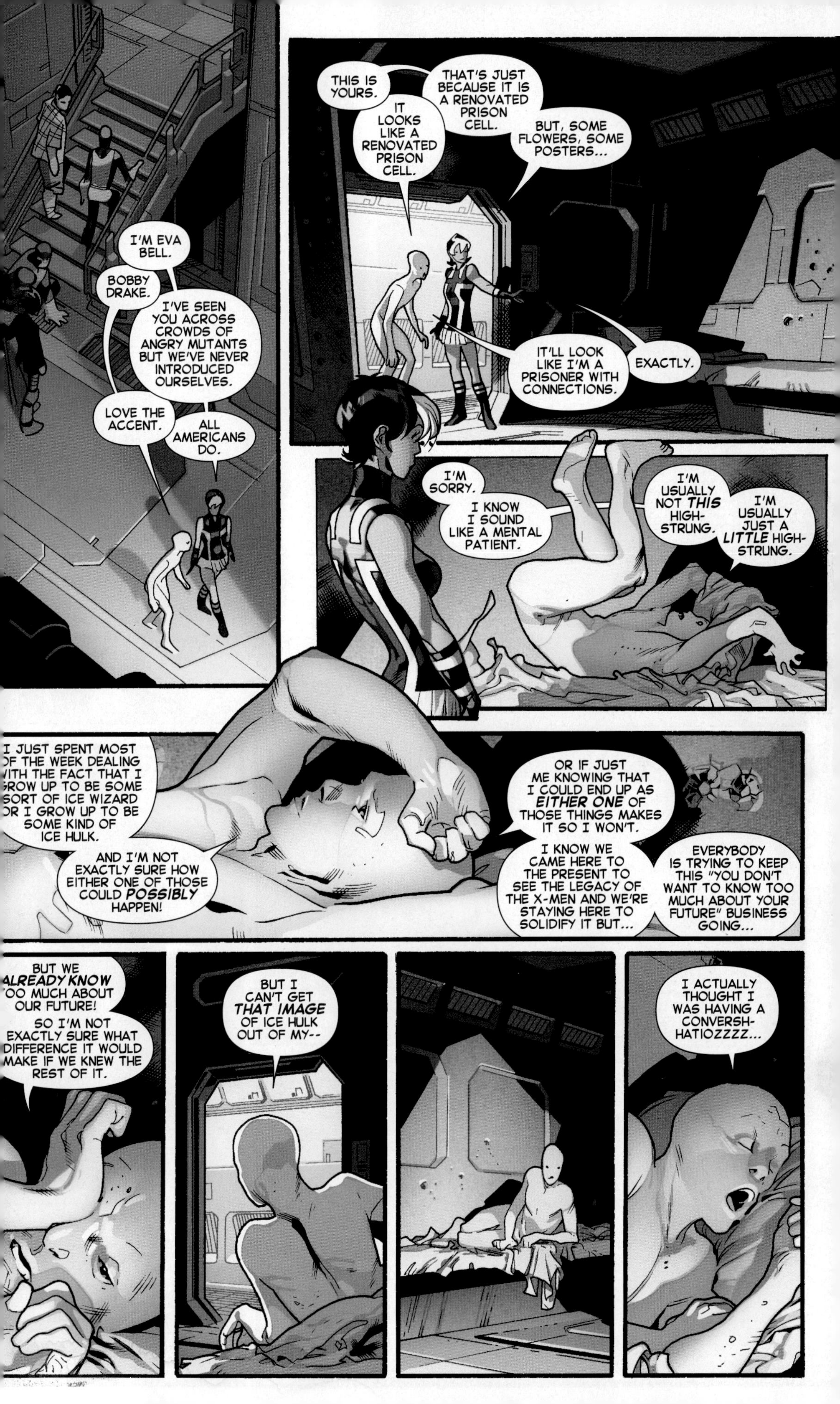

I'M EVA BELL.
BOBBY DRAKE.
I'VE SEEN YOU ACROSS CROWDS OF ANGRY MUTANTS BUT WE'VE NEVER INTRODUCED OURSELVES.
LOVE THE ACCENT.
ALL AMERICANS DO.
THIS IS YOURS.
IT LOOKS LIKE A RENOVATED PRISON CELL.
THAT'S JUST BECAUSE IT IS A RENOVATED PRISON CELL.
BUT, SOME FLOWERS, SOME POSTERS...
IT'LL LOOK LIKE I'M A PRISONER WITH CONNECTIONS.
EXACTLY.
I'M SORRY.
I KNOW I SOUND LIKE A MENTAL PATIENT.
I'M USUALLY NOT THIS HIGH-STRUNG.
I'M USUALLY JUST A LITTLE HIGH-STRUNG.
I JUST SPENT MOST OF THE WEEK DEALING WITH THE FACT THAT I GROW UP TO BE SOME SORT OF ICE WIZARD OR I GROW UP TO BE SOME KIND OF ICE HULK.
AND I'M NOT EXACTLY SURE HOW EITHER ONE OF THOSE COULD POSSIBLY HAPPEN!
OR IF JUST ME KNOWING THAT I COULD END UP AS EITHER ONE OF THOSE THINGS MAKES IT SO I WON'T.
I KNOW WE CAME HERE TO THE PRESENT TO SEE THE LEGACY OF THE X-MEN AND WE'RE STAYING HERE TO SOLIDIFY IT BUT...
EVERYBODY IS TRYING TO KEEP THIS "YOU DON'T WANT TO KNOW TOO MUCH ABOUT YOUR FUTURE" BUSINESS GOING...
BUT WE ALREADY KNOW TOO MUCH ABOUT OUR FUTURE!
SO I'M NOT EXACTLY SURE WHAT DIFFERENCE IT WOULD MAKE IF WE KNEW THE REST OF IT.
BUT I CAN'T GET THAT IMAGE OF ICE HULK OUT OF MY--
I ACTUALLY THOUGHT I WAS HAVING A CONVERSH-HATIOZZZZ...

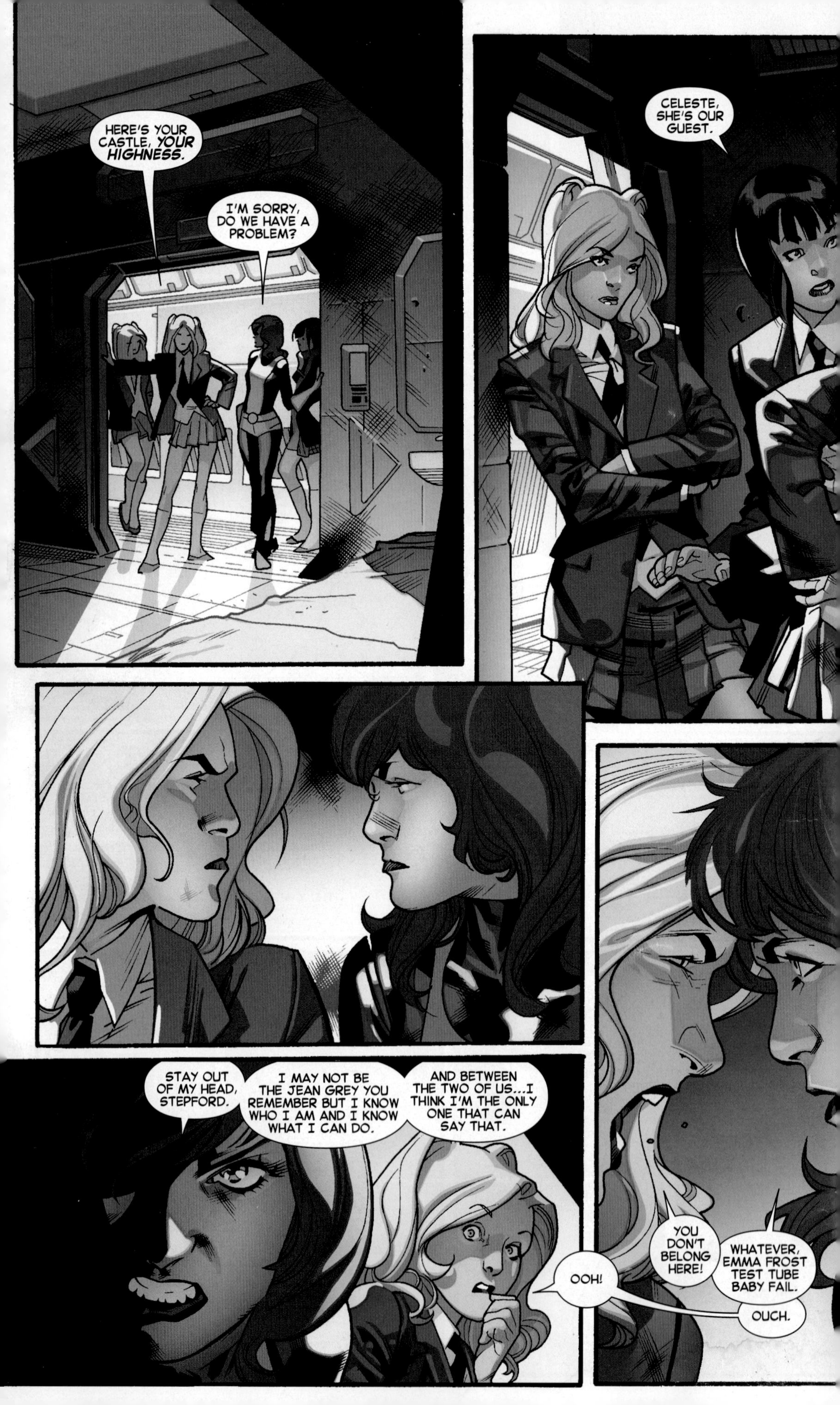
HERE'S YOUR CASTLE, YOUR HIGHNESS.
I'M SORRY, DO WE HAVE A PROBLEM?
CELESTE, SHE'S OUR GUEST.
STAY OUT OF MY HEAD, STEPFORD.
I MAY NOT BE THE JEAN GREY YOU REMEMBER BUT I KNOW WHO I AM AND I KNOW WHAT I CAN DO.
AND BETWEEN THE TWO OF US...I THINK I'M THE ONLY ONE THAT CAN SAY THAT.
YOU DON'T BELONG HERE!
WHATEVER, EMMA FROST TEST TUBE BABY FAIL.
OOH!
OUCH.

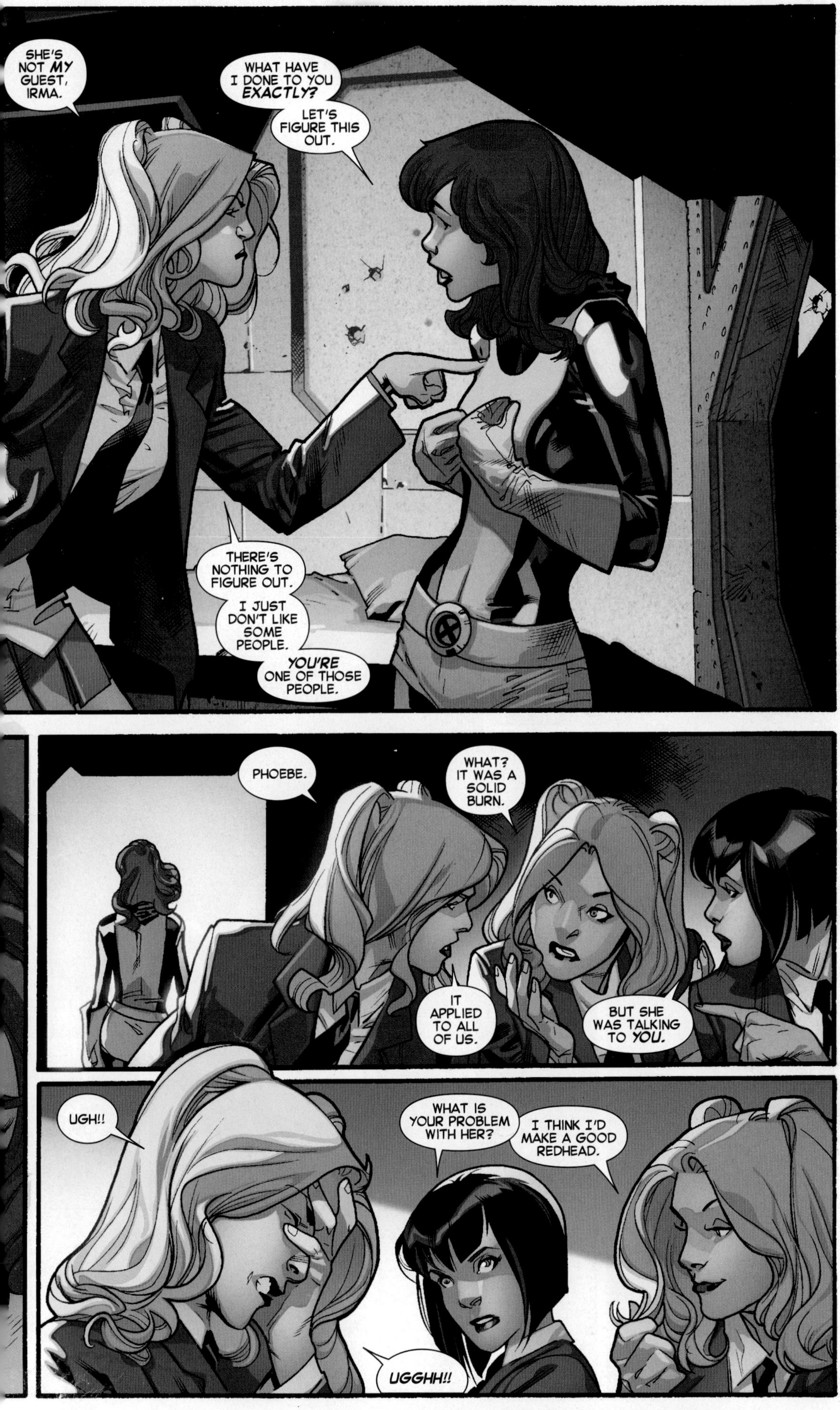

SHE'S NOT MY GUEST, IRMA.
WHAT HAVE I DONE TO YOU EXACTLY?
LET'S FIGURE THIS OUT.
THERE'S NOTHING TO FIGURE OUT.
I JUST DON'T LIKE SOME PEOPLE.
YOU'RE ONE OF THOSE PEOPLE.
PHOEBE.
WHAT? IT WAS A SOLID BURN.
IT APPLIED TO ALL OF US.
BUT SHE WAS TALKING TO YOU.
UGH!!
WHAT IS YOUR PROBLEM WITH HER?
I THINK I'D MAKE A GOOD REDHEAD.
UGGHH!!

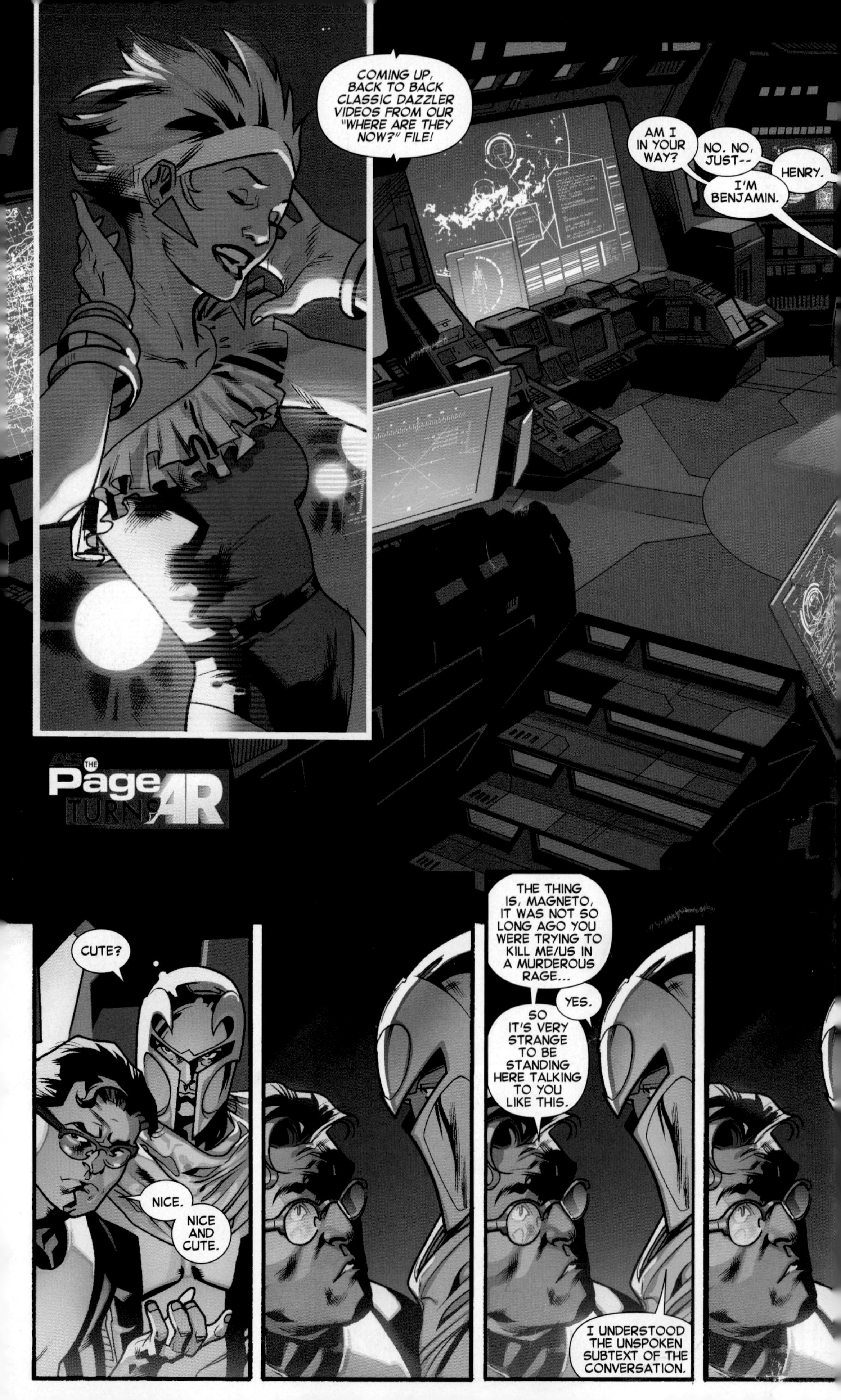
COMING UP, BACK TO BACK CLASSIC DAZZLER VIDEOS FROM OUR "WHERE ARE THEY NOW?" FILE!
AM I IN YOUR WAY?
NO. NO, JUST--
HENRY.
I'M BENJAMIN.
The Page TURNS AR
CUTE?
NICE.
NICE AND CUTE.
THE THING IS, MAGNETO, IT WAS NOT SO LONG AGO YOU WERE TRYING TO KILL ME/US IN A MURDEROUS RAGE...
YES.
SO IT'S VERY STRANGE TO BE STANDING HERE TALKING TO YOU LIKE THIS.
I UNDERSTOOD THE UNSPOKEN SUBTEXT OF THE CONVERSATION.

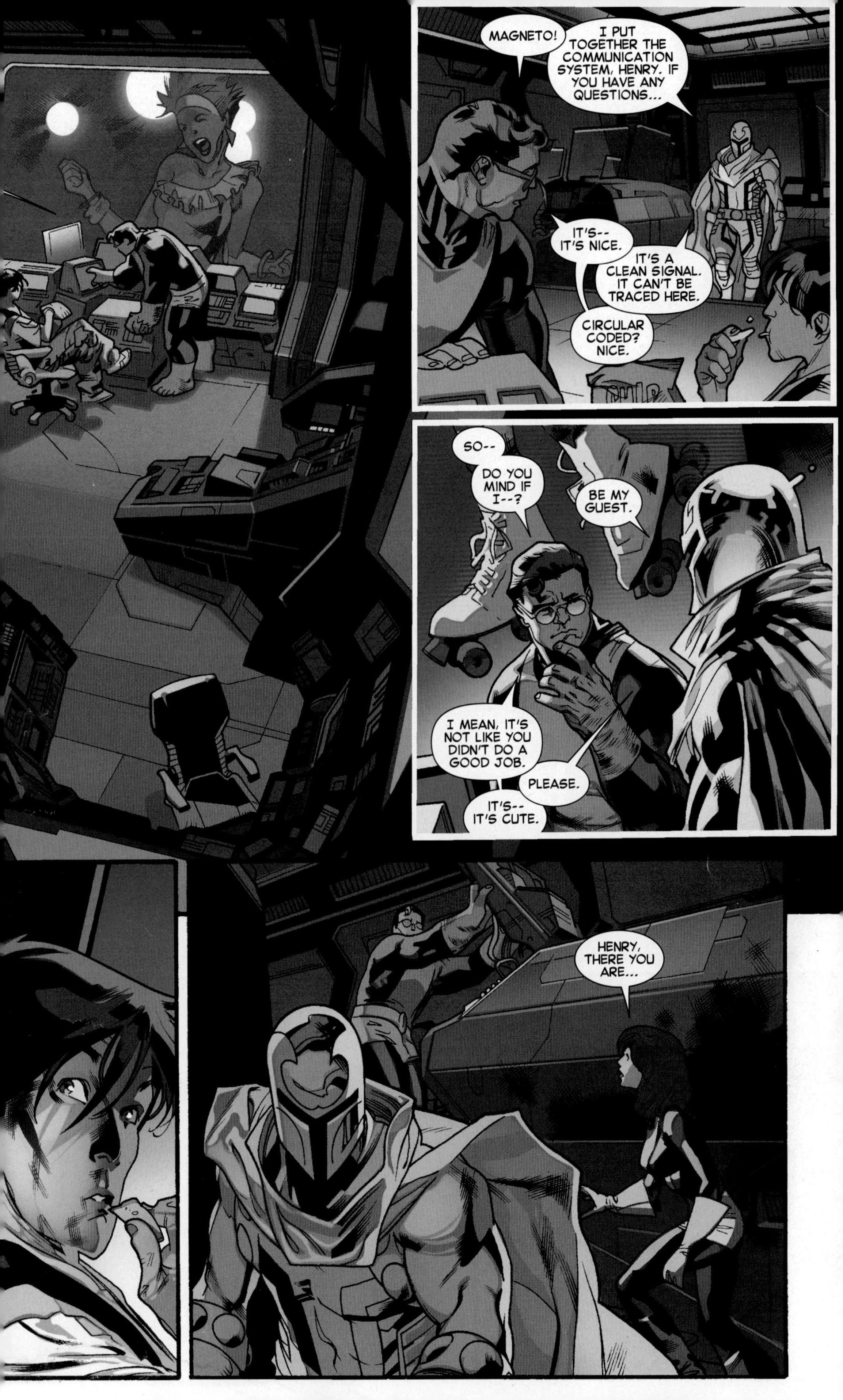
MAGNETO!
I PUT TOGETHER THE COMMUNICATION SYSTEM, HENRY. IF YOU HAVE ANY QUESTIONS...
IT'S-- IT'S NICE.
IT'S A CLEAN SIGNAL. IT CAN'T BE TRACED HERE.
CIRCULAR CODED? NICE.
SO--
DO YOU MIND IF I--?
BE MY GUEST.
I MEAN, IT'S NOT LIKE YOU DIDN'T DO A GOOD JOB.
PLEASE.
IT'S-- IT'S CUTE.
HENRY, THERE YOU ARE...

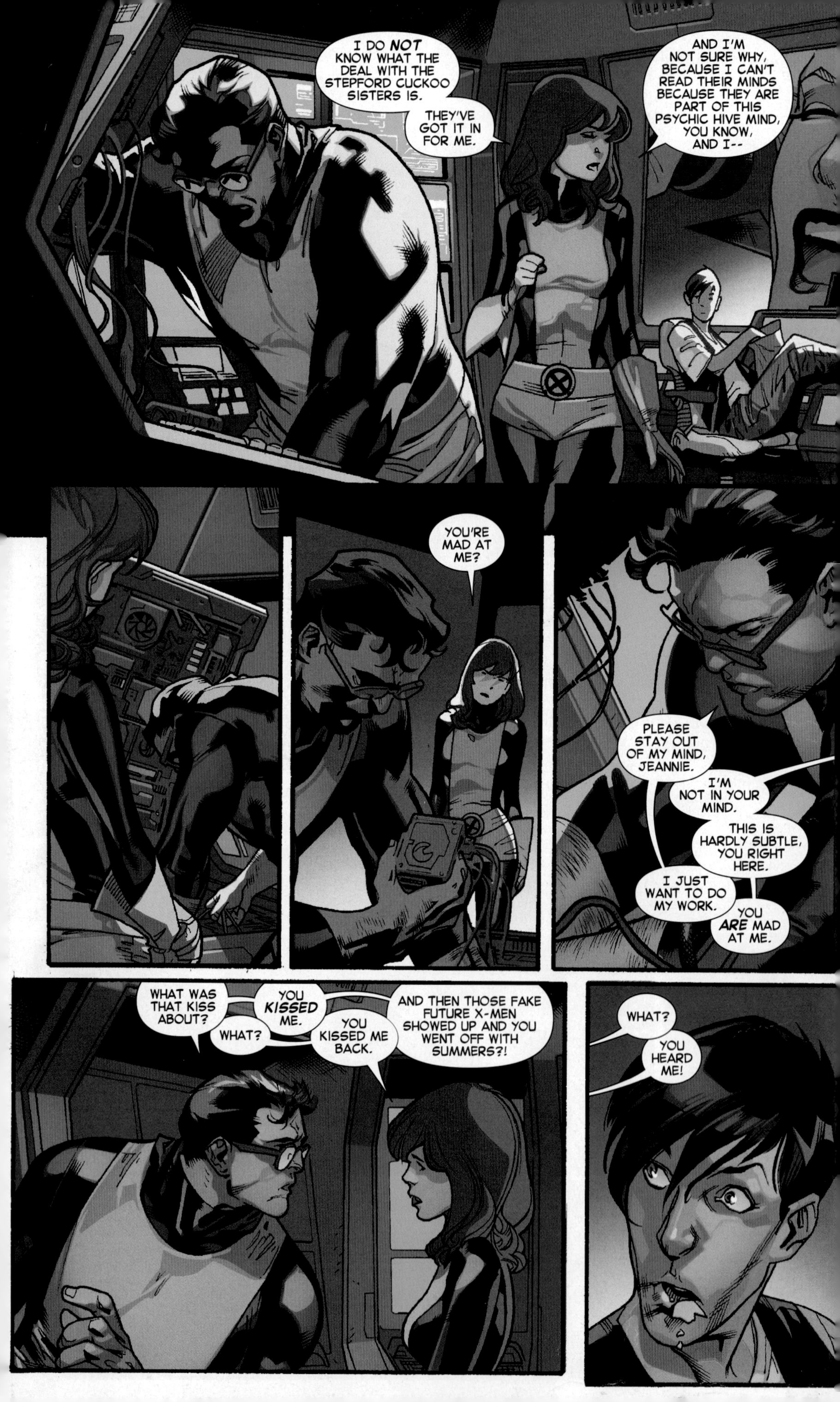

I DO NOT KNOW WHAT THE DEAL WITH THE STEPFORD CUCKOO SISTERS IS.
THEY'VE GOT IT IN FOR ME.
AND I'M NOT SURE WHY, BECAUSE I CAN'T READ THEIR MINDS BECAUSE THEY ARE PART OF THIS PSYCHIC HIVE MIND, YOU KNOW, AND I--
YOU'RE MAD AT ME?
PLEASE STAY OUT OF MY MIND, JEANNIE.
I'M NOT IN YOUR MIND.
THIS IS HARDLY SUBTLE, YOU RIGHT HERE.
I JUST WANT TO DO MY WORK.
YOU ARE MAD AT ME.
WHAT WAS THAT KISS ABOUT?
WHAT?
YOU KISSED ME.
YOU KISSED ME BACK.
AND THEN THOSE FAKE FUTURE X-MEN SHOWED UP AND YOU WENT OFF WITH SUMMERS?!
WHAT?
YOU HEARD ME!

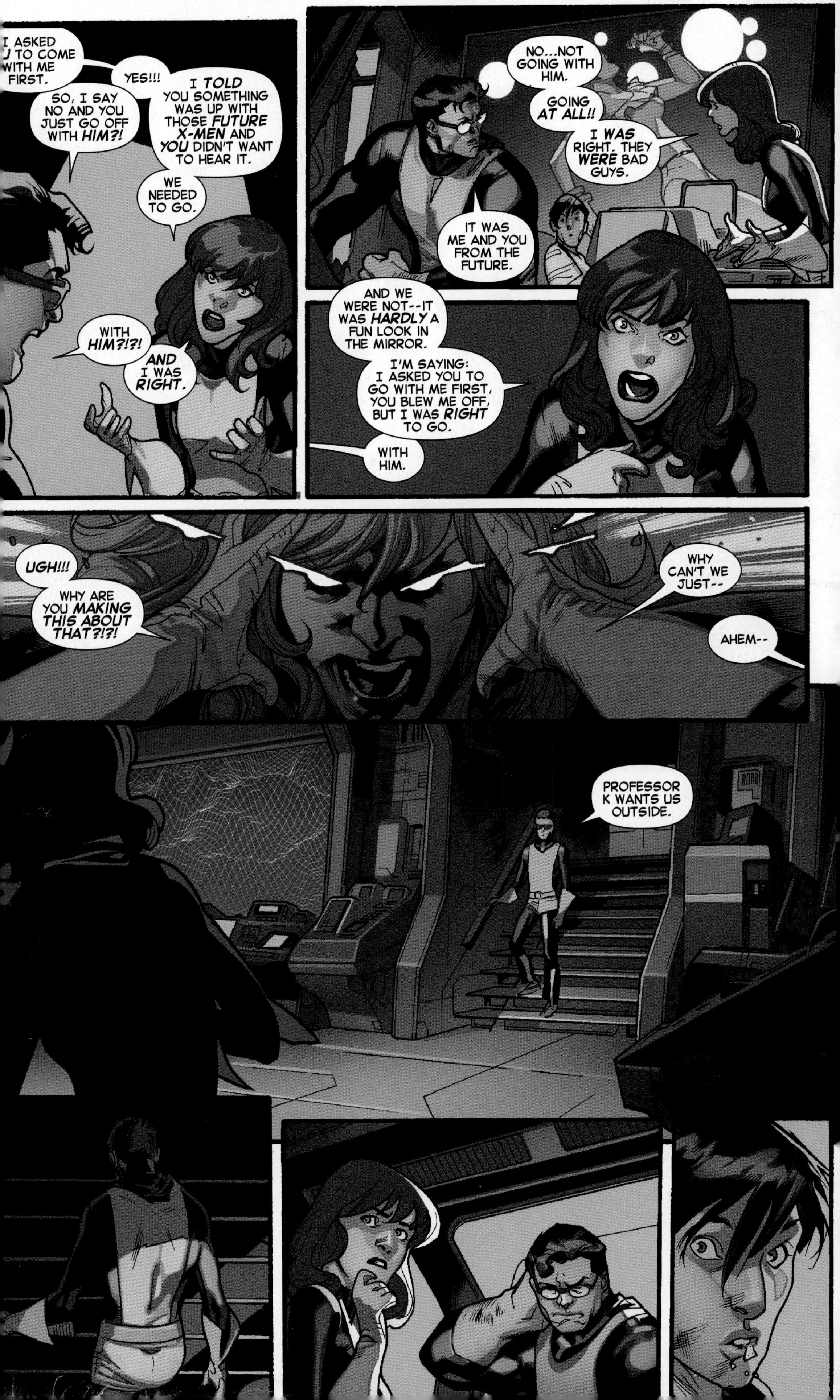
I ASKED
U TO COME
WITH ME
FIRST.
SO, I SAY NO AND YOU JUST GO OFF WITH HIM?!
YES!!!
I TOLD YOU SOMETHING WAS UP WITH THOSE FUTURE X-MEN AND YOU DIDN'T WANT TO HEAR IT.
WE NEEDED TO GO.
WITH HIM?!?!
AND I WAS RIGHT.
NO...NOT GOING WITH HIM.
GOING AT ALL!!
I WAS RIGHT. THEY WERE BAD GUYS.
IT WAS ME AND YOU FROM THE FUTURE.
AND WE WERE NOT--IT WAS HARDLY A FUN LOOK IN THE MIRROR.
I'M SAYING: I ASKED YOU TO GO WITH ME FIRST, YOU BLEW ME OFF, BUT I WAS RIGHT TO GO.
WITH HIM.
UGH!!!
WHY ARE YOU MAKING THIS ABOUT THAT?!?!
WHY CAN'T WE JUST--
AHEM--
PROFESSOR K WANTS US OUTSIDE.

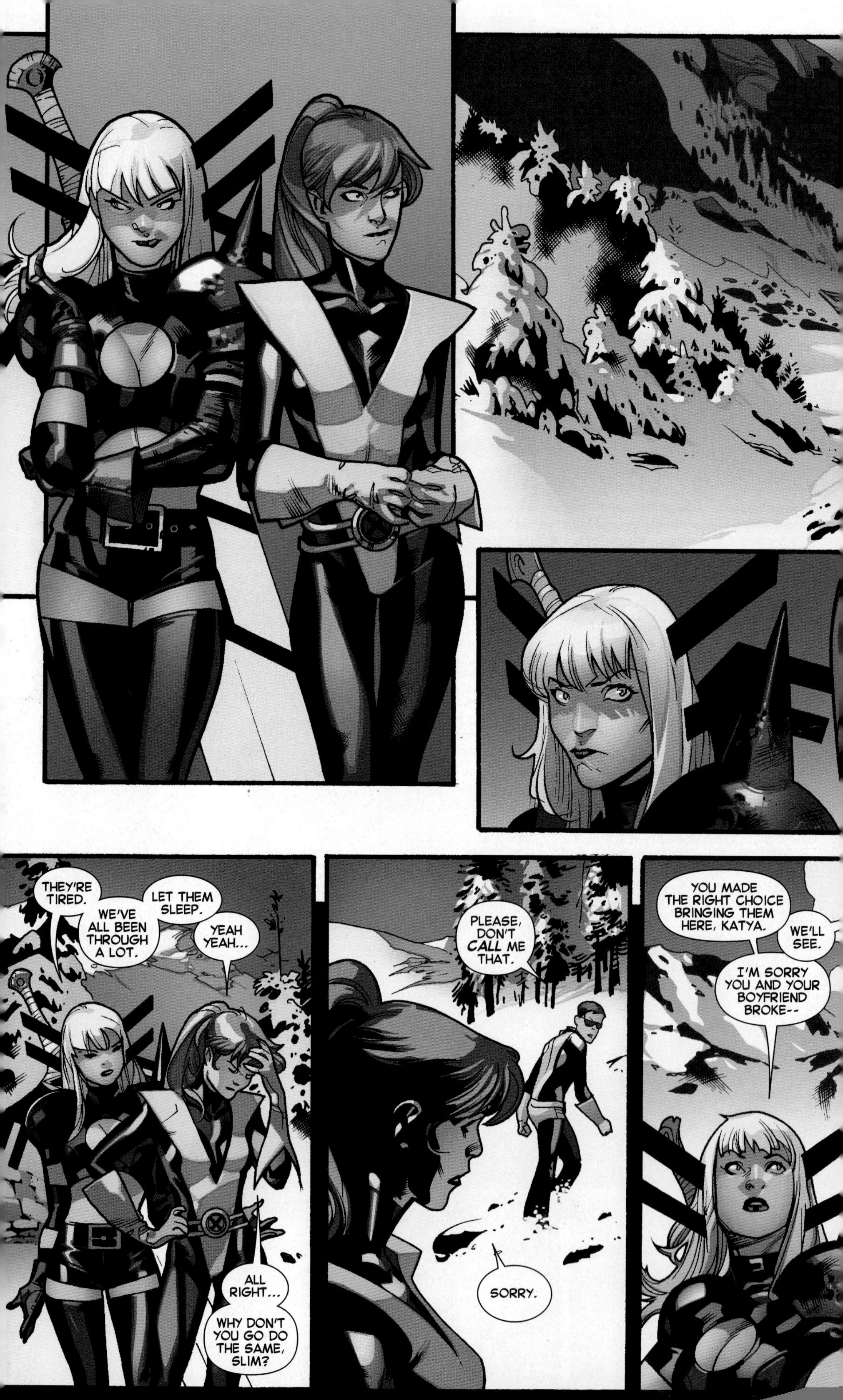
THEY'RE TIRED.
WE'VE ALL BEEN THROUGH A LOT.
LET THEM SLEEP.
YEAH YEAH...
ALL RIGHT...
WHY DON'T YOU GO DO THE SAME, SLIM?
PLEASE, DON'T CALL ME THAT.
SORRY.
YOU MADE THE RIGHT CHOICE BRINGING THEM HERE, KATYA.
WE'LL SEE.
I'M SORRY YOU AND YOUR BOYFRIEND BROKE--

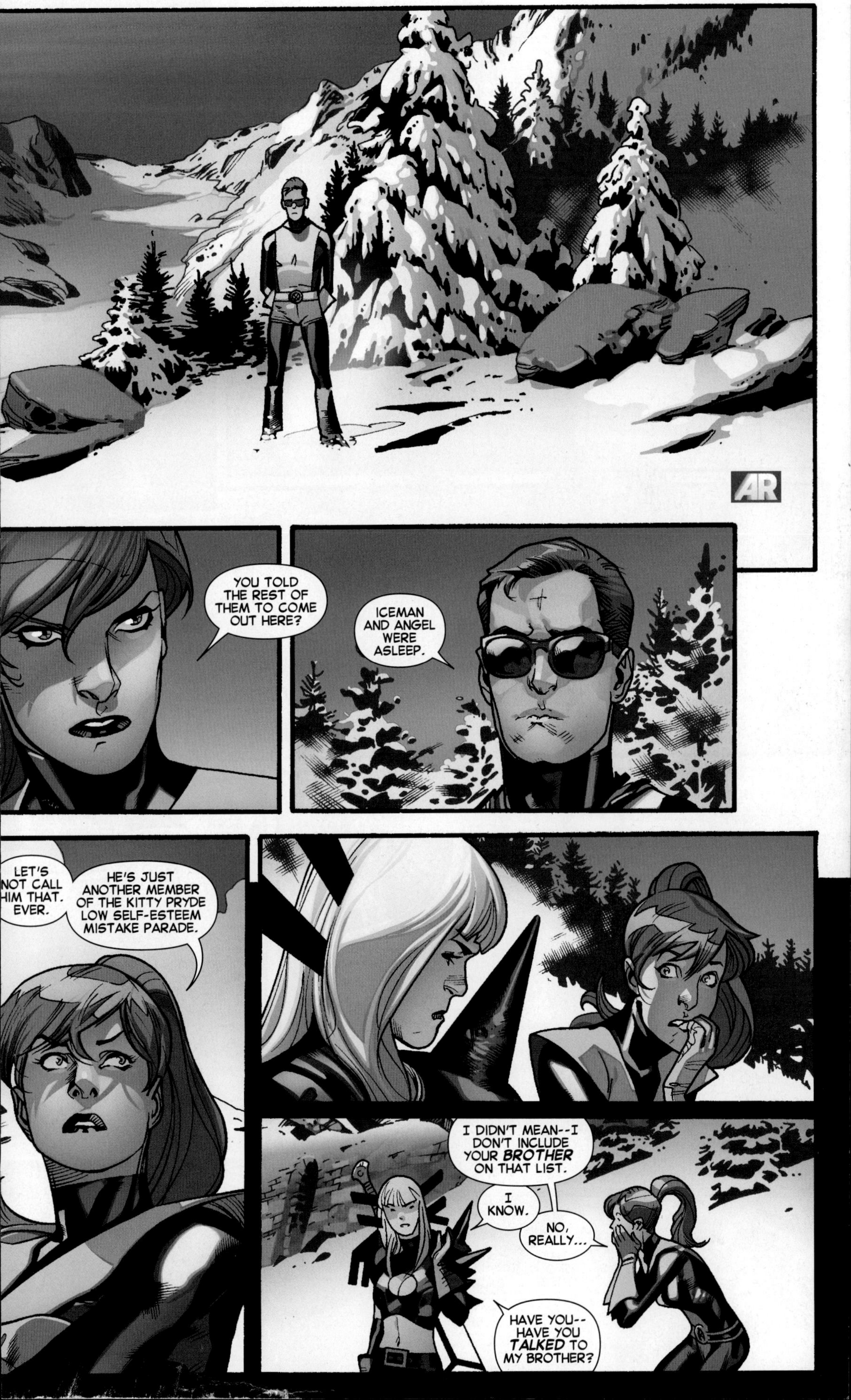
AR
YOU TOLD THE REST OF THEM TO COME OUT HERE?
ICEMAN AND ANGEL WERE ASLEEP.
LET'S NOT CALL HIM THAT. EVER.
HE'S JUST ANOTHER MEMBER OF THE KITTY PRYDE LOW SELF-ESTEEM MISTAKE PARADE.
I DIDN'T MEAN--I DON'T INCLUDE YOUR BROTHER ON THAT LIST.
I KNOW.
NO, REALLY...
HAVE YOU-- HAVE YOU TALKED TO MY BROTHER?

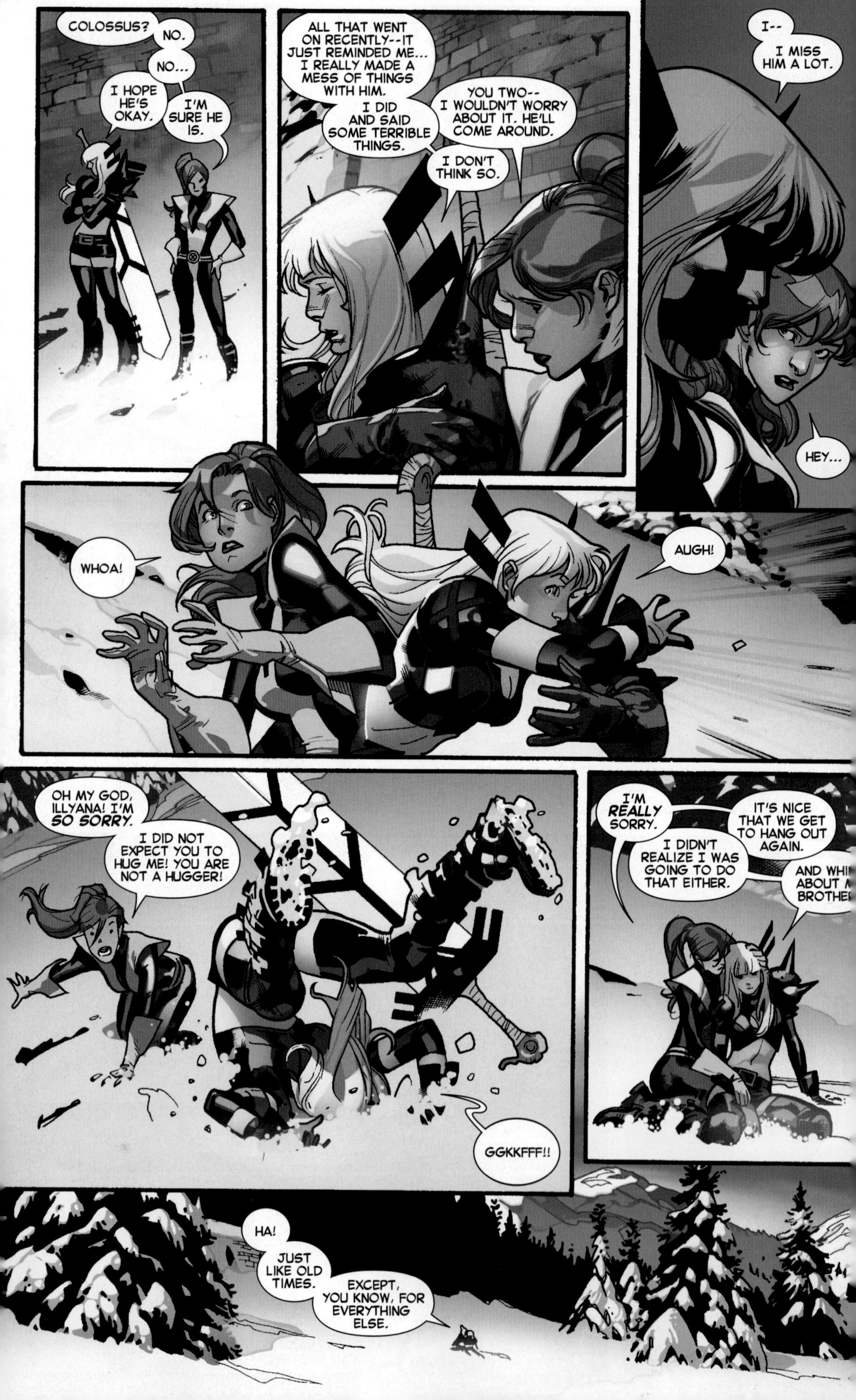

COLOSSUS?
NO.
NO...
I HOPE HE'S OKAY.
I'M SURE HE IS.
ALL THAT WENT ON RECENTLY--IT JUST REMINDED ME... I REALLY MADE A MESS OF THINGS WITH HIM.
I DID AND SAID SOME TERRIBLE THINGS.
YOU TWO-- I WOULDN'T WORRY ABOUT IT. HE'LL COME AROUND.
I DON'T THINK SO.
I--
I MISS HIM A LOT.
HEY...
WHOA!
AUGH!
OH MY GOD, ILLYANA! I'M SO SORRY.
I DID NOT EXPECT YOU TO HUG ME! YOU ARE NOT A HUGGER!
GGKKFFF!!
I'M REALLY SORRY.
I DIDN'T REALIZE I WAS GOING TO DO THAT EITHER.
IT'S NICE THAT WE GET TO HANG OUT AGAIN.
HA!
JUST LIKE OLD TIMES.
EXCEPT, YOU KNOW, FOR EVERYTHING ELSE.

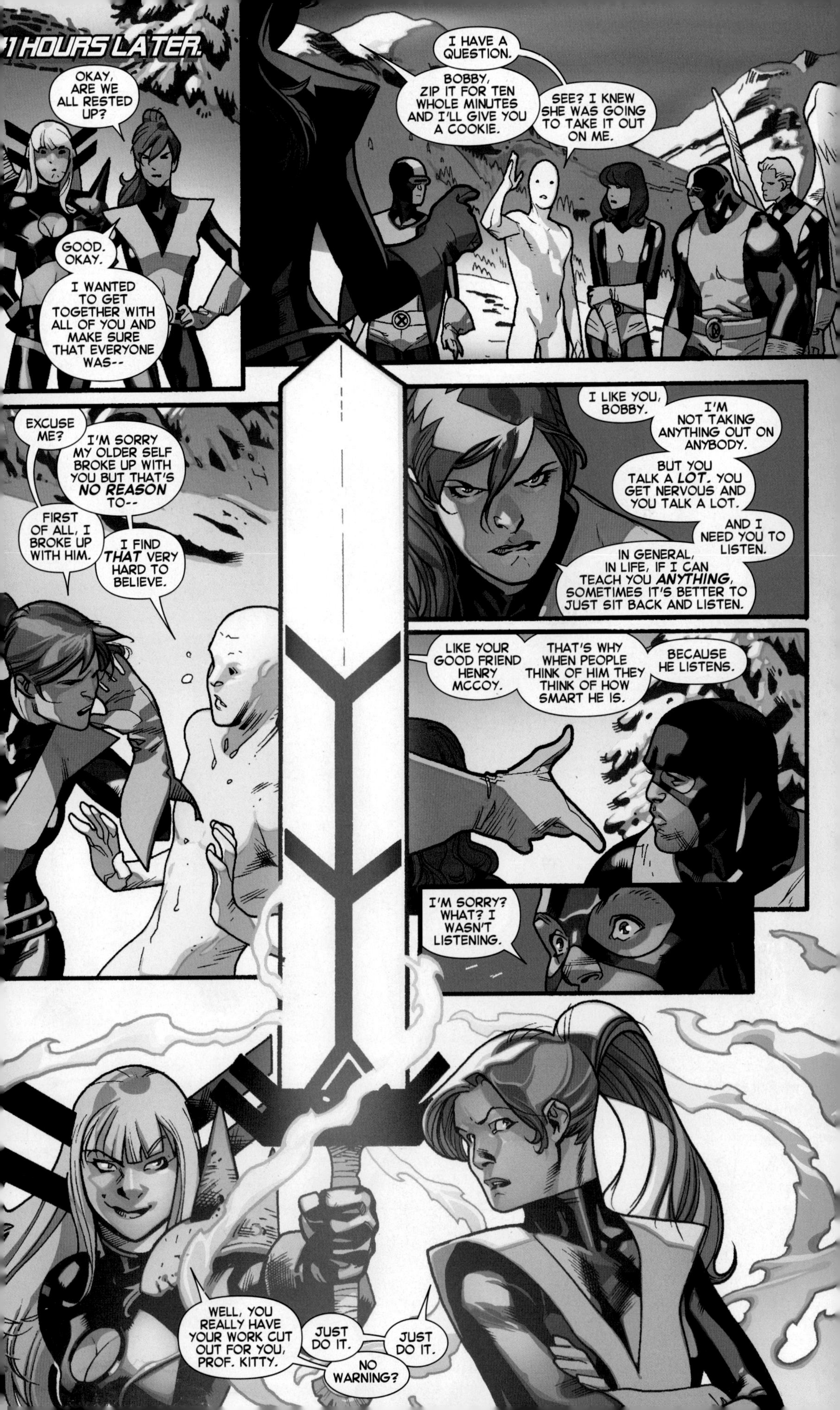

1 HOURS LATER.
OKAY, ARE WE ALL RESTED UP?
GOOD. OKAY.
I WANTED TO GET TOGETHER WITH ALL OF YOU AND MAKE SURE THAT EVERYONE WAS--
I HAVE A QUESTION.
BOBBY, ZIP IT FOR TEN WHOLE MINUTES AND I'LL GIVE YOU A COOKIE.
SEE? I KNEW SHE WAS GOING TO TAKE IT OUT ON ME.
EXCUSE ME?
I'M SORRY MY OLDER SELF BROKE UP WITH YOU BUT THAT'S NO REASON TO--
FIRST OF ALL, I BROKE UP WITH HIM.
I FIND THAT VERY HARD TO BELIEVE.
I LIKE YOU, BOBBY.
I'M NOT TAKING ANYTHING OUT ON ANYBODY.
BUT YOU TALK A LOT. YOU GET NERVOUS AND YOU TALK A LOT.
AND I NEED YOU TO LISTEN.
IN GENERAL, IN LIFE, IF I CAN TEACH YOU ANYTHING, SOMETIMES IT'S BETTER TO JUST SIT BACK AND LISTEN.
LIKE YOUR GOOD FRIEND HENRY McCOY.
THAT'S WHY WHEN PEOPLE THINK OF HIM THEY THINK OF HOW SMART HE IS.
BECAUSE HE LISTENS.
I'M SORRY? WHAT? I WASN'T LISTENING.
WELL, YOU REALLY HAVE YOUR WORK CUT OUT FOR YOU, PROF. KITTY.
JUST DO IT.
JUST DO IT.
NO WARNING?

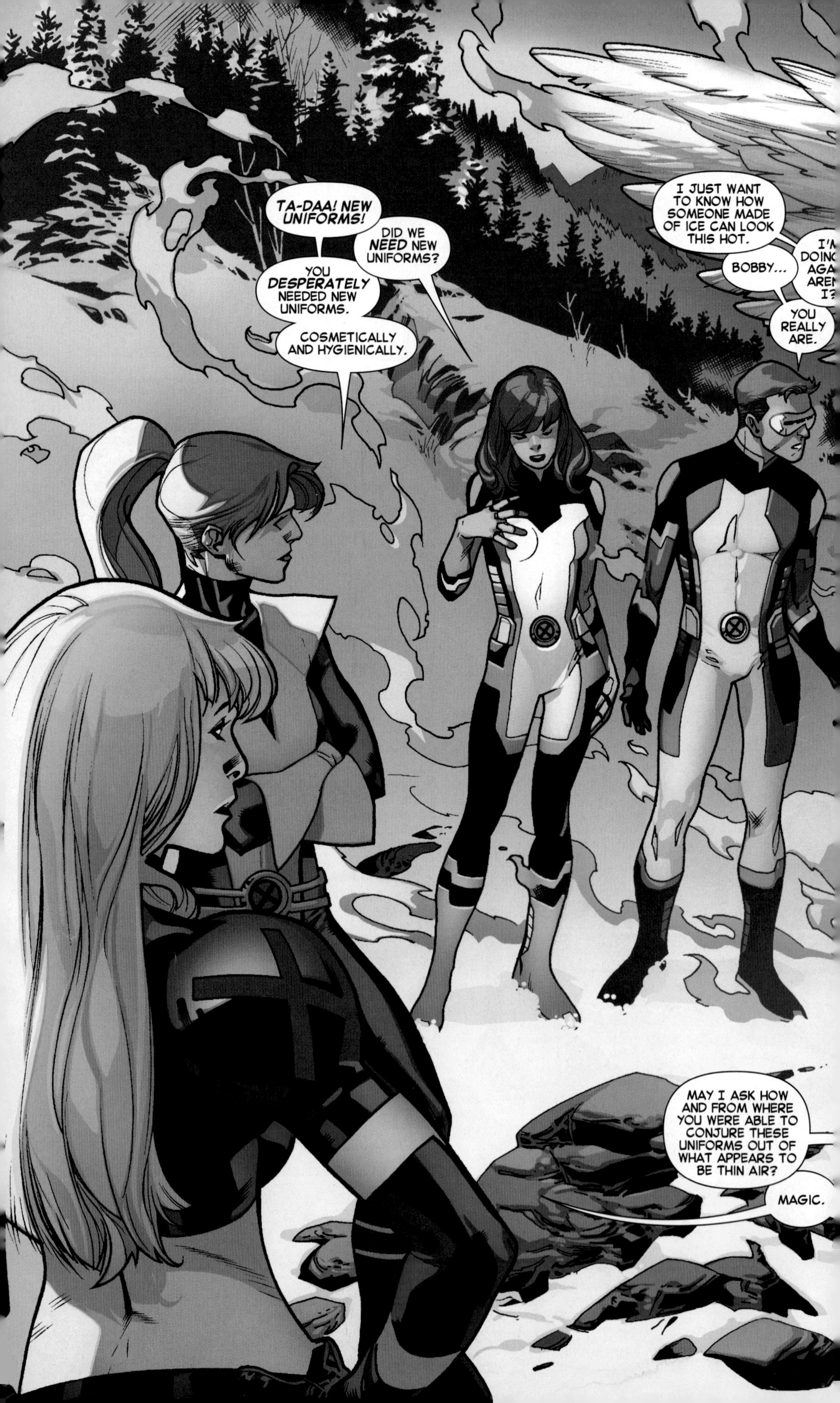
TA-DAA! NEW UNIFORMS!
DID WE NEED NEW UNIFORMS?
YOU DESPERATELY NEEDED NEW UNIFORMS.
COSMETICALLY AND HYGIENICALLY.
I JUST WANT TO KNOW HOW SOMEONE MADE OF ICE CAN LOOK THIS HOT.
BOBBY...
YOU REALLY ARE.
MAY I ASK HOW AND FROM WHERE YOU WERE ABLE TO CONJURE THESE UNIFORMS OUT OF WHAT APPEARS TO BE THIN AIR?
MAGIC.

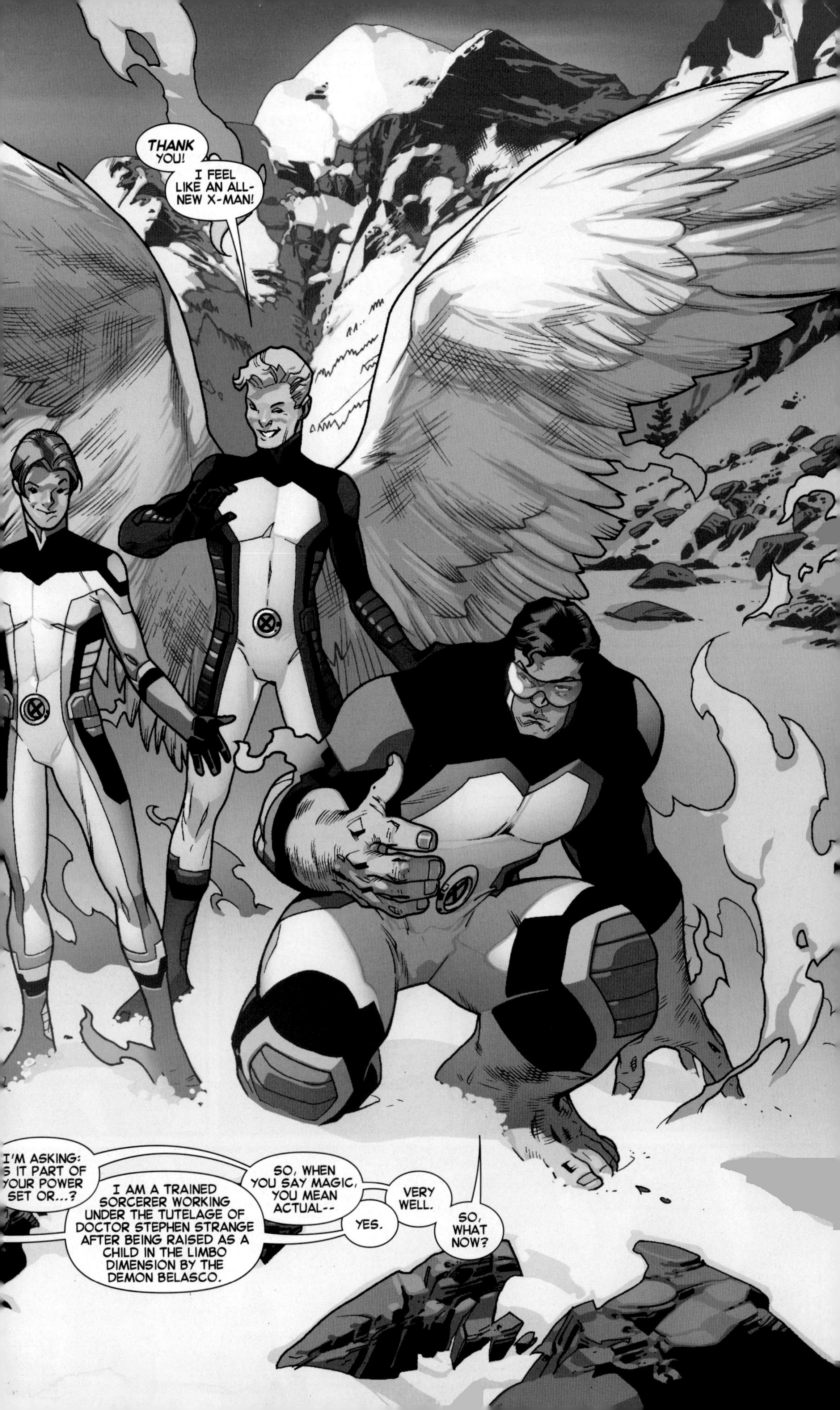
THANK YOU!
I FEEL LIKE AN ALL-NEW X-MAN!
I'M ASKING: S IT PART OF YOUR POWER SET OR...?
I AM A TRAINED SORCERER WORKING UNDER THE TUTELAGE OF DOCTOR STEPHEN STRANGE AFTER BEING RAISED AS A CHILD IN THE LIMBO DIMENSION BY THE DEMON BELASCO.
SO, WHEN YOU SAY MAGIC, YOU MEAN ACTUAL--
YES.
VERY WELL.
SO, WHAT NOW?

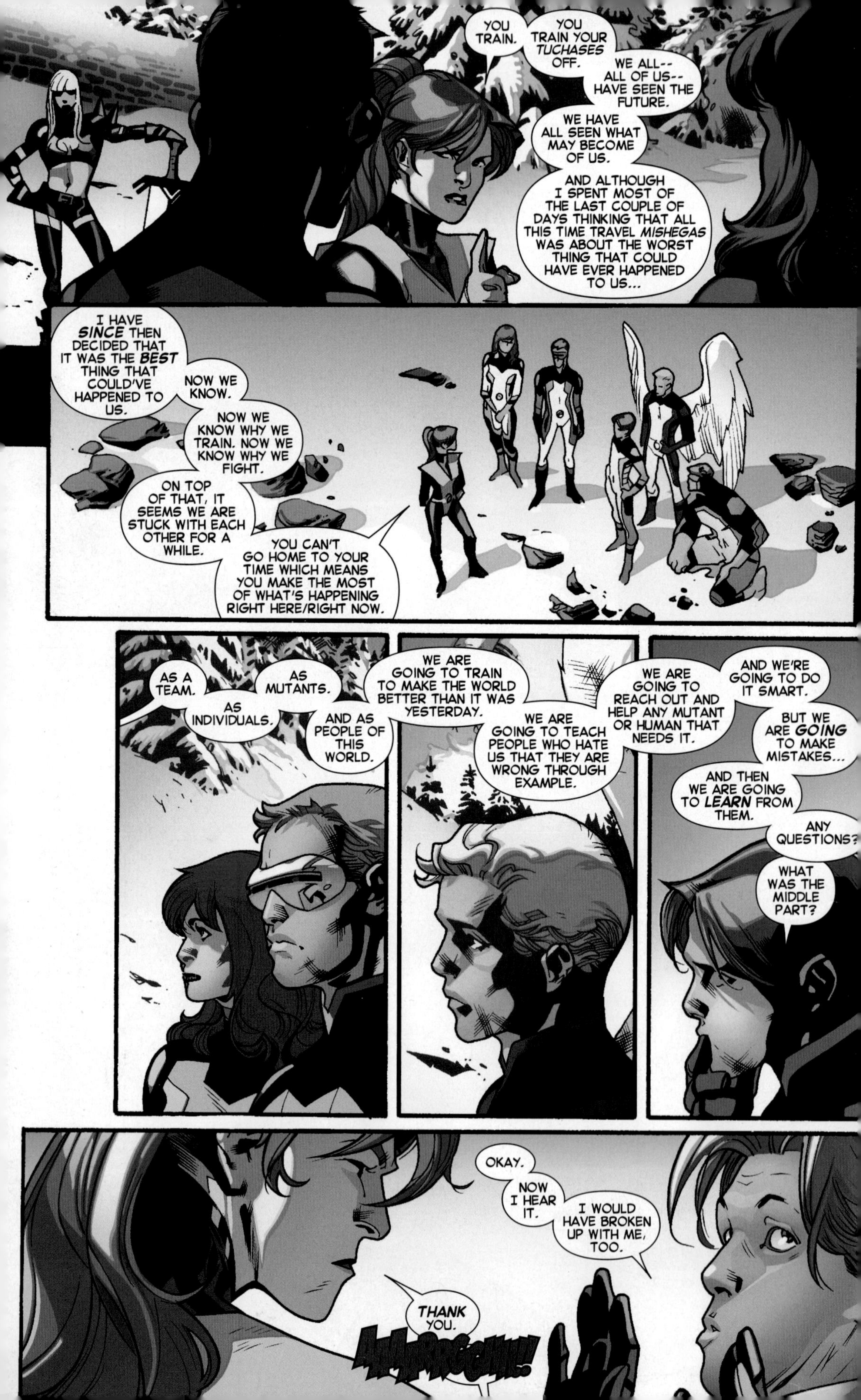
YOU TRAIN.
YOU TRAIN YOUR TUCHASES OFF.
WE ALL-- ALL OF US-- HAVE SEEN THE FUTURE.
WE HAVE ALL SEEN WHAT MAY BECOME OF US.
AND ALTHOUGH I SPENT MOST OF THE LAST COUPLE OF DAYS THINKING THAT ALL THIS TIME TRAVEL MISHEGAS WAS ABOUT THE WORST THING THAT COULD HAVE EVER HAPPENED TO US...
I HAVE SINCE THEN DECIDED THAT IT WAS THE BEST THING THAT COULD'VE HAPPENED TO US.
NOW WE KNOW.
NOW WE KNOW WHY WE TRAIN. NOW WE KNOW WHY WE FIGHT.
ON TOP OF THAT, IT SEEMS WE ARE STUCK WITH EACH OTHER FOR A WHILE.
YOU CAN'T GO HOME TO YOUR TIME WHICH MEANS YOU MAKE THE MOST OF WHAT'S HAPPENING RIGHT HERE/RIGHT NOW.
AS A TEAM.
AS INDIVIDUALS.
AS MUTANTS.
AND AS PEOPLE OF THIS WORLD.
WE ARE GOING TO TRAIN TO MAKE THE WORLD BETTER THAN IT WAS YESTERDAY.
WE ARE GOING TO TEACH PEOPLE WHO HATE US THAT THEY ARE WRONG THROUGH EXAMPLE.
WE ARE GOING TO REACH OUT AND HELP ANY MUTANT OR HUMAN THAT NEEDS IT.
AND WE'RE GOING TO DO IT SMART.
BUT WE ARE GOING TO MAKE MISTAKES...
AND THEN WE ARE GOING TO LEARN FROM THEM.
ANY QUESTIONS?
WHAT WAS THE MIDDLE PART?
OKAY.
NOW I HEAR IT.
I WOULD HAVE BROKEN UP WITH ME, TOO.
THANK YOU.

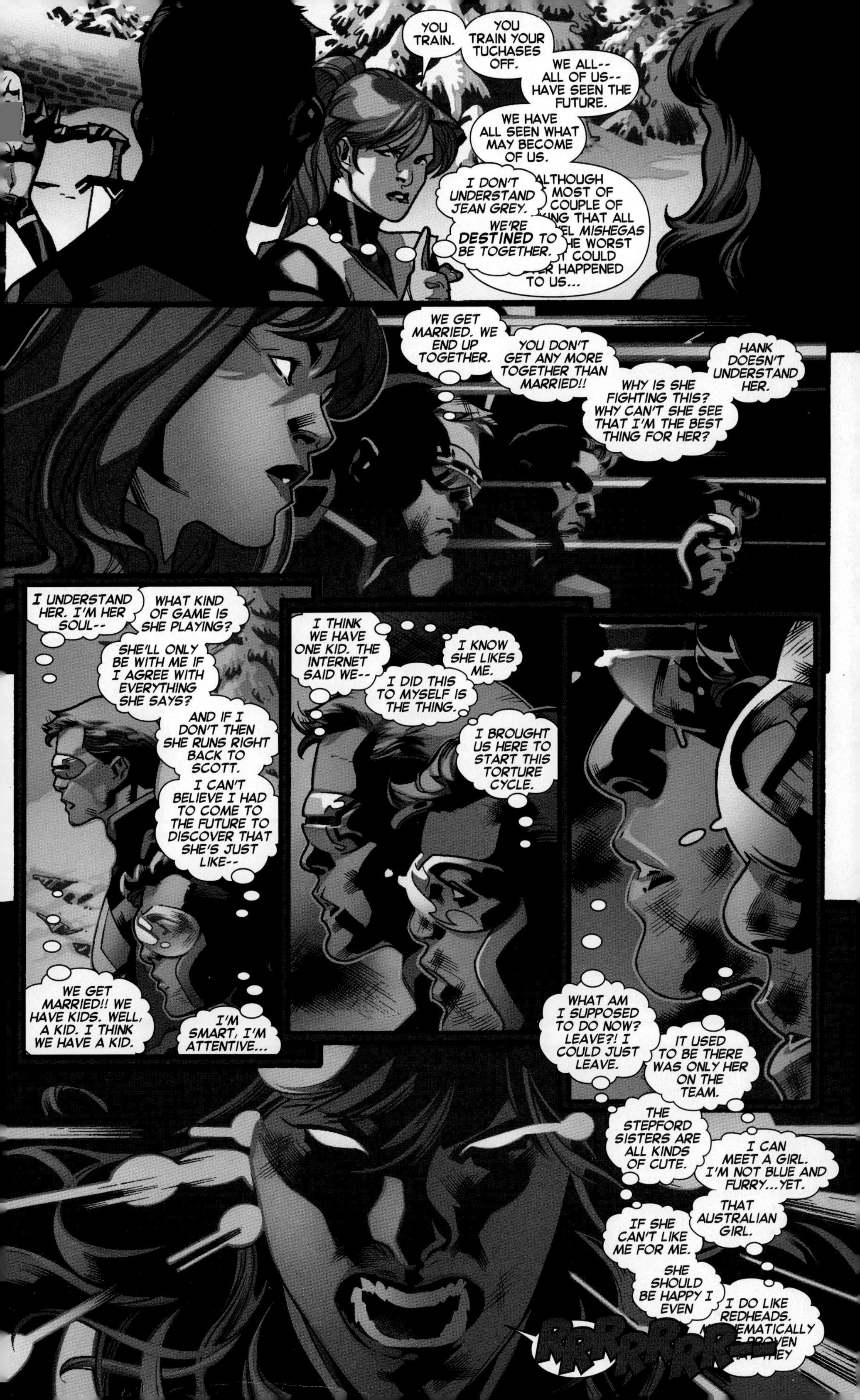
YOU TRAIN.
YOU TRAIN YOUR TUCHASES OFF.
WE ALL-- ALL OF US-- HAVE SEEN THE FUTURE.
WE HAVE ALL SEEN WHAT MAY BECOME OF US.
ALTHOUGH MOST OF COUPLE OF THAT ALL MISHEGAS THE WORST COULD HAPPENED TO US...
I DON'T UNDERSTAND JEAN GREY.
WE'RE **DESTINED** TO BE TOGETHER.
WE GET MARRIED. WE END UP TOGETHER.
YOU DON'T GET ANY MORE TOGETHER THAN MARRIED!!
WHY IS SHE FIGHTING THIS? WHY CAN'T SHE SEE THAT I'M THE BEST THING FOR HER?
HANK DOESN'T UNDERSTAND HER.
I UNDERSTAND HER. I'M HER SOUL--
WHAT KIND OF GAME IS SHE PLAYING?
SHE'LL ONLY BE WITH ME IF I AGREE WITH EVERYTHING SHE SAYS?
AND IF I DON'T THEN SHE RUNS RIGHT BACK TO SCOTT.
I CAN'T BELIEVE I HAD TO COME TO THE FUTURE TO DISCOVER THAT SHE'S JUST LIKE--
WE GET MARRIED!! WE HAVE KIDS. WELL, A KID. I THINK WE HAVE A KID.
I'M SMART, I'M ATTENTIVE...
I THINK WE HAVE ONE KID. THE INTERNET SAID WE--
I KNOW SHE LIKES ME.
I DID THIS TO MYSELF IS THE THING.
I BROUGHT US HERE TO START THIS TORTURE CYCLE.
WHAT AM I SUPPOSED TO DO NOW? LEAVE?! I COULD JUST LEAVE.
IT USED TO BE THERE WAS ONLY HER ON THE TEAM.
THE STEPFORD SISTERS ARE ALL KINDS OF CUTE.
I CAN MEET A GIRL. I'M NOT BLUE AND FURRY...YET.
THAT AUSTRALIAN GIRL.
IF SHE CAN'T LIKE ME FOR ME.
SHE SHOULD BE HAPPY I EVEN
I DO LIKE REDHEADS.
RRRRRRR--

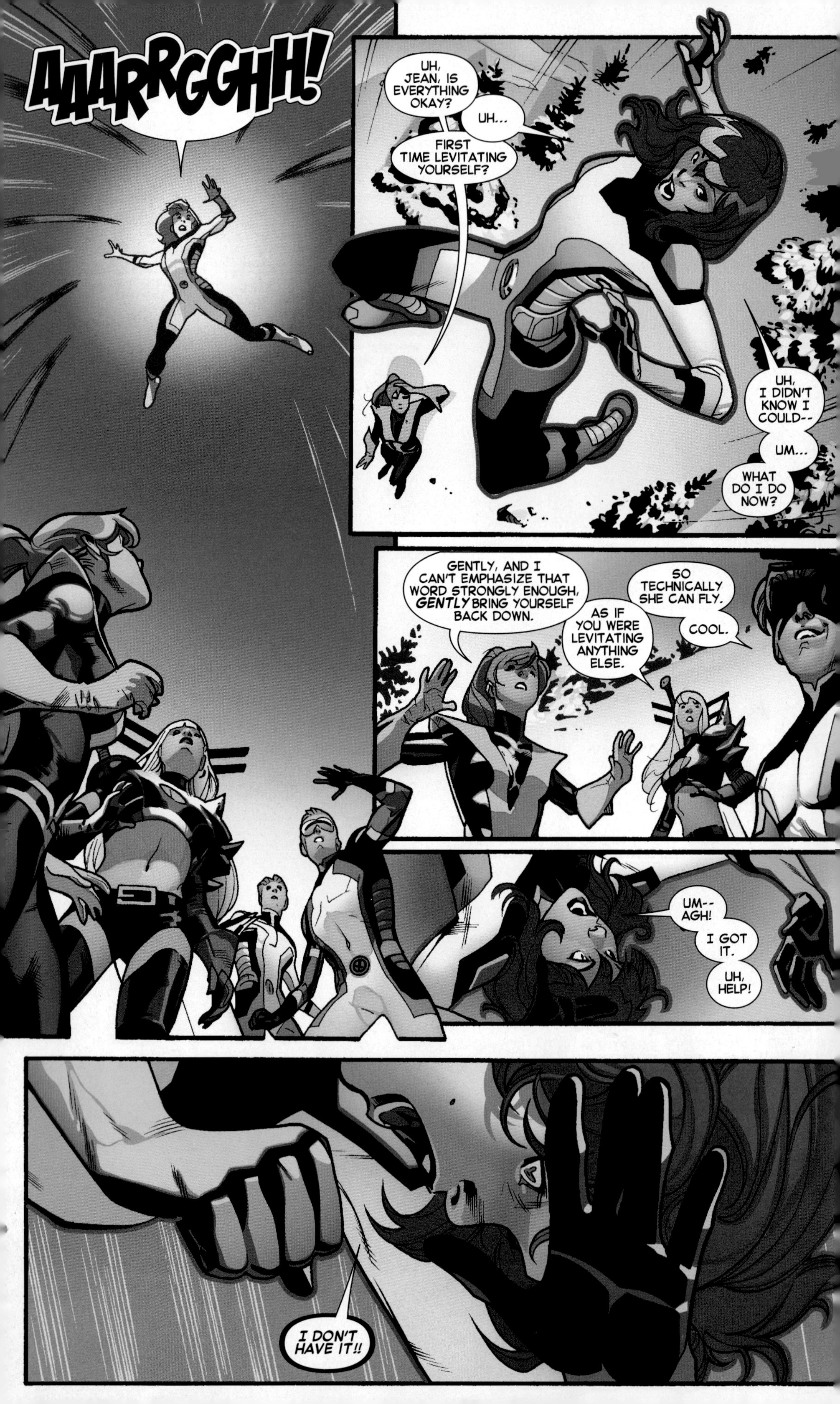
AAARRGGHH!
UH, JEAN, IS EVERYTHING OKAY?
UH...
FIRST TIME LEVITATING YOURSELF?
UH, I DIDN'T KNOW I COULD--
UM...
WHAT DO I DO NOW?
GENTLY, AND I CAN'T EMPHASIZE THAT WORD STRONGLY ENOUGH, GENTLY BRING YOURSELF BACK DOWN.
AS IF YOU WERE LEVITATING ANYTHING ELSE.
SO TECHNICALLY SHE CAN FLY.
COOL.
UM-- AGH!
I GOT IT.
UH, HELP!
I DON'T HAVE IT!!

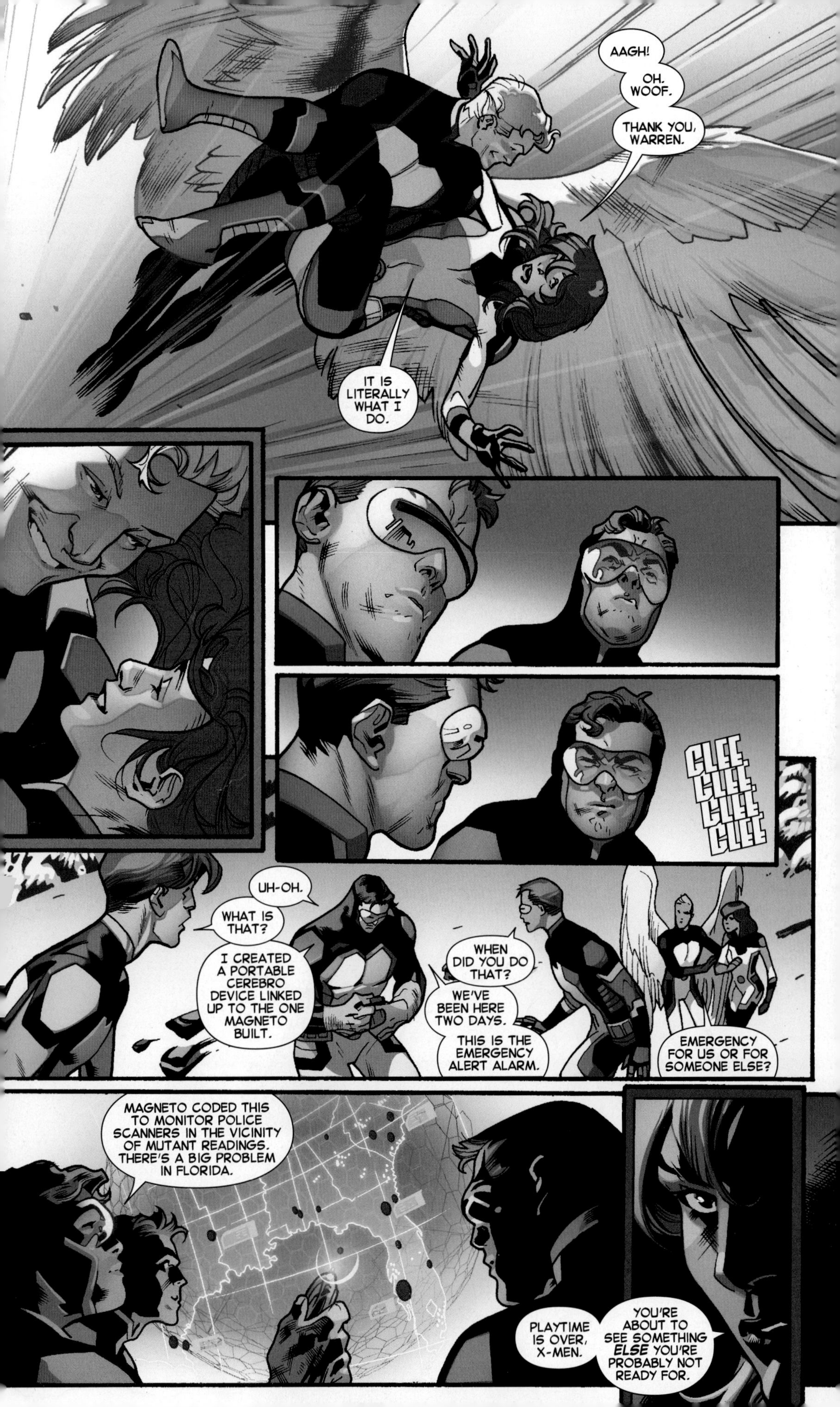
AAGH!
OH. WOOF.
THANK YOU, WARREN.
IT IS LITERALLY WHAT I DO.
CLEE CLEE CLEE CLEE
UH-OH.
WHAT IS THAT?
I CREATED A PORTABLE CEREBRO DEVICE LINKED UP TO THE ONE MAGNETO BUILT.
WHEN DID YOU DO THAT?
WE'VE BEEN HERE TWO DAYS.
THIS IS THE EMERGENCY ALERT ALARM.
EMERGENCY FOR US OR FOR SOMEONE ELSE?
MAGNETO CODED THIS TO MONITOR POLICE SCANNERS IN THE VICINITY OF MUTANT READINGS. THERE'S A BIG PROBLEM IN FLORIDA.
PLAYTIME IS OVER, X-MEN.
YOU'RE ABOUT TO SEE SOMETHING *ELSE* YOU'RE PROBABLY NOT READY FOR.

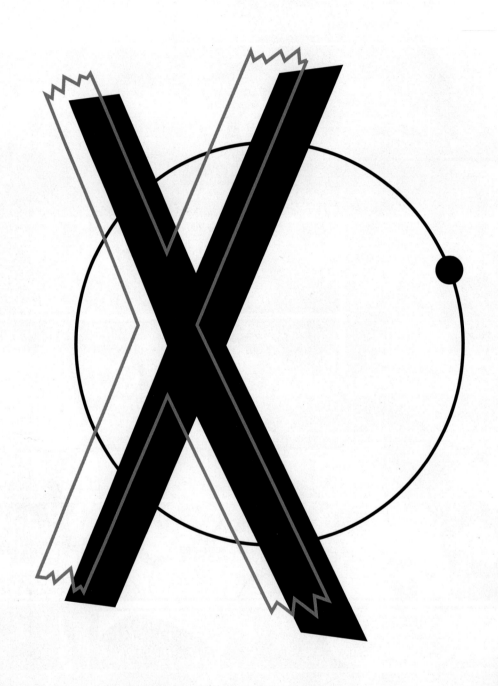

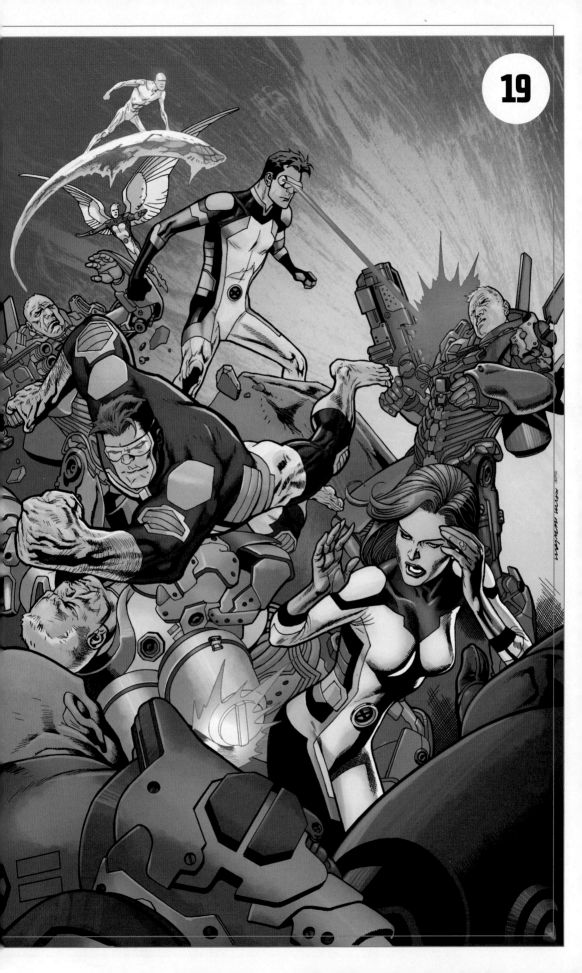

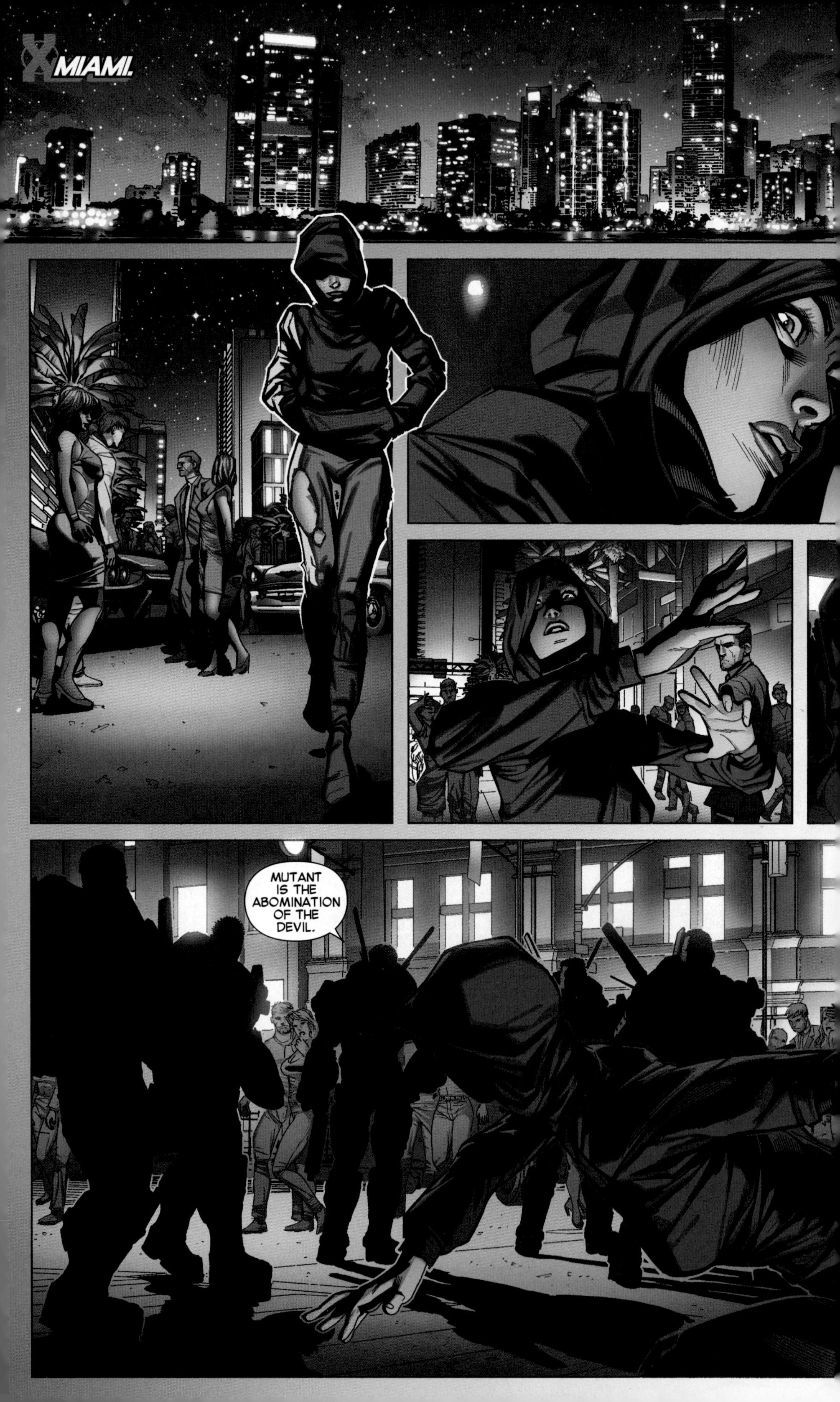
MIAMI.
MUTANT IS THE ABOMINATION OF THE DEVIL.

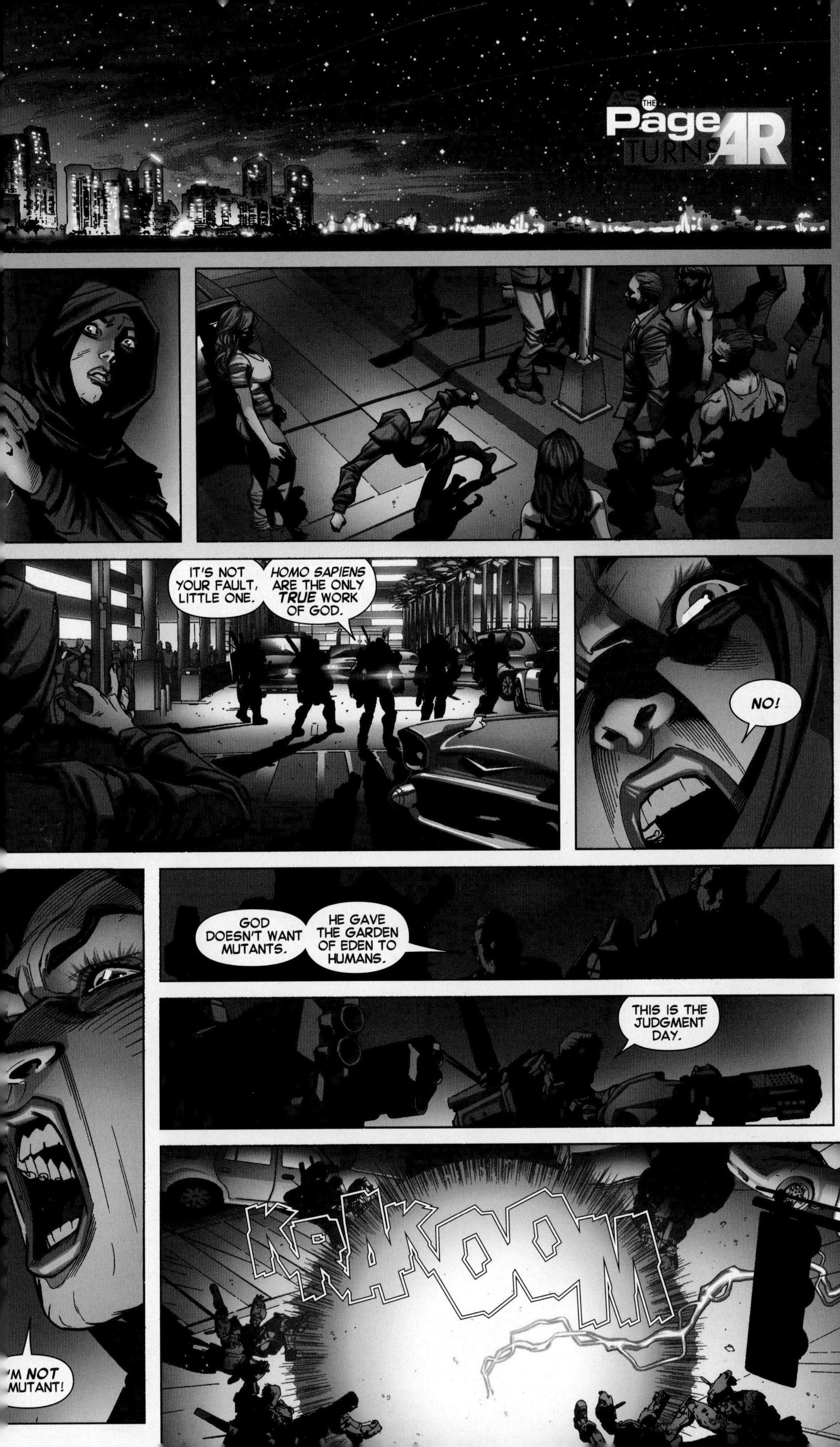

AS THE Page TURNS AR
IT'S NOT YOUR FAULT, LITTLE ONE.
HOMO SAPIENS ARE THE ONLY TRUE WORK OF GOD.
NO!
GOD DOESN'T WANT MUTANTS.
HE GAVE THE GARDEN OF EDEN TO HUMANS.
THIS IS THE JUDGMENT DAY.
KRAKOOM
'M NOT MUTANT!

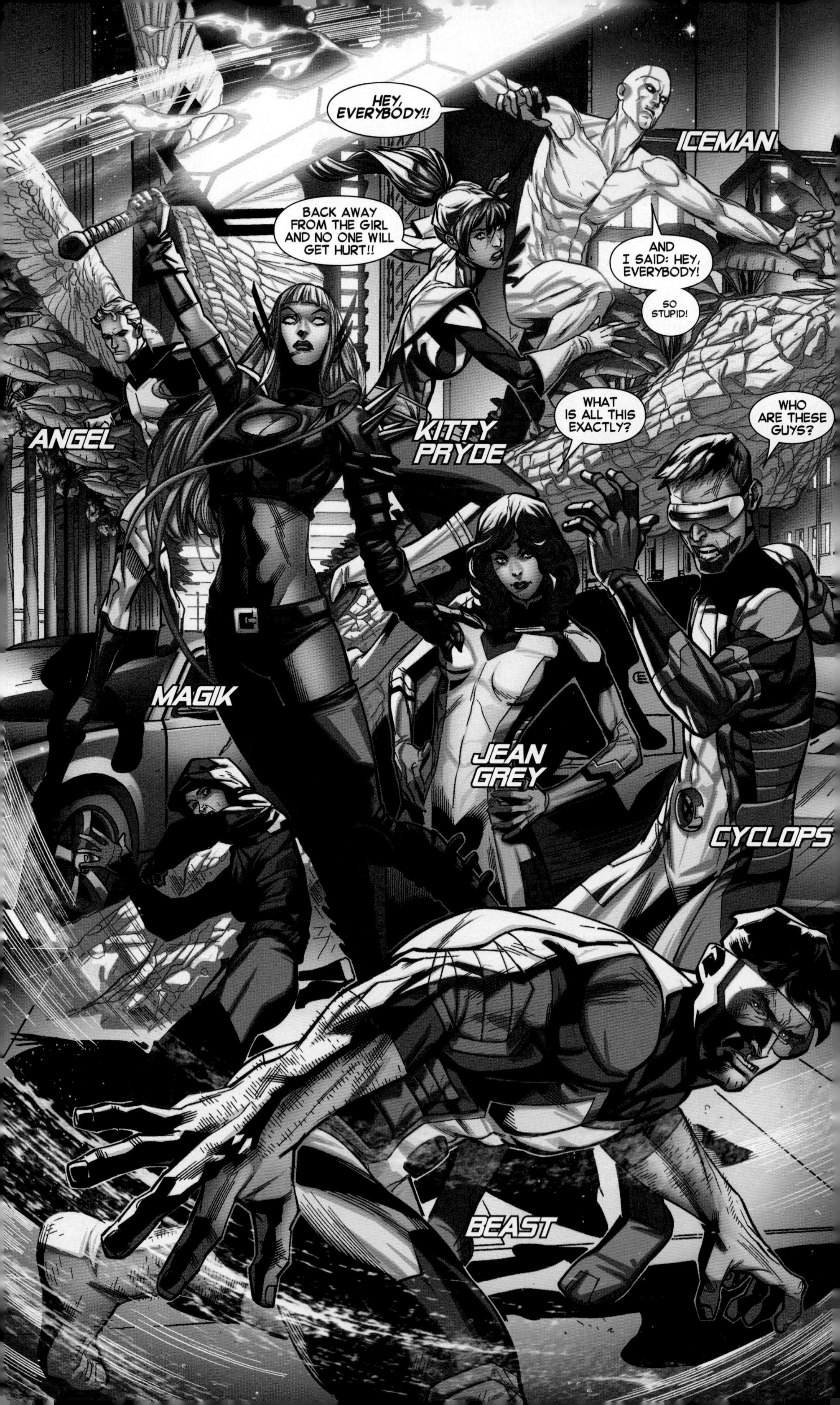
HEY, EVERYBODY!!
ICEMAN
BACK AWAY FROM THE GIRL AND NO ONE WILL GET HURT!!
AND I SAID: HEY, EVERYBODY!
SO STUPID!
WHAT IS ALL THIS EXACTLY?
WHO ARE THESE GUYS?
ANGEL
KITTY PRYDE
MAGIK
JEAN GREY
CYCLOPS
BEAST

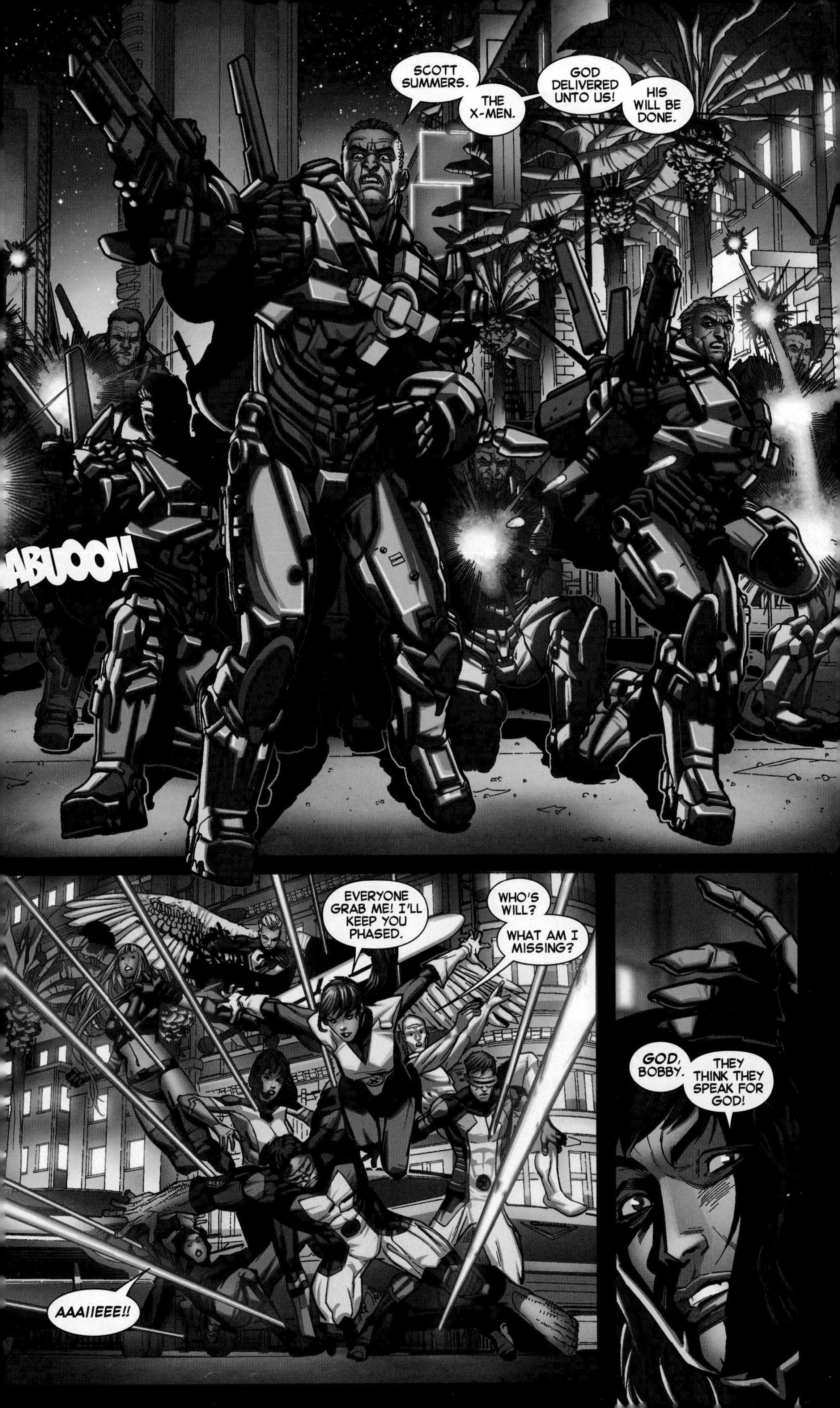
SCOTT SUMMERS.
THE X-MEN.
GOD DELIVERED UNTO US!
HIS WILL BE DONE.
ABUOOM
EVERYONE GRAB ME! I'LL KEEP YOU PHASED.
WHO'S WILL?
WHAT AM I MISSING?
AAAIIEEE!!
GOD, BOBBY.
THEY THINK THEY SPEAK FOR GOD!

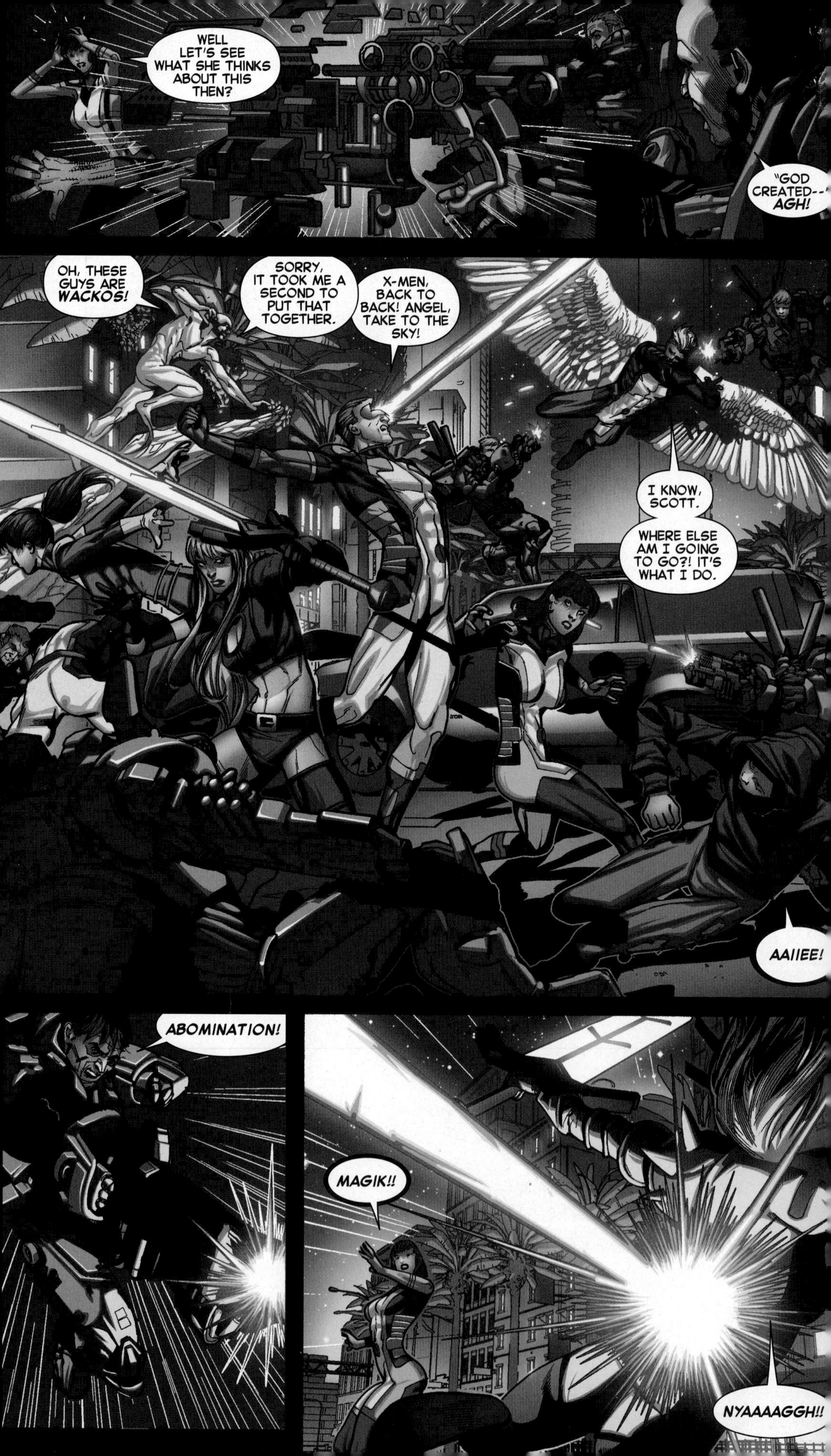
WELL LET'S SEE WHAT SHE THINKS ABOUT THIS THEN?
"GOD CREATED-- AGH!
OH, THESE GUYS ARE WACKOS!
SORRY, IT TOOK ME A SECOND TO PUT THAT TOGETHER.
X-MEN, BACK TO BACK! ANGEL, TAKE TO THE SKY!
I KNOW, SCOTT.
WHERE ELSE AM I GOING TO GO?! IT'S WHAT I DO.
AAIIEE!
ABOMINATION!
MAGIK!!
NYAAAAGGH!!

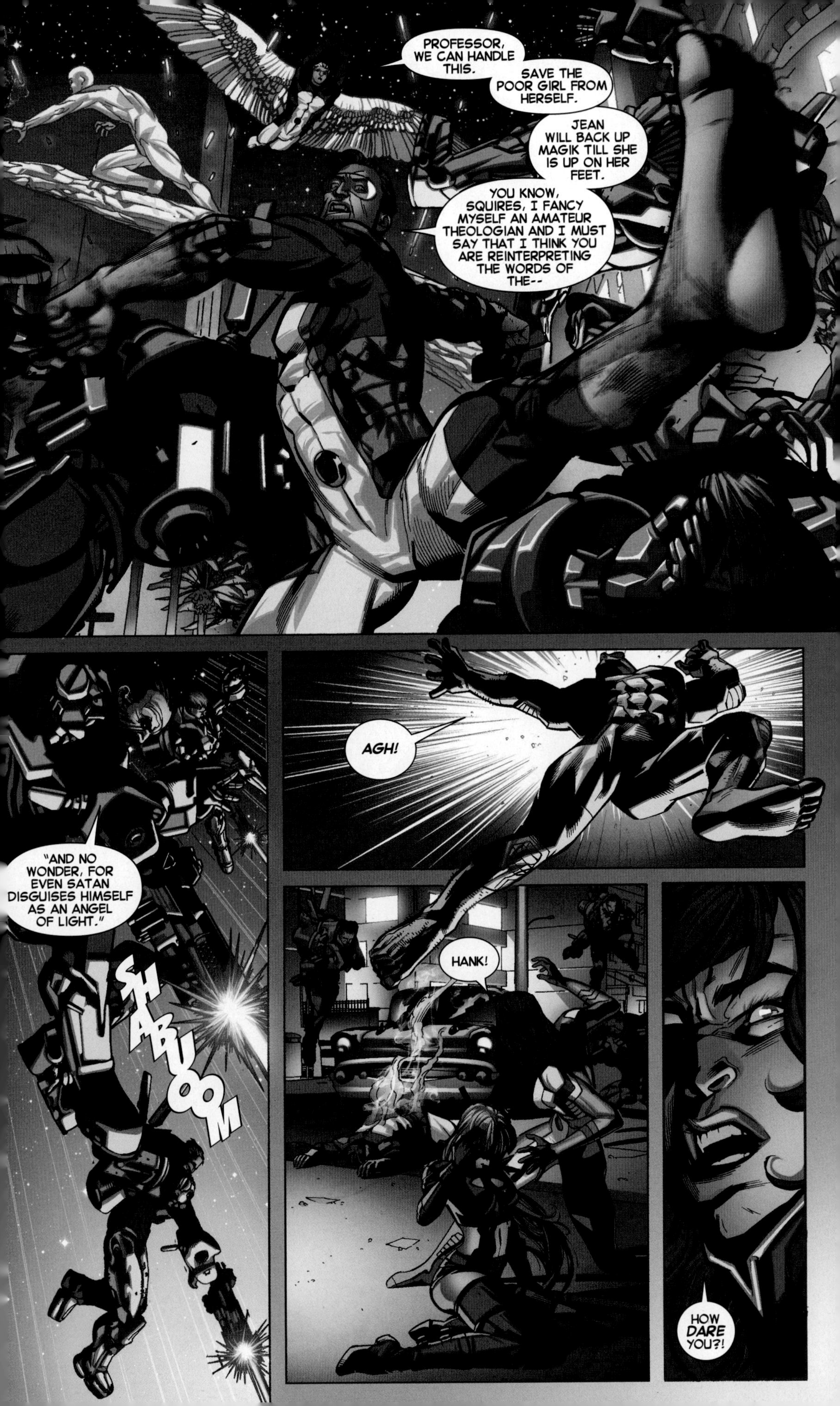

PROFESSOR, WE CAN HANDLE THIS.
SAVE THE POOR GIRL FROM HERSELF.
JEAN WILL BACK UP MAGIK TILL SHE IS UP ON HER FEET.
YOU KNOW, SQUIRES, I FANCY MYSELF AN AMATEUR THEOLOGIAN AND I MUST SAY THAT I THINK YOU ARE REINTERPRETING THE WORDS OF THE--
"AND NO WONDER, FOR EVEN SATAN DISGUISES HIMSELF AS AN ANGEL OF LIGHT."
SHABUOOM
AGH!
HANK!
HOW DARE YOU?!

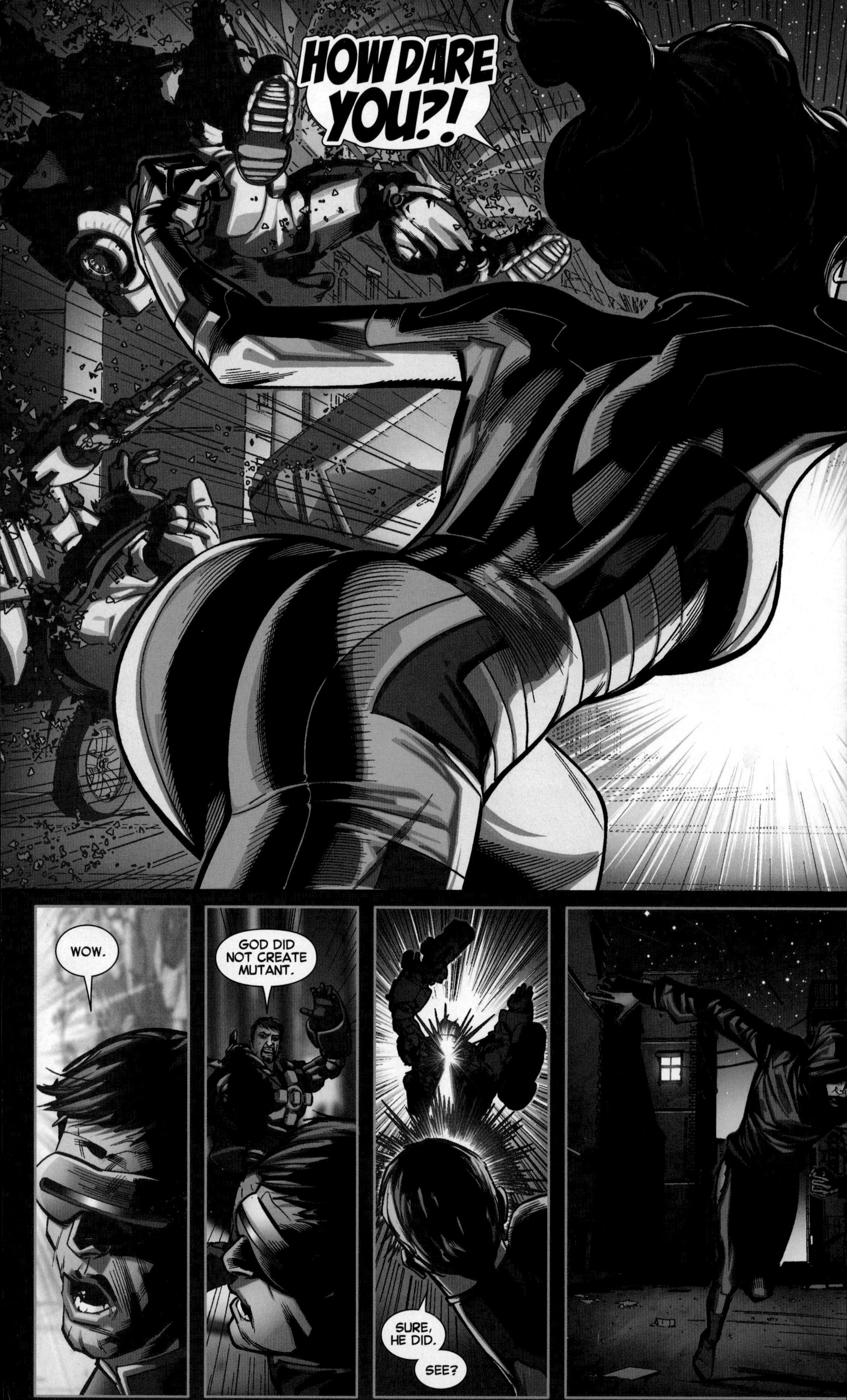
HOW DARE YOU?!
WOW.
GOD DID NOT CREATE MUTANT.
SURE, HE DID.
SEE?

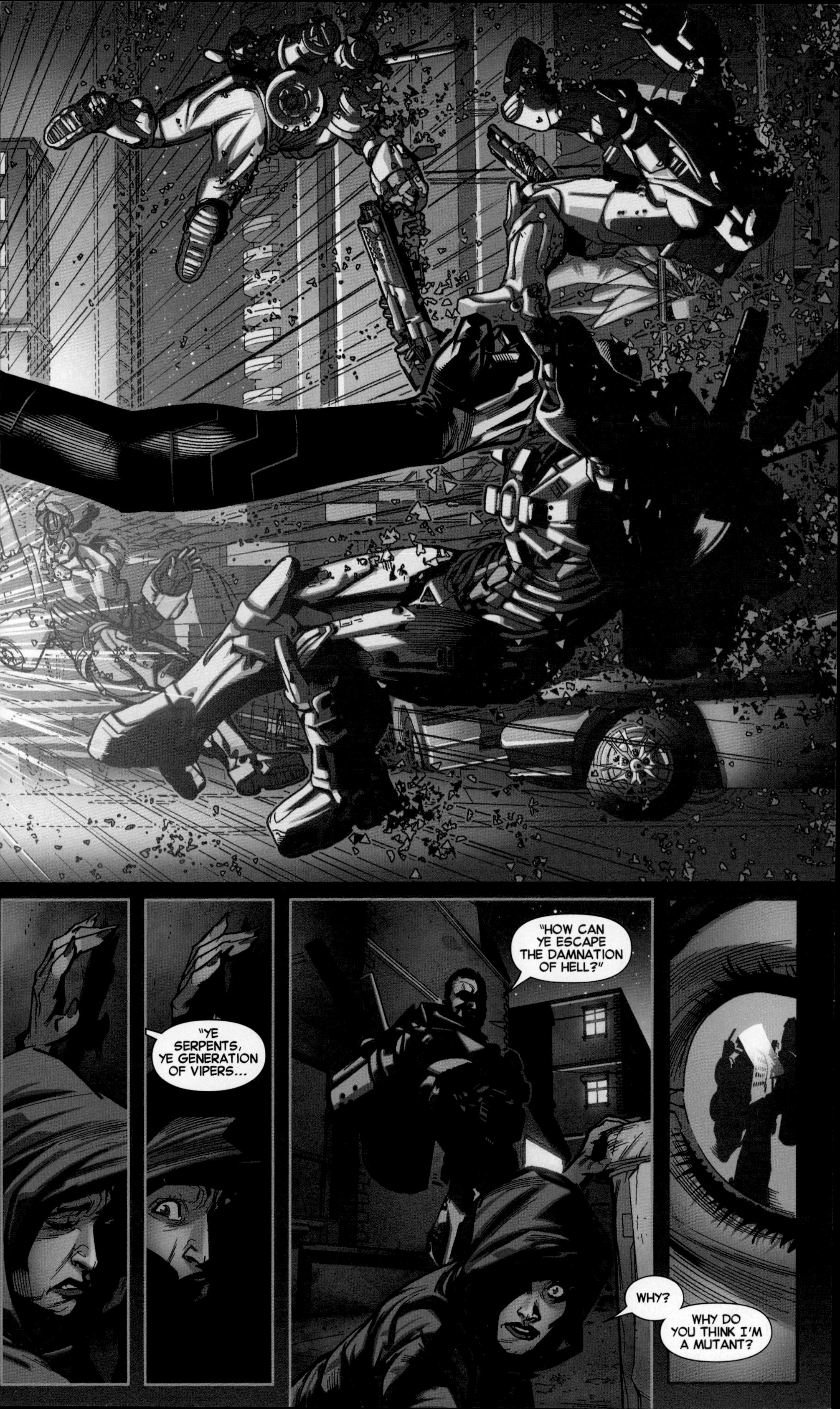

"YE SERPENTS, YE GENERATION OF VIPERS...
"HOW CAN YE ESCAPE THE DAMNATION OF HELL?"
WHY?
WHY DO YOU THINK I'M A MUTANT?

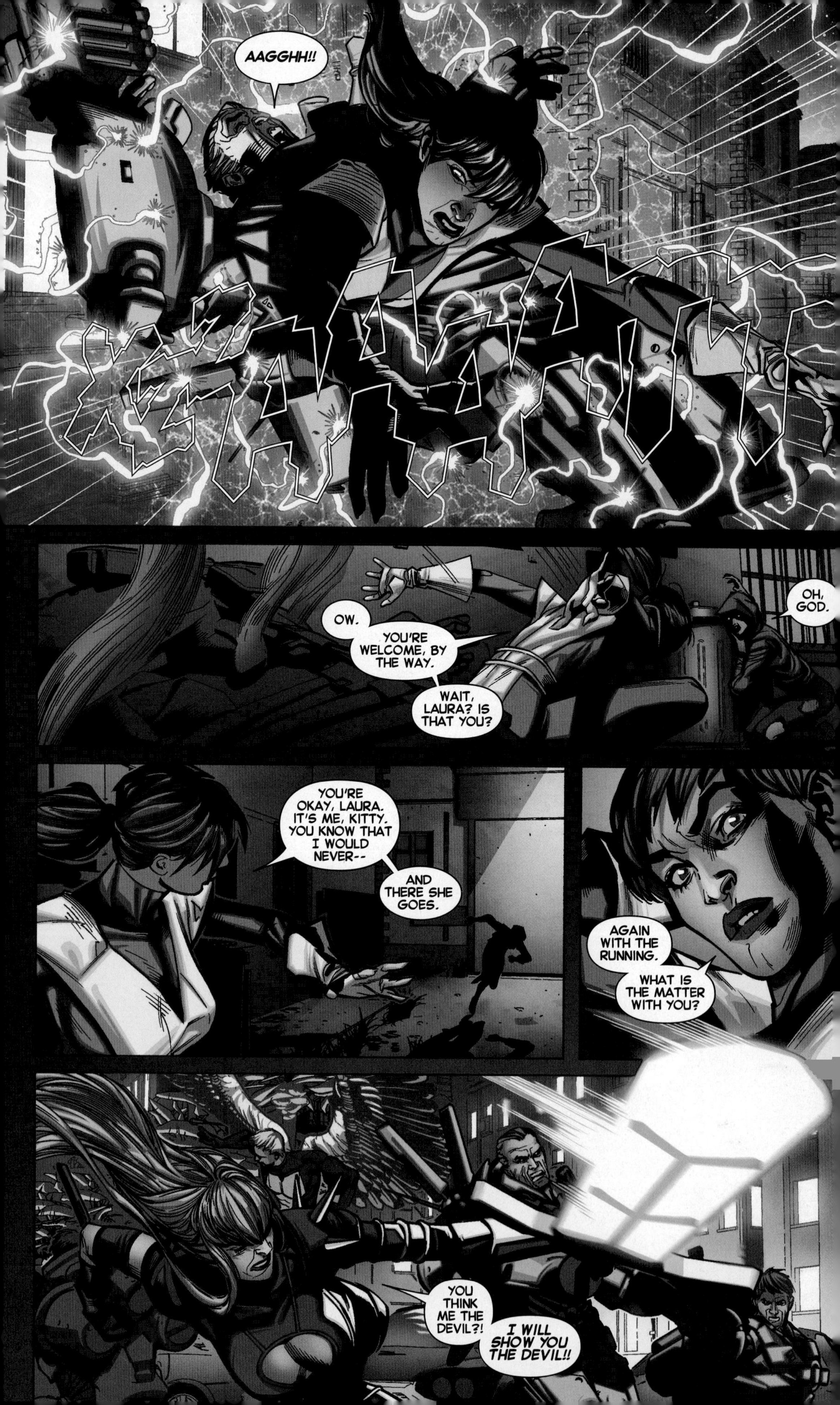
AAGGHH!!
OW.
YOU'RE WELCOME, BY THE WAY.
WAIT, LAURA? IS THAT YOU?
OH, GOD.
YOU'RE OKAY, LAURA. IT'S ME, KITTY. YOU KNOW THAT I WOULD NEVER--
AND THERE SHE GOES.
AGAIN WITH THE RUNNING.
WHAT IS THE MATTER WITH YOU?
YOU THINK ME THE DEVIL?!
I WILL SHOW YOU THE DEVIL!!

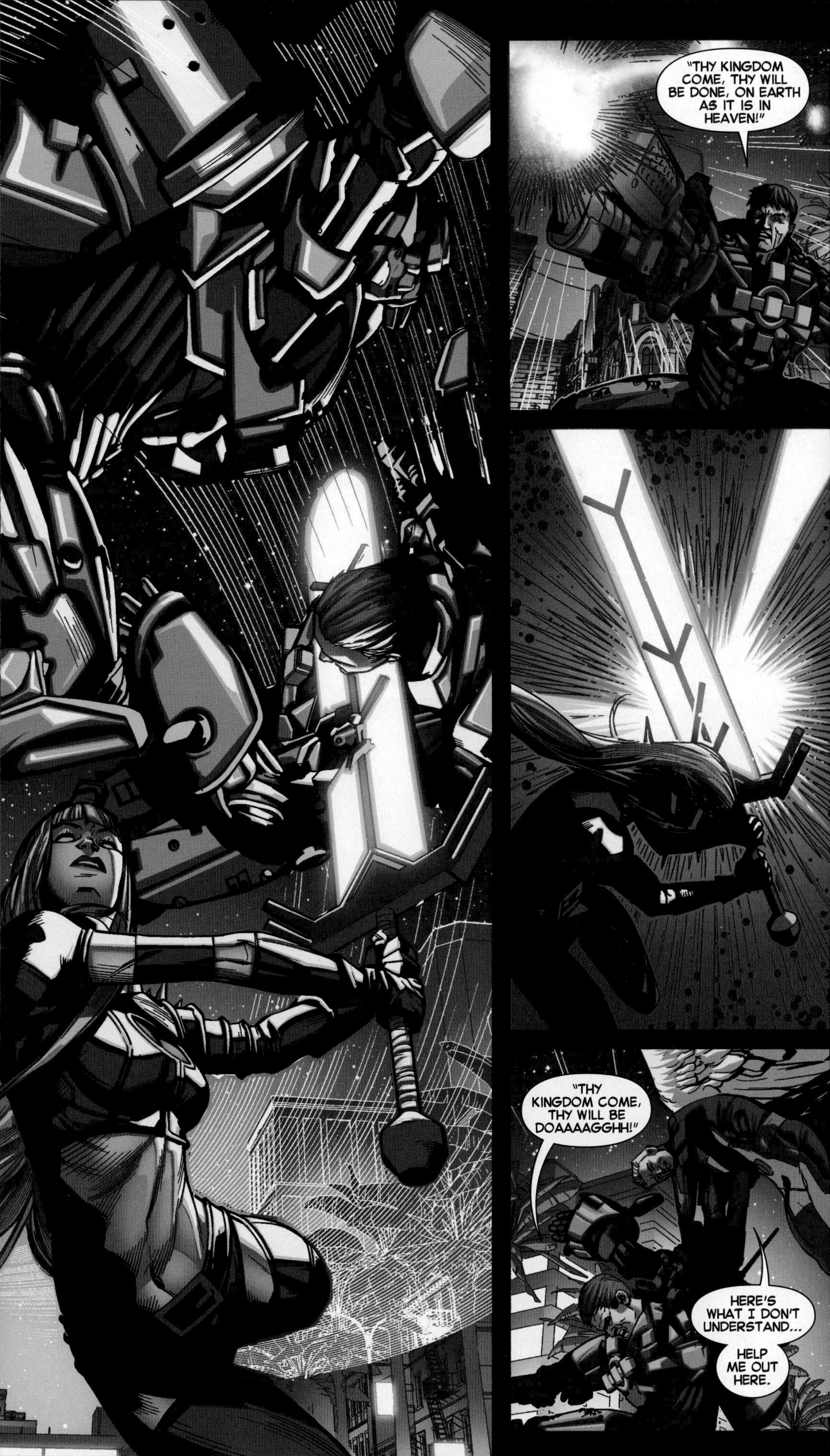
"THY KINGDOM COME, THY WILL BE DONE, ON EARTH AS IT IS IN HEAVEN!"
"THY KINGDOM COME, THY WILL BE DOAAAAGGHH!"
HERE'S WHAT I DON'T UNDERSTAND...
HELP ME OUT HERE.

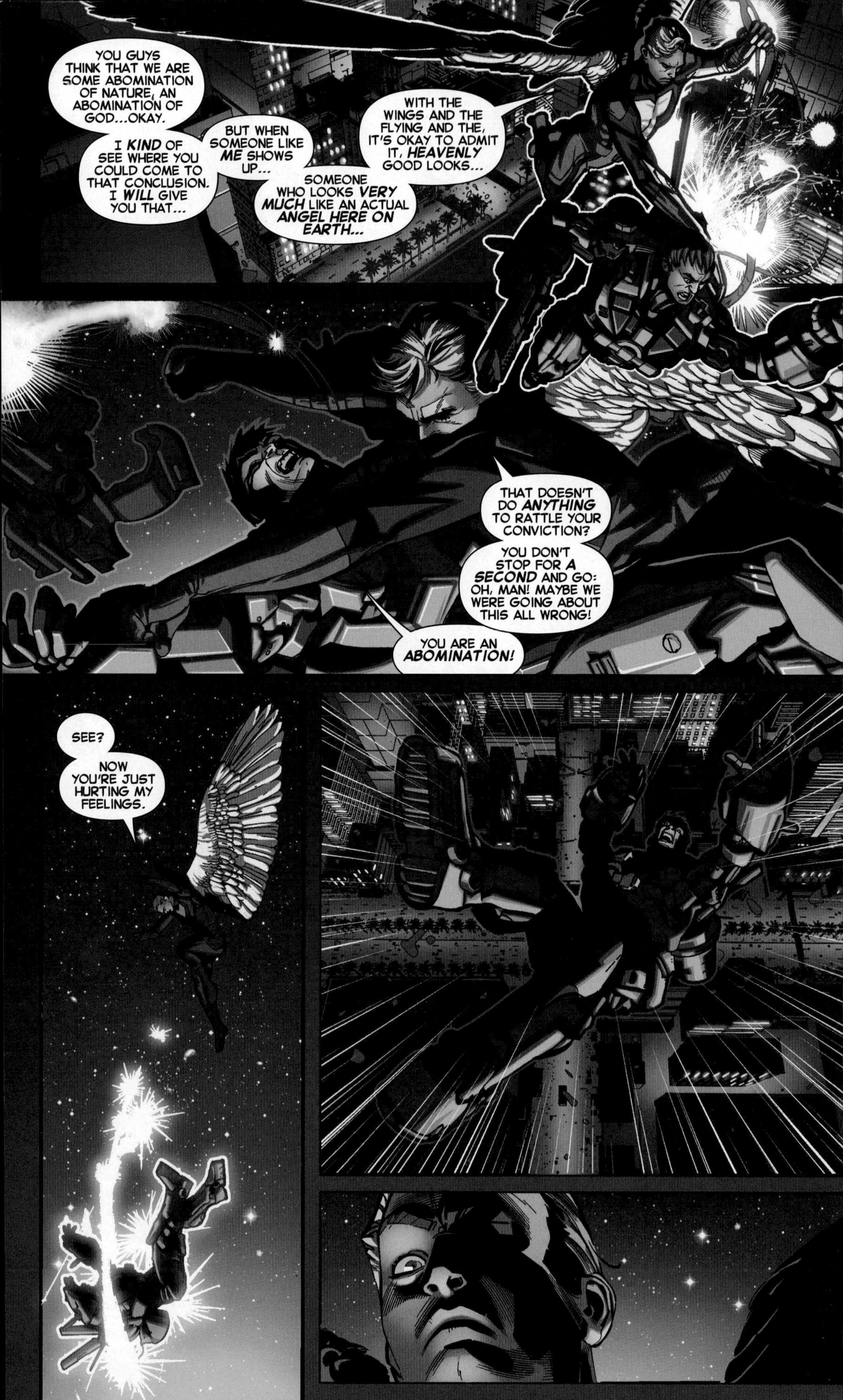
YOU GUYS THINK THAT WE ARE SOME ABOMINATION OF NATURE, AN ABOMINATION OF GOD...OKAY.
I KIND OF SEE WHERE YOU COULD COME TO THAT CONCLUSION. I WILL GIVE YOU THAT...
BUT WHEN SOMEONE LIKE ME SHOWS UP...
SOMEONE WHO LOOKS VERY MUCH LIKE AN ACTUAL ANGEL HERE ON EARTH...
WITH THE WINGS AND THE FLYING AND THE, IT'S OKAY TO ADMIT IT, HEAVENLY GOOD LOOKS...
THAT DOESN'T DO ANYTHING TO RATTLE YOUR CONVICTION?
YOU DON'T STOP FOR A SECOND AND GO: OH, MAN! MAYBE WE WERE GOING ABOUT THIS ALL WRONG!
YOU ARE AN ABOMINATION!
SEE?
NOW YOU'RE JUST HURTING MY FEELINGS.

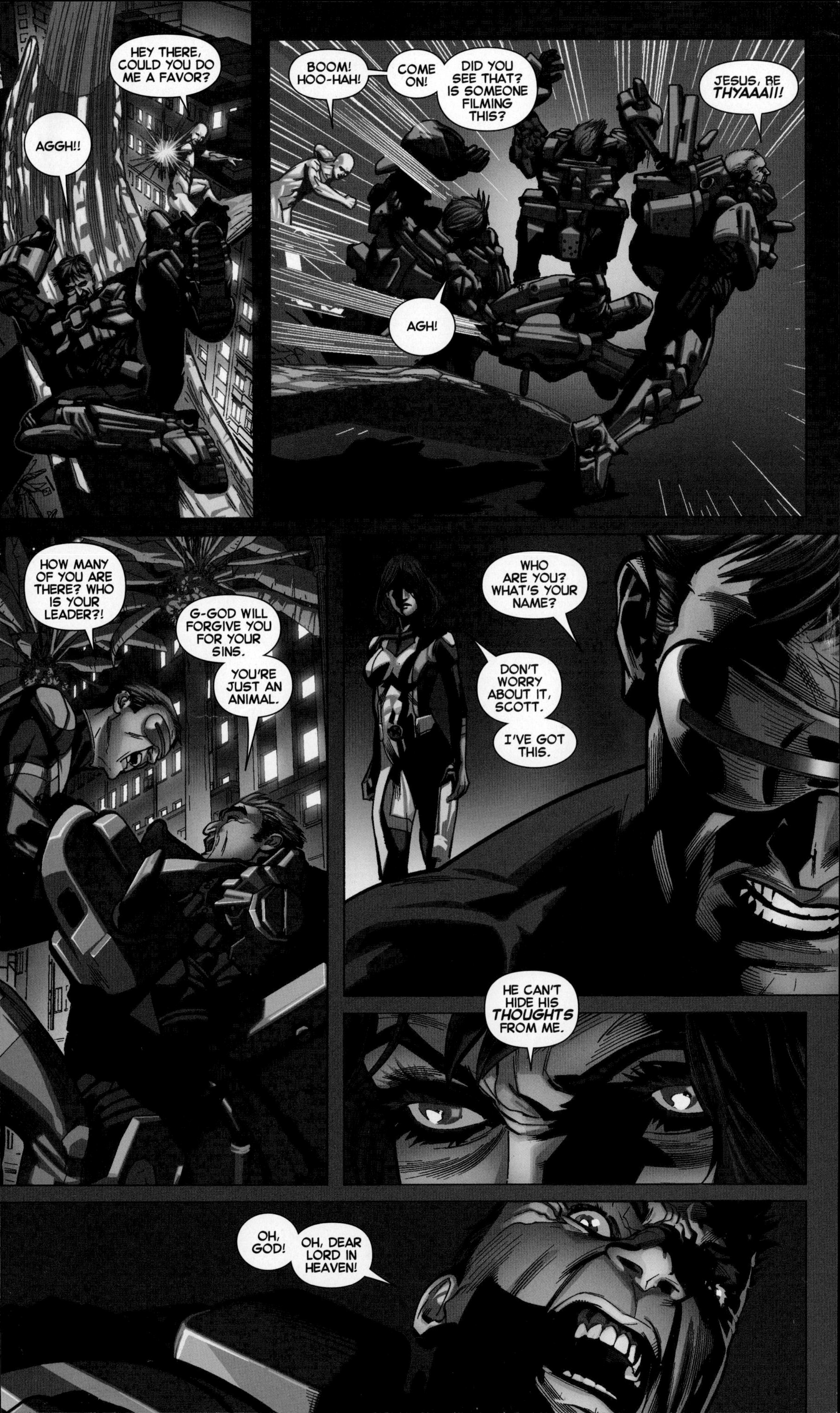
HEY THERE, COULD YOU DO ME A FAVOR?
AGGH!!
BOOM! HOO-HAH!
COME ON!
DID YOU SEE THAT? IS SOMEONE FILMING THIS?
JESUS, BE THYAAAII!
AGH!
HOW MANY OF YOU ARE THERE? WHO IS YOUR LEADER?!
G-GOD WILL FORGIVE YOU FOR YOUR SINS.
YOU'RE JUST AN ANIMAL.
WHO ARE YOU? WHAT'S YOUR NAME?
DON'T WORRY ABOUT IT, SCOTT.
I'VE GOT THIS.
HE CAN'T HIDE HIS THOUGHTS FROM ME.
OH, GOD!
OH, DEAR LORD IN HEAVEN!

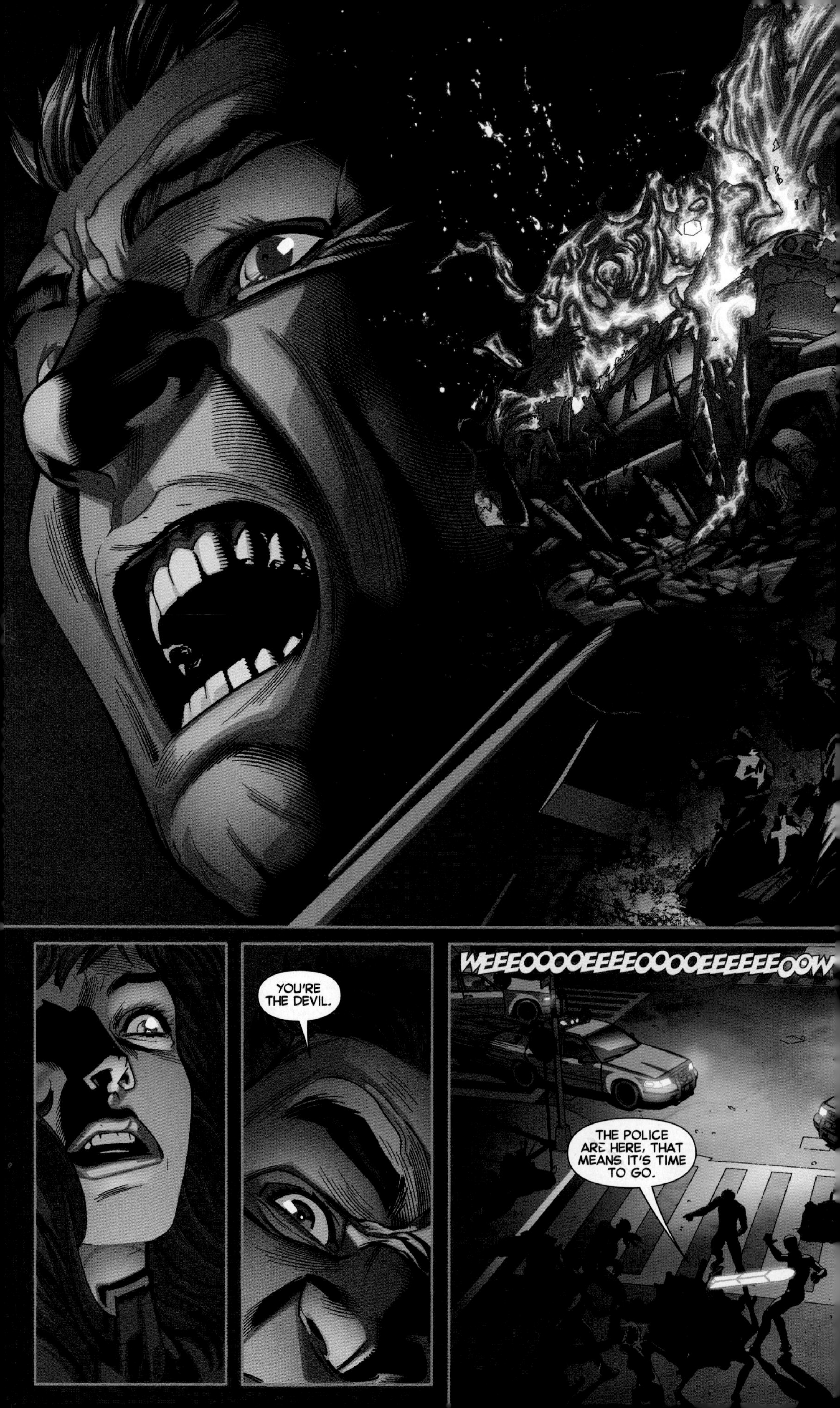
YOU'RE THE DEVIL.
WEEEOOOOEEEEOOOOEEEEEEOOW
THE POLICE ARE HERE, THAT MEANS IT'S TIME TO GO.

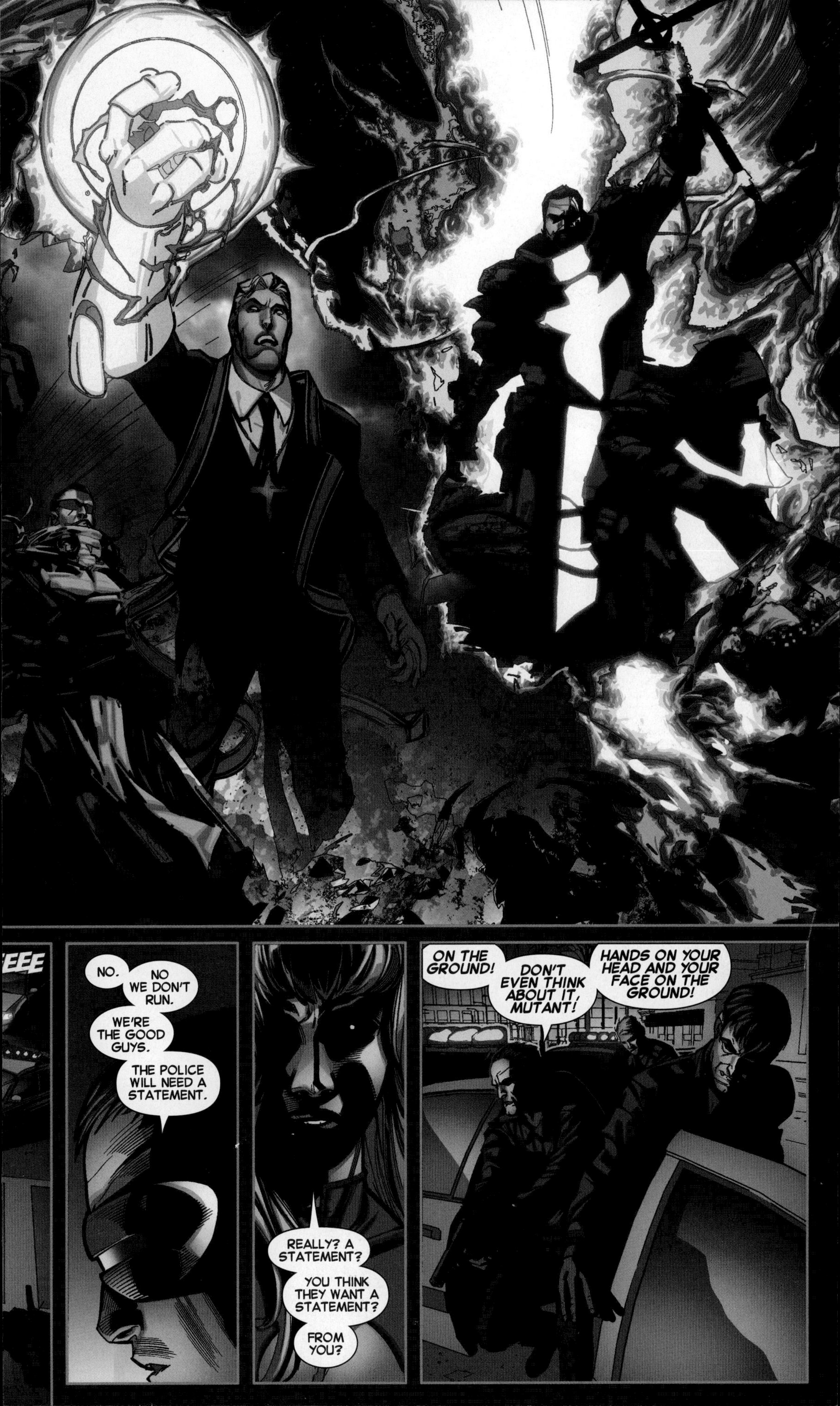
EEEE
NO.
NO WE DON'T RUN.
WE'RE THE GOOD GUYS.
THE POLICE WILL NEED A STATEMENT.
REALLY? A STATEMENT?
YOU THINK THEY WANT A STATEMENT?
FROM YOU?
ON THE GROUND!
DON'T EVEN THINK ABOUT IT, MUTANT!
HANDS ON YOUR HEAD AND YOUR FACE ON THE GROUND!

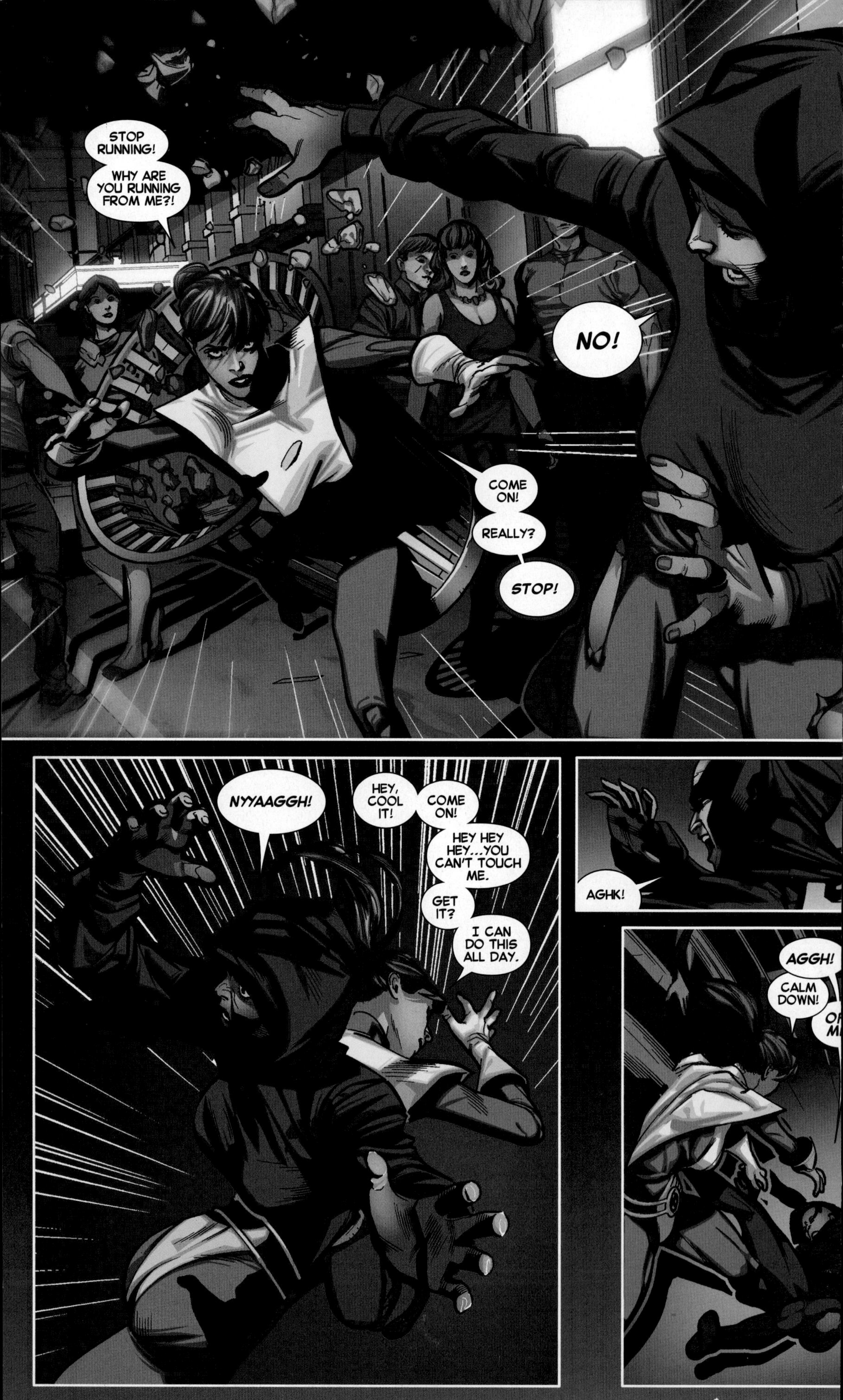

STOP RUNNING!
WHY ARE YOU RUNNING FROM ME?!
NO!
COME ON!
REALLY?
STOP!
NYYAAGGH!
HEY, COOL IT!
COME ON!
HEY HEY HEY...YOU CAN'T TOUCH ME.
GET IT?
I CAN DO THIS ALL DAY.
AGHK!
AGGH!
CALM DOWN!

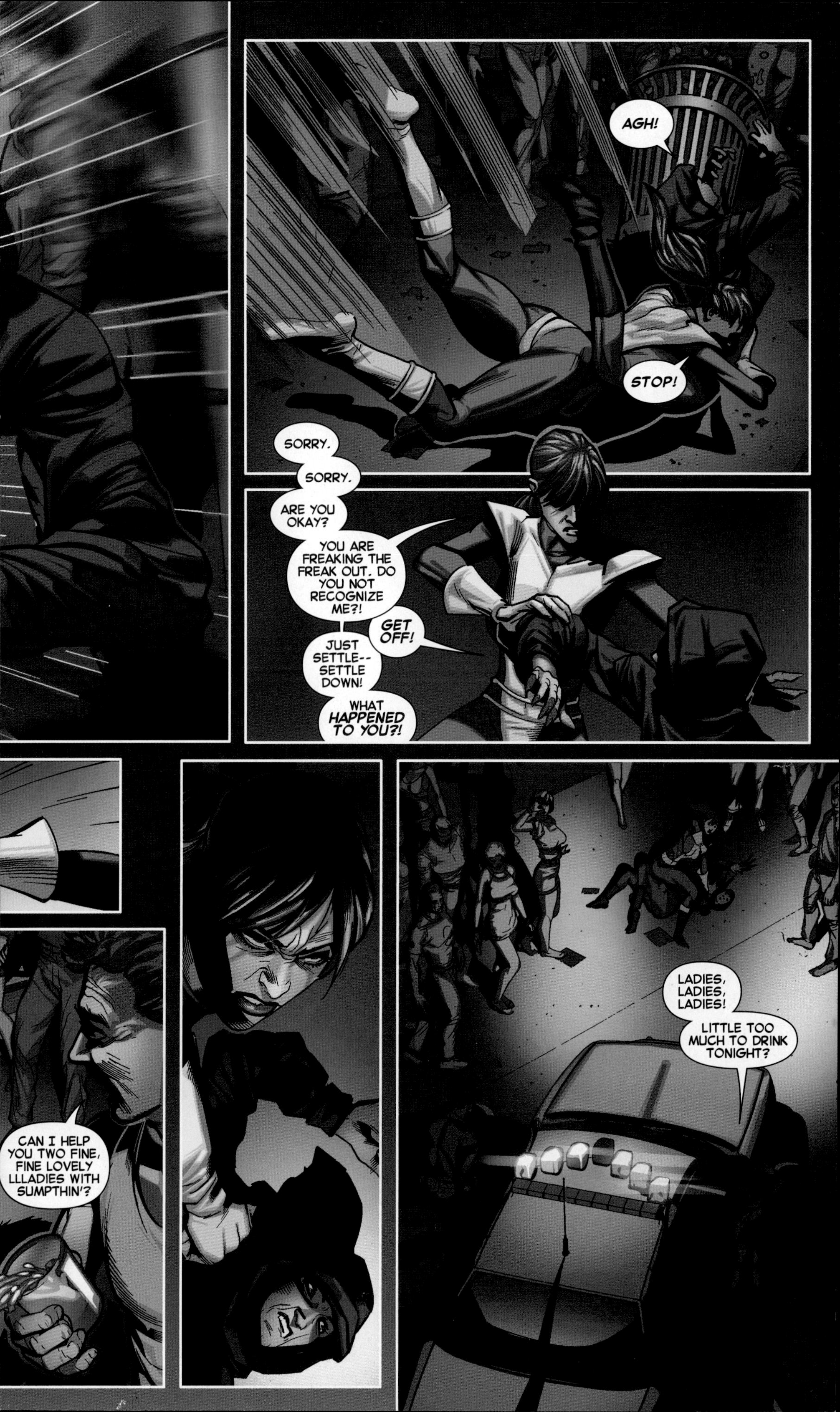
AGH!
STOP!
SORRY.
SORRY.
ARE YOU OKAY?
YOU ARE FREAKING THE FREAK OUT. DO YOU NOT RECOGNIZE ME?!
GET OFF!
JUST SETTLE-- SETTLE DOWN!
WHAT HAPPENED TO YOU?!
CAN I HELP YOU TWO FINE, FINE LOVELY LLLADIES WITH SUMPTHIN'?
LADIES, LADIES, LADIES!
LITTLE TOO MUCH TO DRINK TONIGHT?

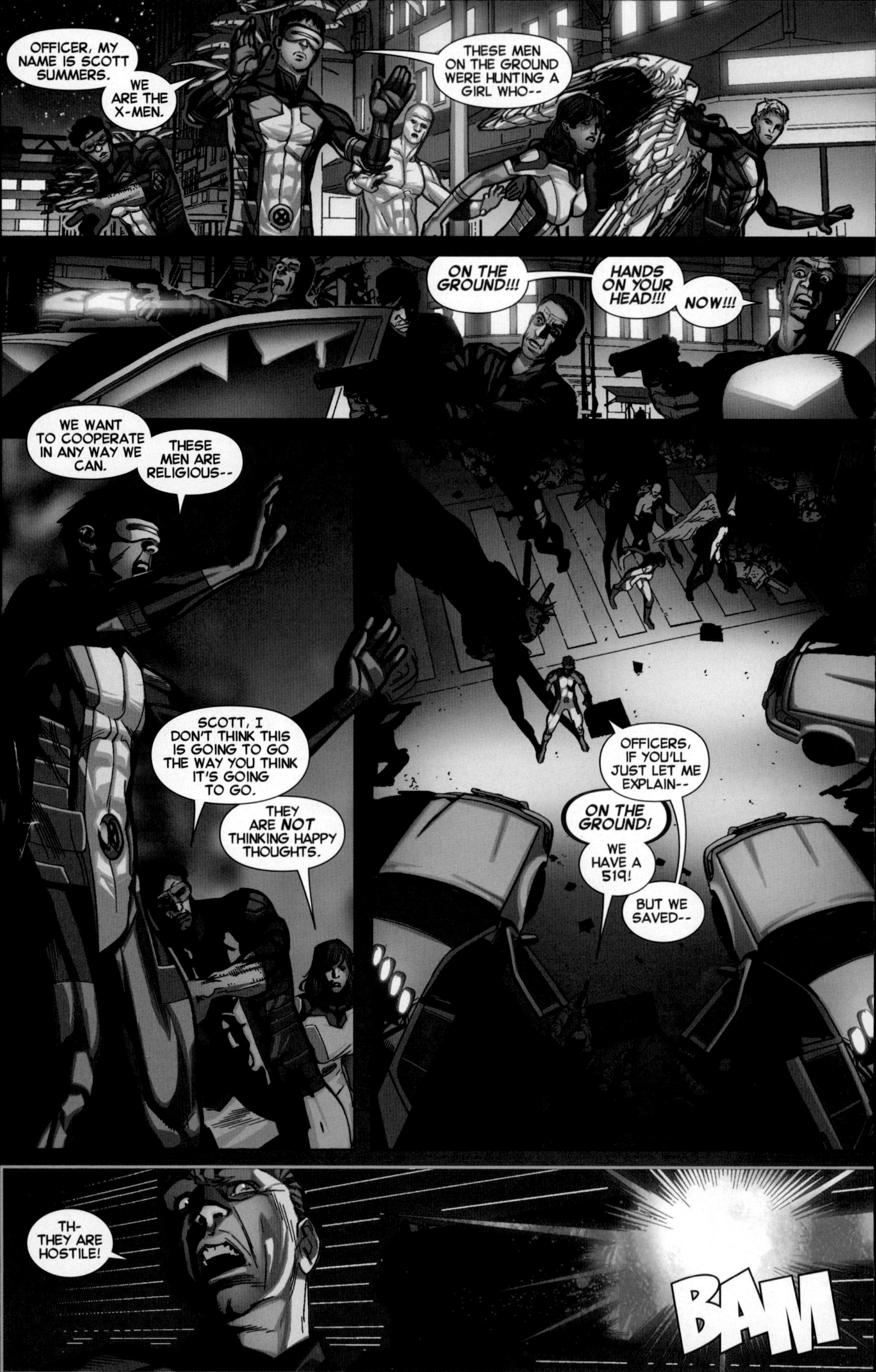
OFFICER, MY NAME IS SCOTT SUMMERS.
WE ARE THE X-MEN.
THESE MEN ON THE GROUND WERE HUNTING A GIRL WHO--
ON THE GROUND!!!
HANDS ON YOUR HEAD!!!
NOW!!!
WE WANT TO COOPERATE IN ANY WAY WE CAN.
THESE MEN ARE RELIGIOUS--
SCOTT, I DON'T THINK THIS IS GOING TO GO THE WAY YOU THINK IT'S GOING TO GO.
THEY ARE NOT THINKING HAPPY THOUGHTS.
OFFICERS, IF YOU'LL JUST LET ME EXPLAIN--
ON THE GROUND!
WE HAVE A 519!
BUT WE SAVED--
TH- THEY ARE HOSTILE!
BAM

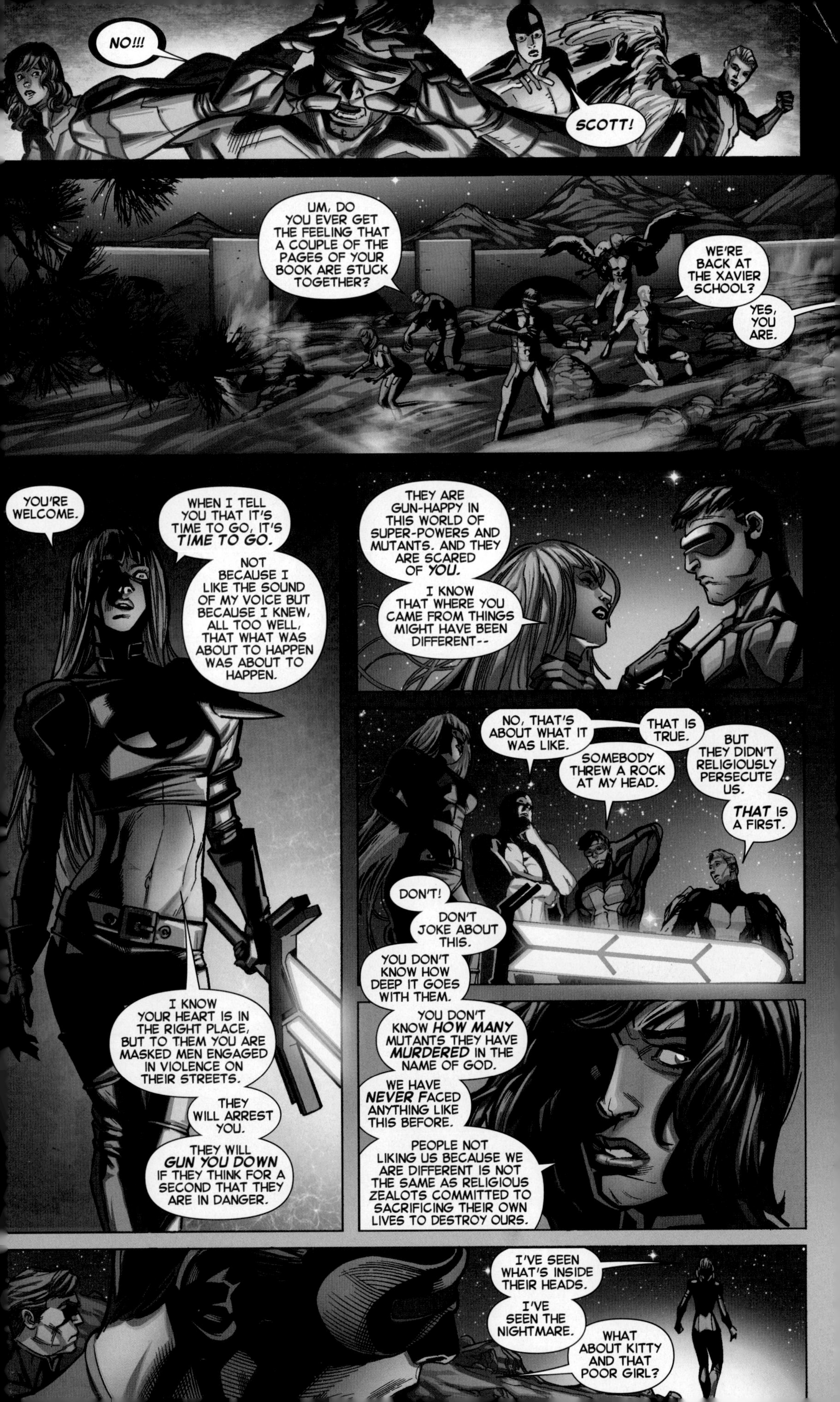
NO!!!
SCOTT!
UM, DO YOU EVER GET THE FEELING THAT A COUPLE OF THE PAGES OF YOUR BOOK ARE STUCK TOGETHER?
WE'RE BACK AT THE XAVIER SCHOOL?
YES, YOU ARE.
YOU'RE WELCOME.
WHEN I TELL YOU THAT IT'S TIME TO GO, IT'S TIME TO GO.
NOT BECAUSE I LIKE THE SOUND OF MY VOICE BUT BECAUSE I KNEW, ALL TOO WELL, THAT WHAT WAS ABOUT TO HAPPEN WAS ABOUT TO HAPPEN.
THEY ARE GUN-HAPPY IN THIS WORLD OF SUPER-POWERS AND MUTANTS. AND THEY ARE SCARED OF YOU.
I KNOW THAT WHERE YOU CAME FROM THINGS MIGHT HAVE BEEN DIFFERENT--
NO, THAT'S ABOUT WHAT IT WAS LIKE.
THAT IS TRUE.
SOMEBODY THREW A ROCK AT MY HEAD.
BUT THEY DIDN'T RELIGIOUSLY PERSECUTE US.
THAT IS A FIRST.
DON'T!
DON'T JOKE ABOUT THIS.
YOU DON'T KNOW HOW DEEP IT GOES WITH THEM.
YOU DON'T KNOW HOW MANY MUTANTS THEY HAVE MURDERED IN THE NAME OF GOD.
WE HAVE NEVER FACED ANYTHING LIKE THIS BEFORE.
PEOPLE NOT LIKING US BECAUSE WE ARE DIFFERENT IS NOT THE SAME AS RELIGIOUS ZEALOTS COMMITTED TO SACRIFICING THEIR OWN LIVES TO DESTROY OURS.
I KNOW YOUR HEART IS IN THE RIGHT PLACE, BUT TO THEM YOU ARE MASKED MEN ENGAGED IN VIOLENCE ON THEIR STREETS.
THEY WILL ARREST YOU.
THEY WILL GUN YOU DOWN IF THEY THINK FOR A SECOND THAT THEY ARE IN DANGER.
I'VE SEEN WHAT'S INSIDE THEIR HEADS.
I'VE SEEN THE NIGHTMARE.
WHAT ABOUT KITTY AND THAT POOR GIRL?

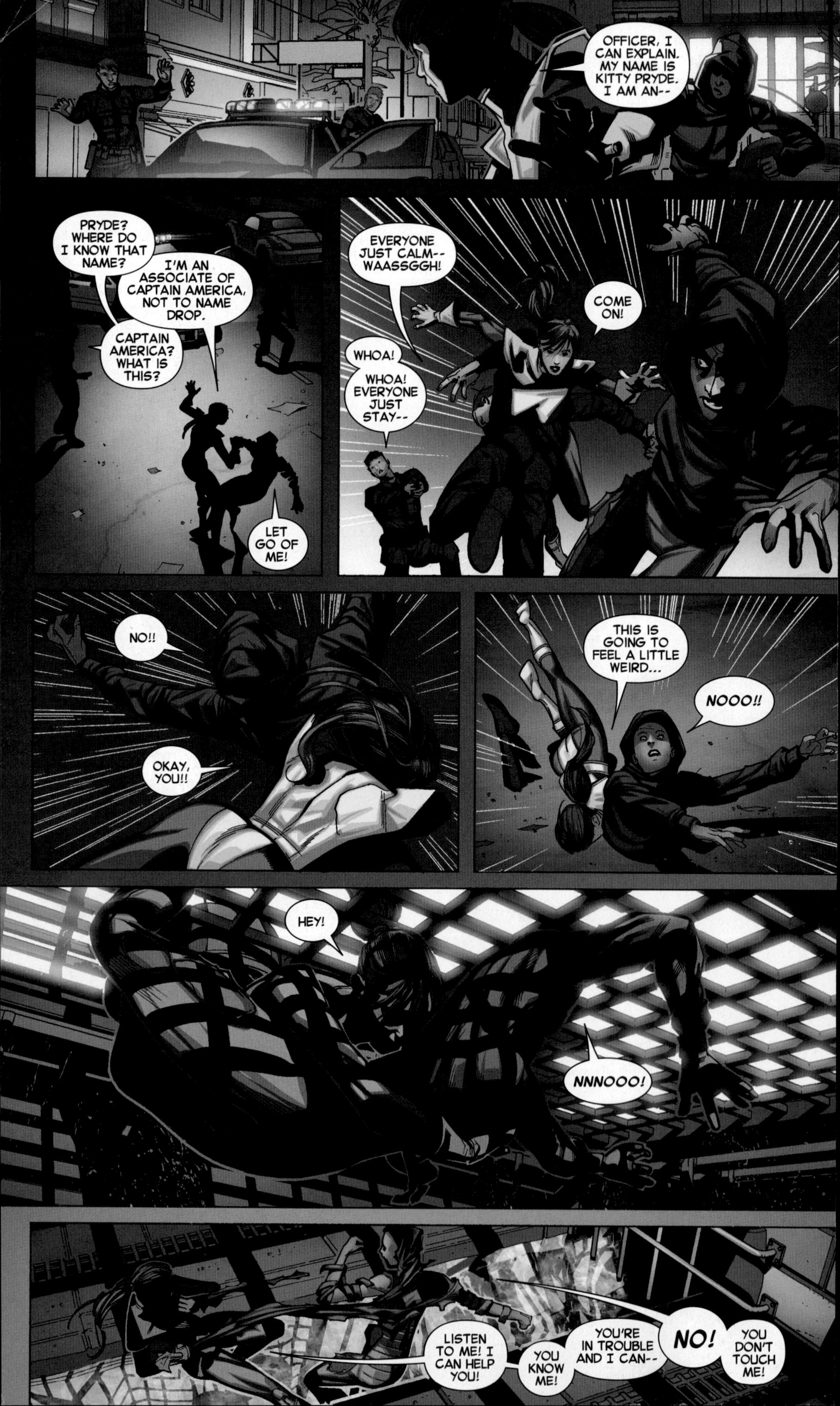

OFFICER, I CAN EXPLAIN. MY NAME IS KITTY PRYDE. I AM AN--
PRYDE? WHERE DO I KNOW THAT NAME?
I'M AN ASSOCIATE OF CAPTAIN AMERICA, NOT TO NAME DROP.
CAPTAIN AMERICA? WHAT IS THIS?
LET GO OF ME!
EVERYONE JUST CALM-- WAASSGGH!
COME ON!
WHOA!
WHOA! EVERYONE JUST STAY--
NO!!
OKAY, YOU!!
THIS IS GOING TO FEEL A LITTLE WEIRD...
NOOO!!
HEY!
NNNOOO!
LISTEN TO ME! I CAN HELP YOU!
YOU KNOW ME!
YOU'RE IN TROUBLE AND I CAN--
NO!
YOU DON'T TOUCH ME!

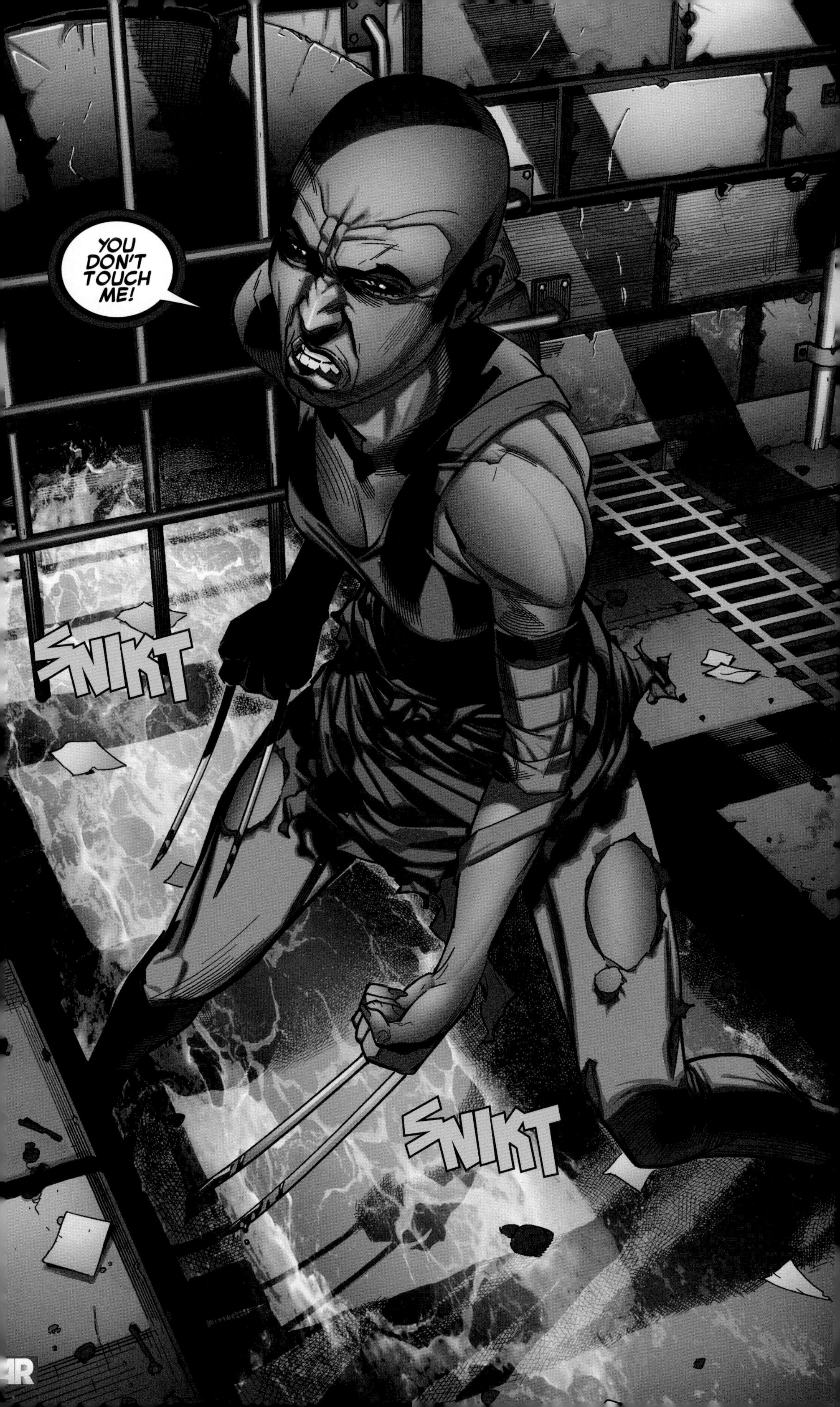
YOU DON'T TOUCH ME!
SNIKT
SNIKT

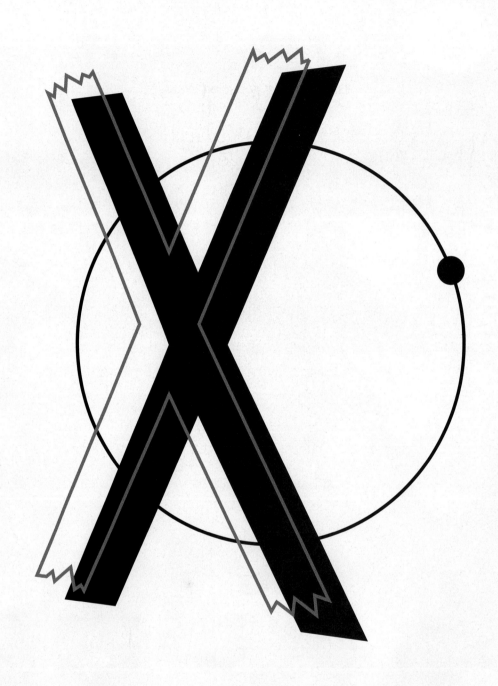

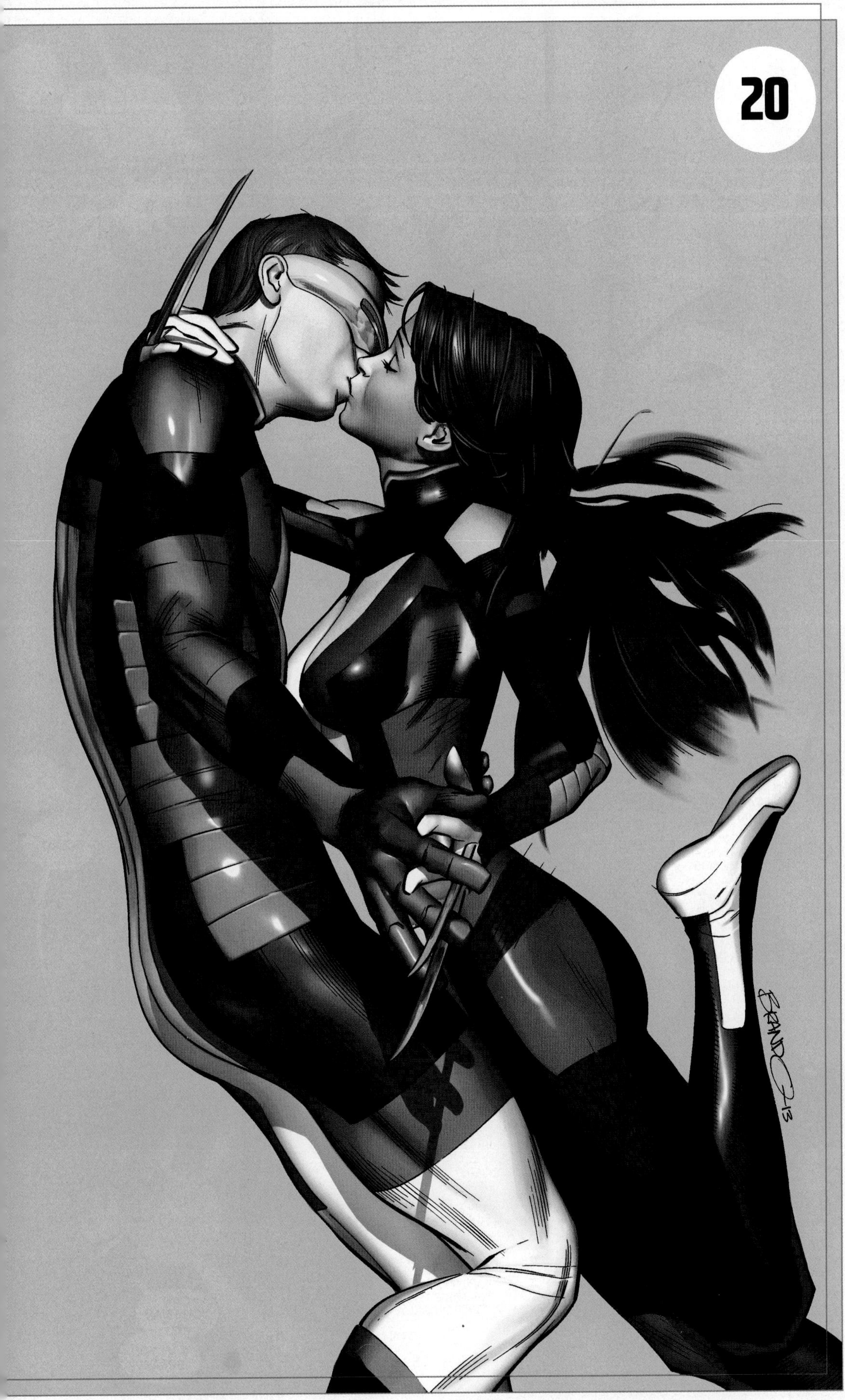
20

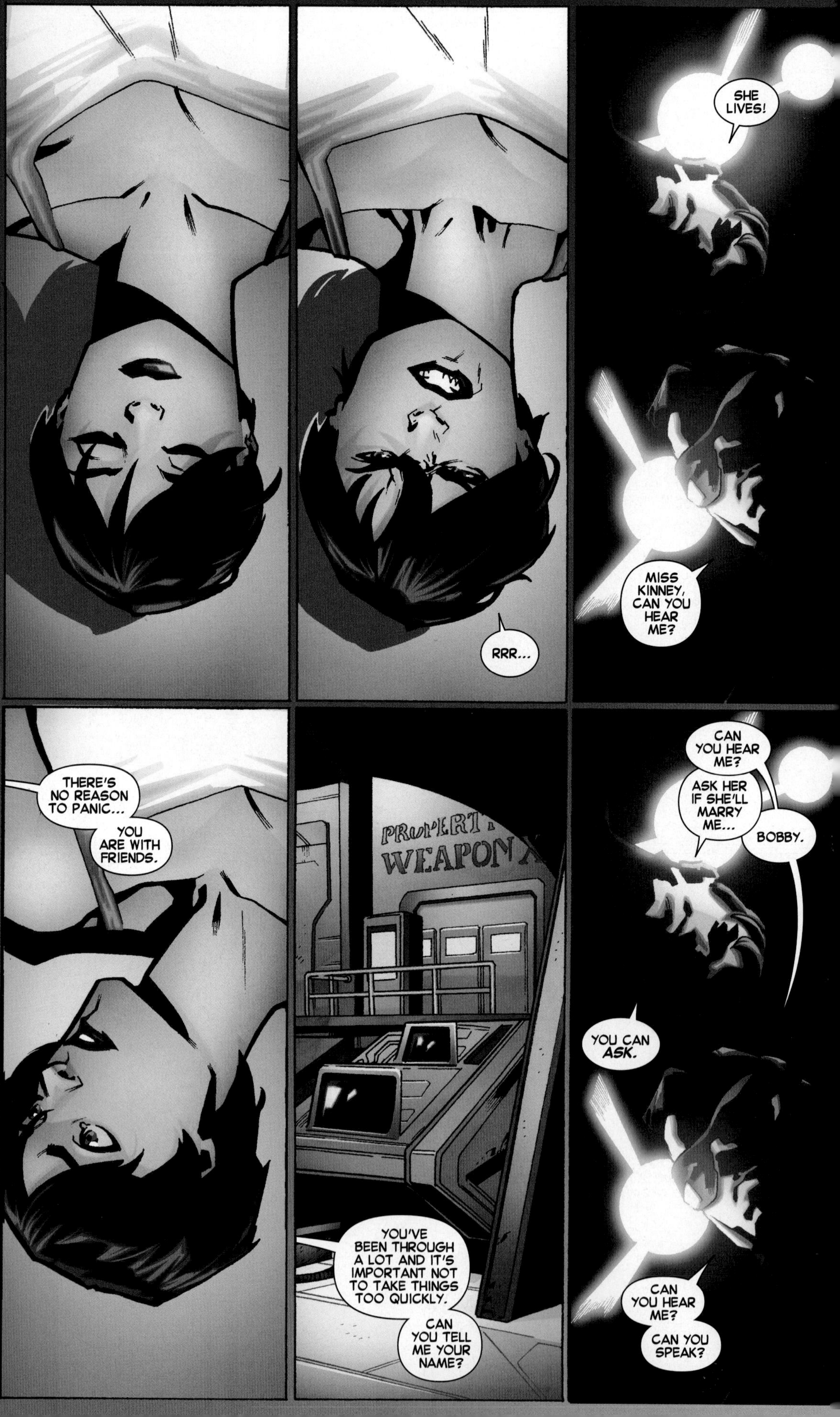

RRR...
SHE LIVES!
MISS KINNEY, CAN YOU HEAR ME?
THERE'S NO REASON TO PANIC...
YOU ARE WITH FRIENDS.
PROPERTY OF WEAPON X
YOU'VE BEEN THROUGH A LOT AND IT'S IMPORTANT NOT TO TAKE THINGS TOO QUICKLY.
CAN YOU TELL ME YOUR NAME?
CAN YOU HEAR ME?
ASK HER IF SHE'LL MARRY ME...
BOBBY.
YOU CAN ASK.
CAN YOU HEAR ME?
CAN YOU SPEAK?

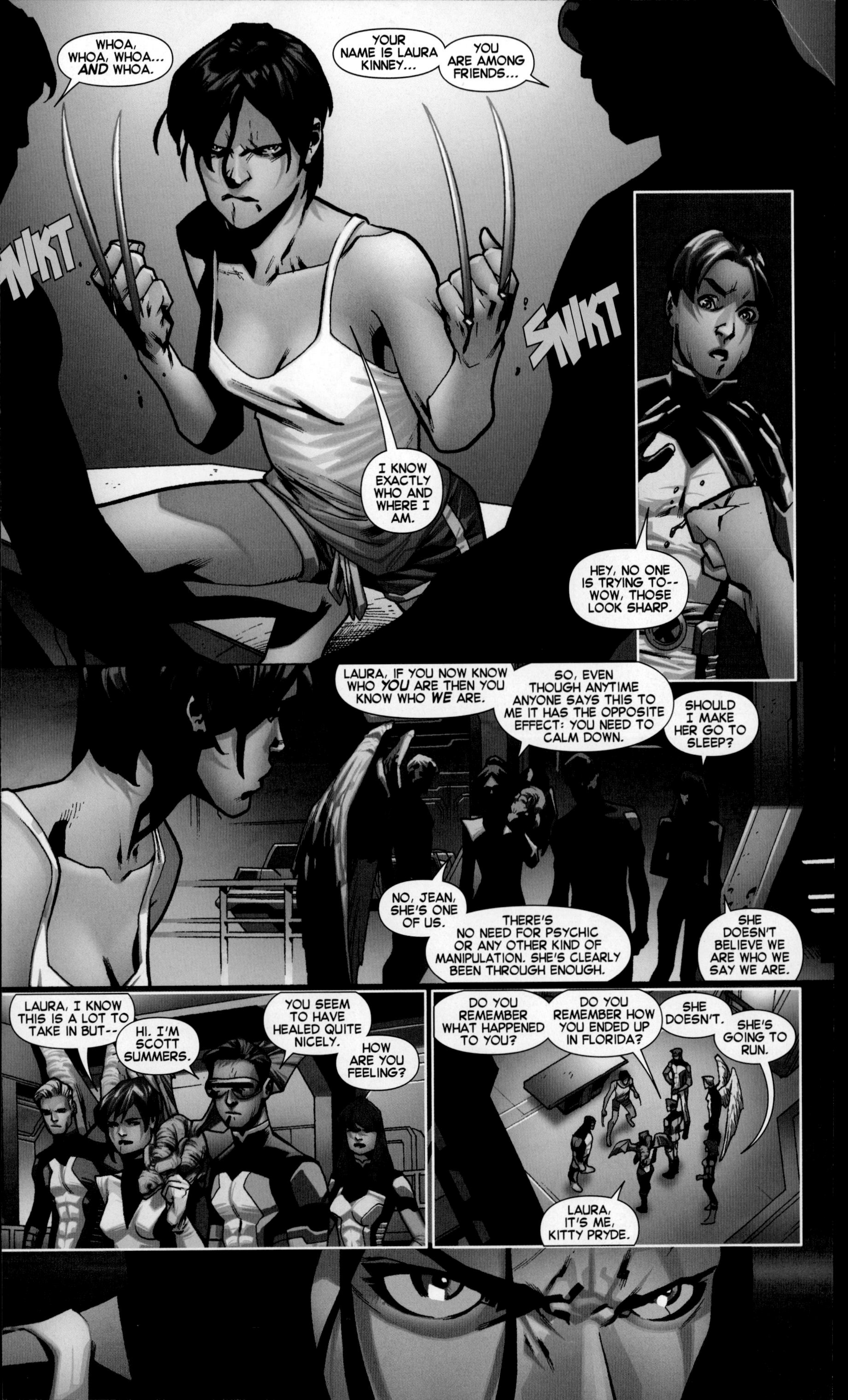
WHOA, WHOA, WHOA... AND WHOA.
YOUR NAME IS LAURA KINNEY...
YOU ARE AMONG FRIENDS...
SNIKT
SNIKT
I KNOW EXACTLY WHO AND WHERE I AM.
HEY, NO ONE IS TRYING TO-- WOW, THOSE LOOK SHARP.
LAURA, IF YOU NOW KNOW WHO YOU ARE THEN YOU KNOW WHO WE ARE.
SO, EVEN THOUGH ANYTIME ANYONE SAYS THIS TO ME IT HAS THE OPPOSITE EFFECT: YOU NEED TO CALM DOWN.
SHOULD I MAKE HER GO TO SLEEP?
NO, JEAN, SHE'S ONE OF US.
THERE'S NO NEED FOR PSYCHIC OR ANY OTHER KIND OF MANIPULATION. SHE'S CLEARLY BEEN THROUGH ENOUGH.
SHE DOESN'T BELIEVE WE ARE WHO WE SAY WE ARE.
LAURA, I KNOW THIS IS A LOT TO TAKE IN BUT--
HI. I'M SCOTT SUMMERS.
YOU SEEM TO HAVE HEALED QUITE NICELY.
HOW ARE YOU FEELING?
DO YOU REMEMBER WHAT HAPPENED TO YOU?
DO YOU REMEMBER HOW YOU ENDED UP IN FLORIDA?
SHE DOESN'T.
SHE'S GOING TO RUN.
LAURA, IT'S ME, KITTY PRYDE.

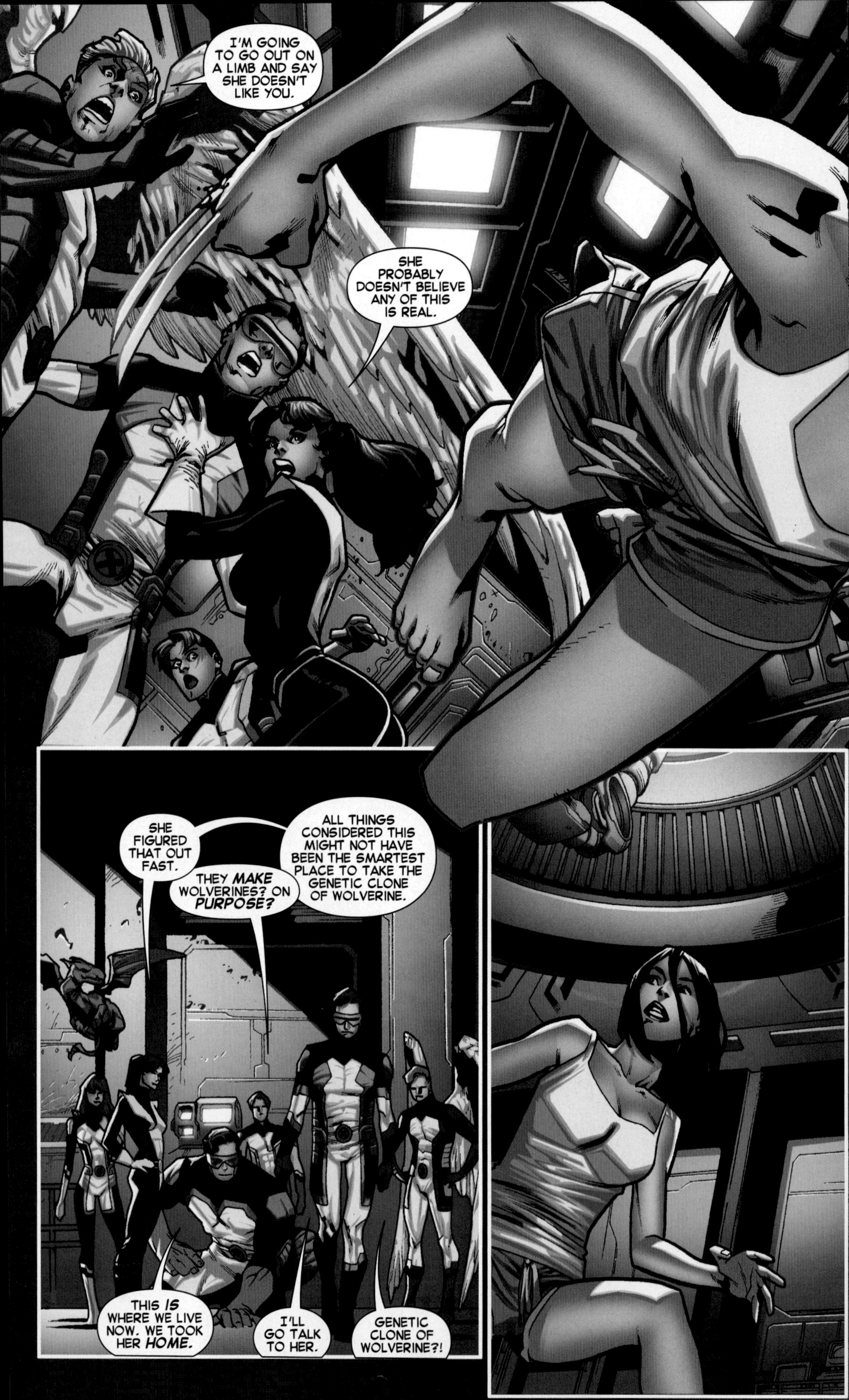
I'M GOING TO GO OUT ON A LIMB AND SAY SHE DOESN'T LIKE YOU.
SHE PROBABLY DOESN'T BELIEVE ANY OF THIS IS REAL.
SHE FIGURED THAT OUT FAST.
ALL THINGS CONSIDERED THIS MIGHT NOT HAVE BEEN THE SMARTEST PLACE TO TAKE THE GENETIC CLONE OF WOLVERINE.
THEY *MAKE* WOLVERINES? ON *PURPOSE?*
THIS *IS* WHERE WE LIVE NOW. WE TOOK HER *HOME.*
I'LL GO TALK TO HER.
GENETIC CLONE OF WOLVERINE?!

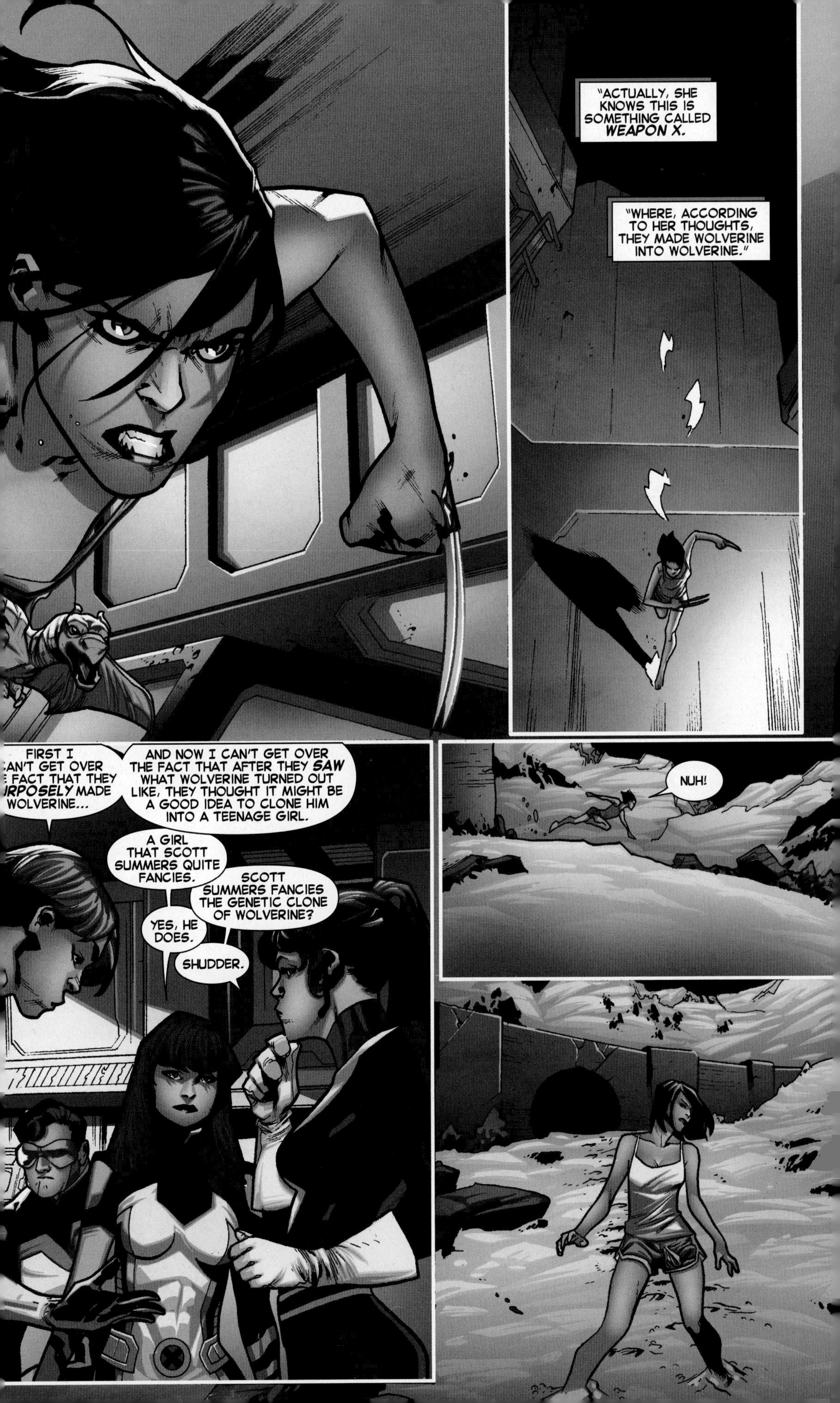

"ACTUALLY, SHE KNOWS THIS IS SOMETHING CALLED **WEAPON X.**
"WHERE, ACCORDING TO HER THOUGHTS, THEY MADE WOLVERINE INTO WOLVERINE."
FIRST I CAN'T GET OVER THE FACT THAT THEY PURPOSELY MADE WOLVERINE...
AND NOW I CAN'T GET OVER THE FACT THAT AFTER THEY *SAW* WHAT WOLVERINE TURNED OUT LIKE, THEY THOUGHT IT MIGHT BE A GOOD IDEA TO CLONE HIM INTO A TEENAGE GIRL.
A GIRL THAT SCOTT SUMMERS QUITE FANCIES.
SCOTT SUMMERS FANCIES THE GENETIC CLONE OF WOLVERINE?
YES, HE DOES.
SHUDDER.
NUH!

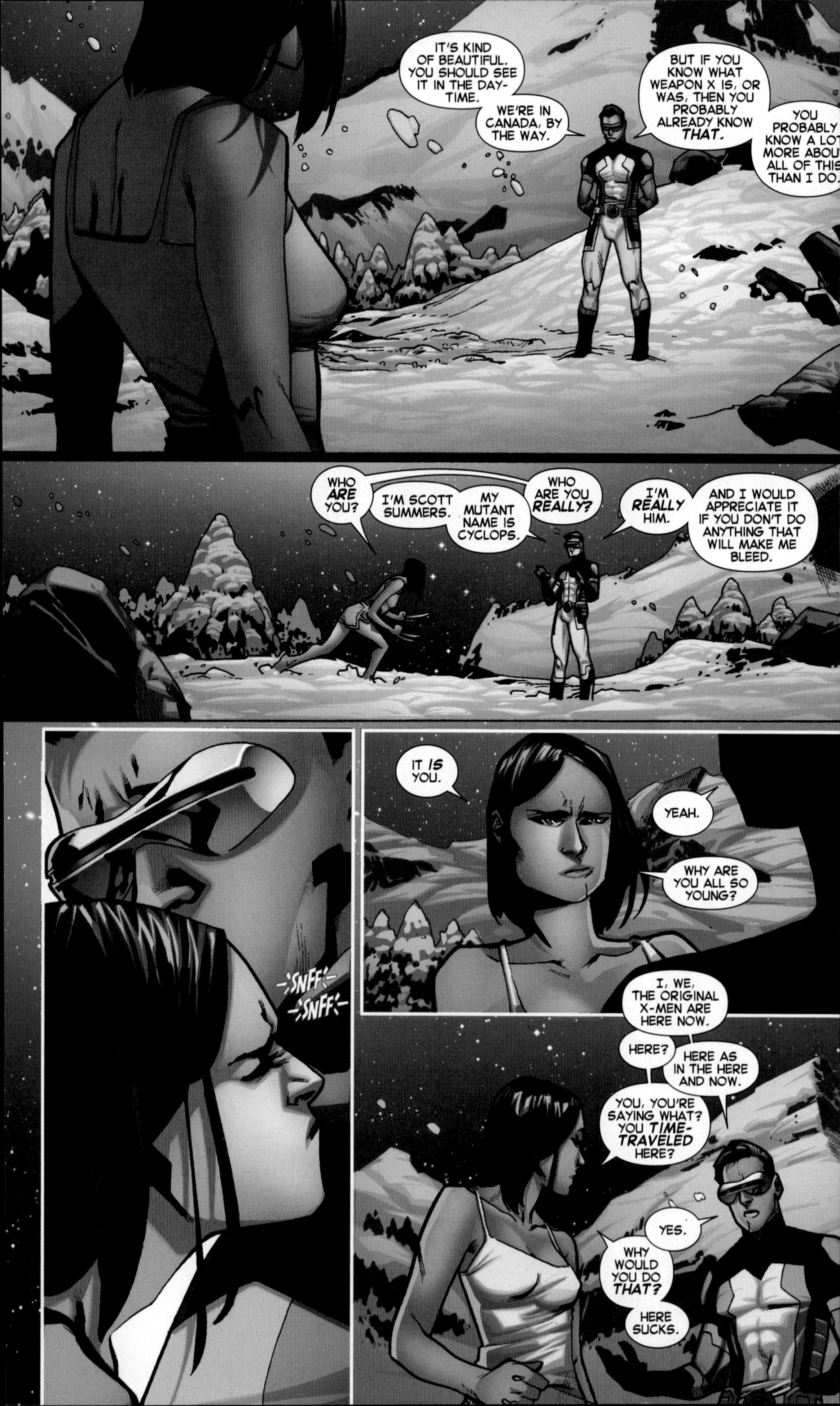
IT'S KIND OF BEAUTIFUL. YOU SHOULD SEE IT IN THE DAY-TIME.
WE'RE IN CANADA, BY THE WAY.
BUT IF YOU KNOW WHAT WEAPON X IS, OR WAS, THEN YOU PROBABLY ALREADY KNOW THAT.
YOU PROBABLY KNOW A LOT MORE ABOUT ALL OF THIS THAN I DO.
WHO ARE YOU?
I'M SCOTT SUMMERS.
MY MUTANT NAME IS CYCLOPS.
WHO ARE YOU REALLY?
I'M REALLY HIM.
AND I WOULD APPRECIATE IT IF YOU DON'T DO ANYTHING THAT WILL MAKE ME BLEED.
SNFF
SNFF
IT IS YOU.
YEAH.
WHY ARE YOU ALL SO YOUNG?
I, WE, THE ORIGINAL X-MEN ARE HERE NOW.
HERE?
HERE AS IN THE HERE AND NOW.
YOU, YOU'RE SAYING WHAT? YOU TIME-TRAVELED HERE?
YES.
WHY WOULD YOU DO THAT?
HERE SUCKS.

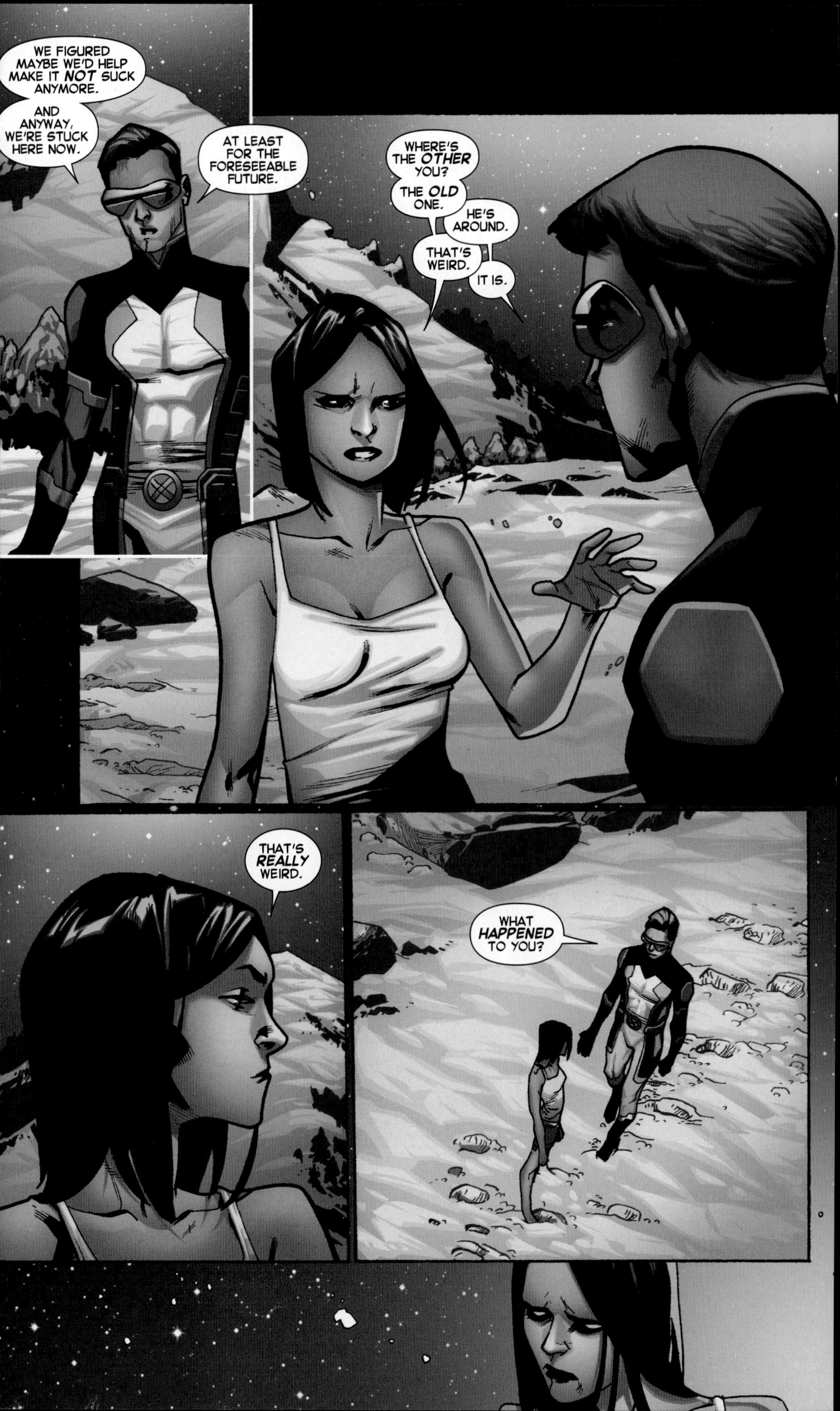
WE FIGURED MAYBE WE'D HELP MAKE IT NOT SUCK ANYMORE.
AND ANYWAY, WE'RE STUCK HERE NOW.
AT LEAST FOR THE FORESEEABLE FUTURE.
WHERE'S THE OTHER YOU?
THE OLD ONE.
HE'S AROUND.
THAT'S WEIRD.
IT IS.
THAT'S REALLY WEIRD.
WHAT HAPPENED TO YOU?

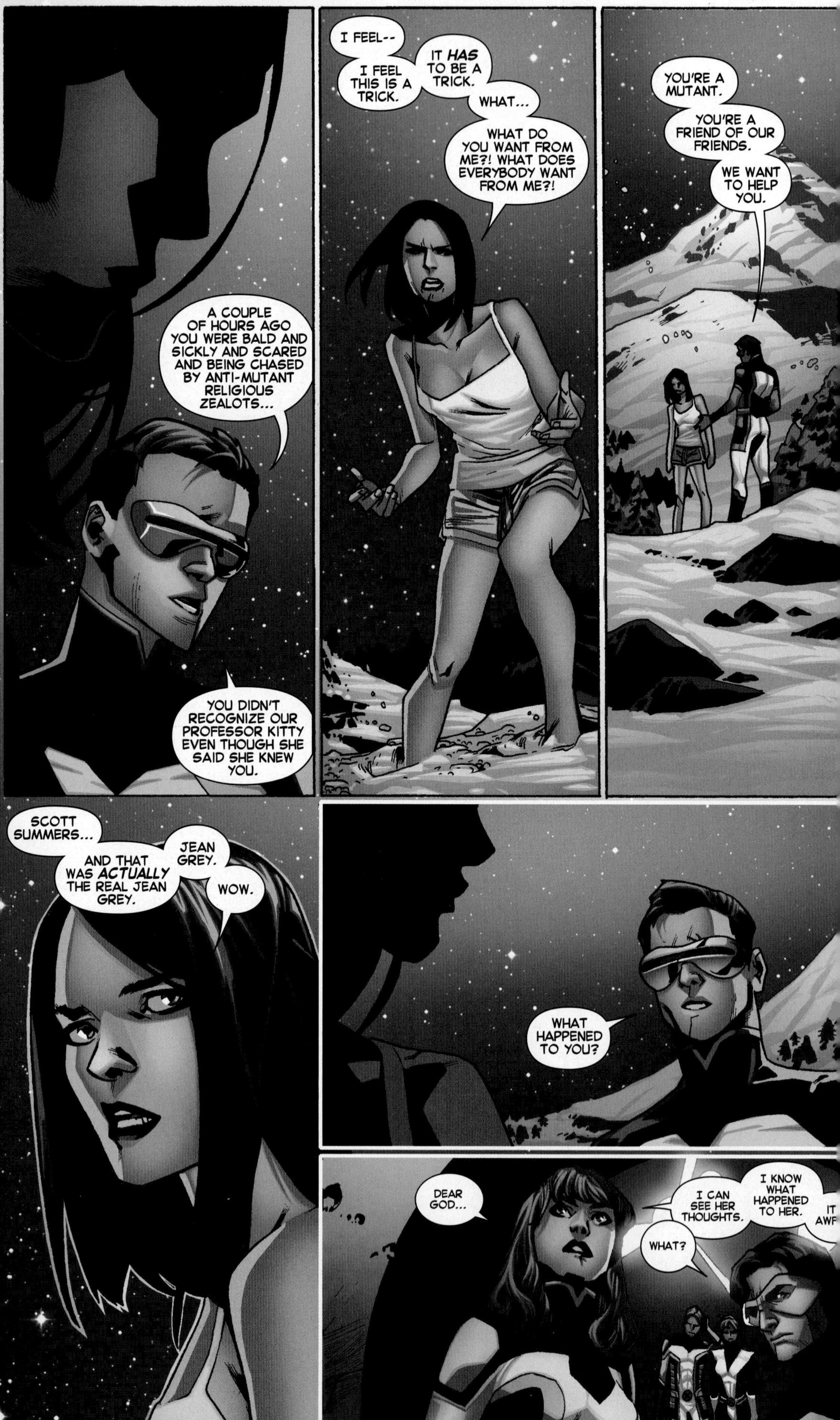
A COUPLE OF HOURS AGO YOU WERE BALD AND SICKLY AND SCARED AND BEING CHASED BY ANTI-MUTANT RELIGIOUS ZEALOTS...
YOU DIDN'T RECOGNIZE OUR PROFESSOR KITTY EVEN THOUGH SHE SAID SHE KNEW YOU.
I FEEL--
I FEEL THIS IS A TRICK.
IT HAS TO BE A TRICK.
WHAT...
WHAT DO YOU WANT FROM ME?! WHAT DOES EVERYBODY WANT FROM ME?!
YOU'RE A MUTANT.
YOU'RE A FRIEND OF OUR FRIENDS.
WE WANT TO HELP YOU.
SCOTT SUMMERS...
AND THAT WAS ACTUALLY THE REAL JEAN GREY.
JEAN GREY.
WOW.
WHAT HAPPENED TO YOU?
DEAR GOD...
I CAN SEE HER THOUGHTS.
WHAT?
I KNOW WHAT HAPPENED TO HER.

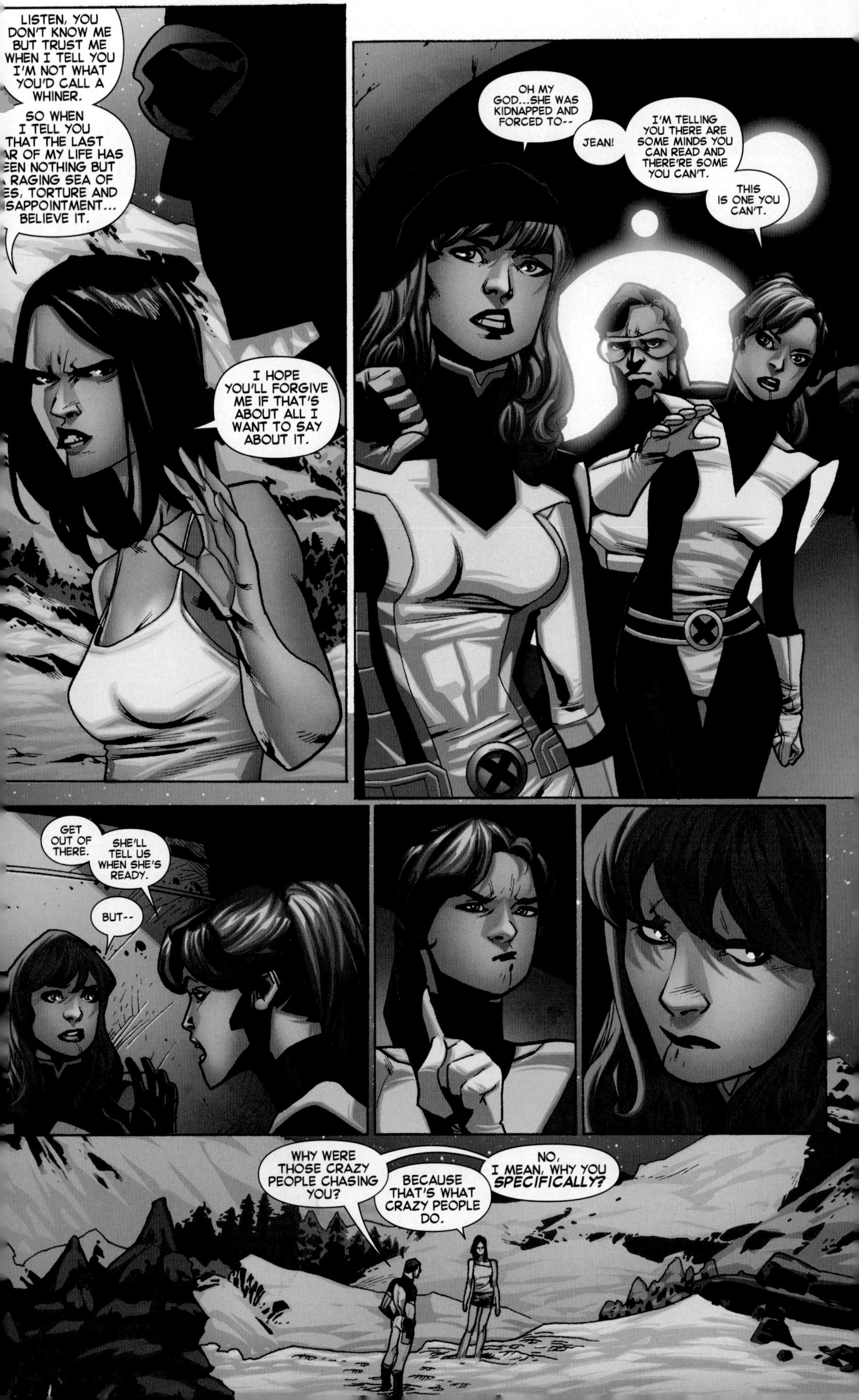
LISTEN, YOU DON'T KNOW ME BUT TRUST ME WHEN I TELL YOU I'M NOT WHAT YOU'D CALL A WHINER.
SO WHEN I TELL YOU THAT THE LAST AR OF MY LIFE HAS EEN NOTHING BUT RAGING SEA OF ES, TORTURE AND SAPPOINTMENT... BELIEVE IT.
I HOPE YOU'LL FORGIVE ME IF THAT'S ABOUT ALL I WANT TO SAY ABOUT IT.
OH MY GOD...SHE WAS KIDNAPPED AND FORCED TO--
JEAN!
I'M TELLING YOU THERE ARE SOME MINDS YOU CAN READ AND THERE'RE SOME YOU CAN'T.
THIS IS ONE YOU CAN'T.
GET OUT OF THERE.
SHE'LL TELL US WHEN SHE'S READY.
BUT--
WHY WERE THOSE CRAZY PEOPLE CHASING YOU?
BECAUSE THAT'S WHAT CRAZY PEOPLE DO.
NO, I MEAN, WHY YOU *SPECIFICALLY?*

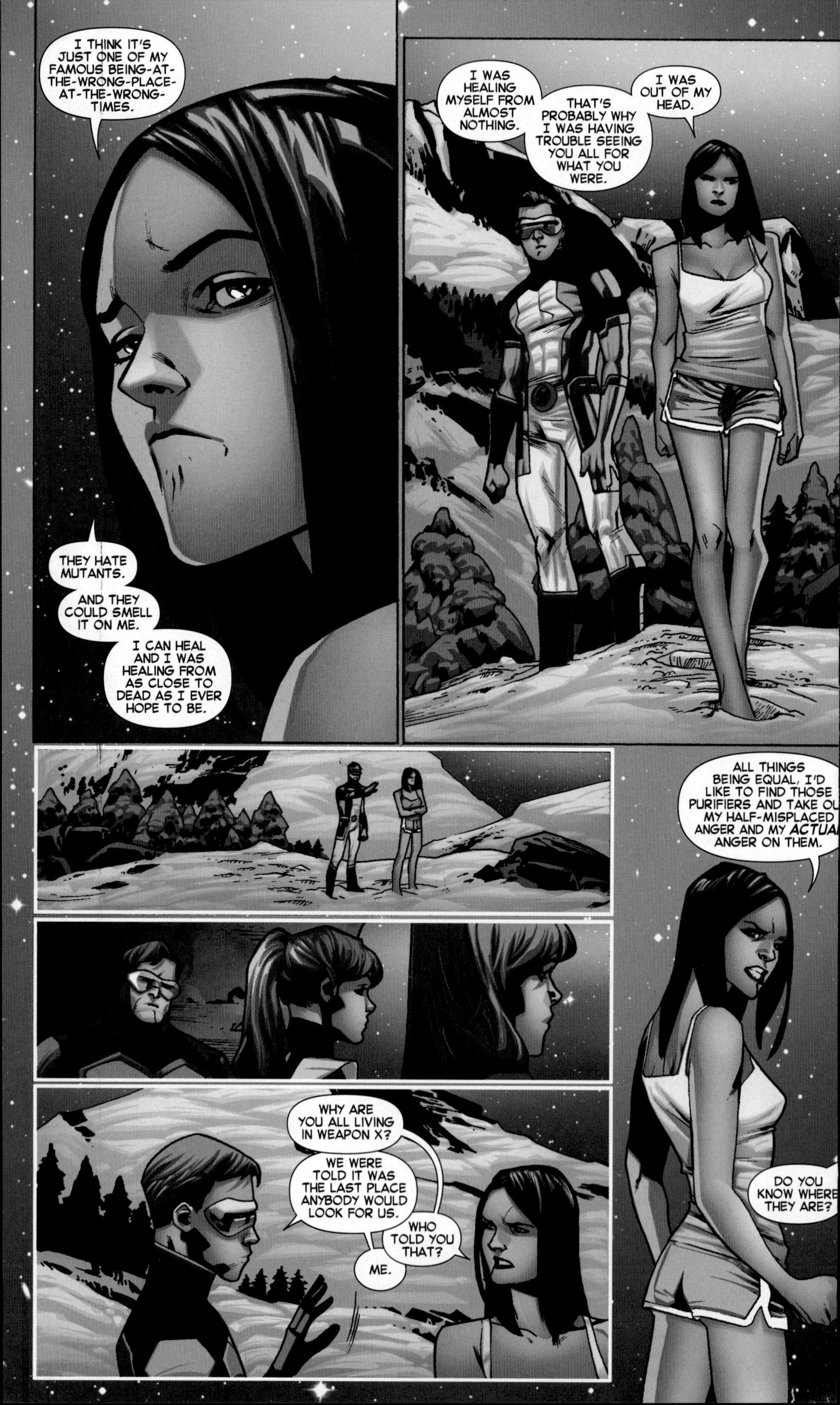

I THINK IT'S JUST ONE OF MY FAMOUS BEING-AT-THE-WRONG-PLACE-AT-THE-WRONG-TIMES.
THEY HATE MUTANTS.
AND THEY COULD SMELL IT ON ME.
I CAN HEAL AND I WAS HEALING FROM AS CLOSE TO DEAD AS I EVER HOPE TO BE.
I WAS HEALING MYSELF FROM ALMOST NOTHING.
THAT'S PROBABLY WHY I WAS HAVING TROUBLE SEEING YOU ALL FOR WHAT YOU WERE.
I WAS OUT OF MY HEAD.
ALL THINGS BEING EQUAL, I'D LIKE TO FIND THOSE PURIFIERS AND TAKE OU MY HALF-MISPLACED ANGER AND MY ACTUAL ANGER ON THEM.
WHY ARE YOU ALL LIVING IN WEAPON X?
WE WERE TOLD IT WAS THE LAST PLACE ANYBODY WOULD LOOK FOR US.
WHO TOLD YOU THAT?
ME.
DO YOU KNOW WHERE THEY ARE?

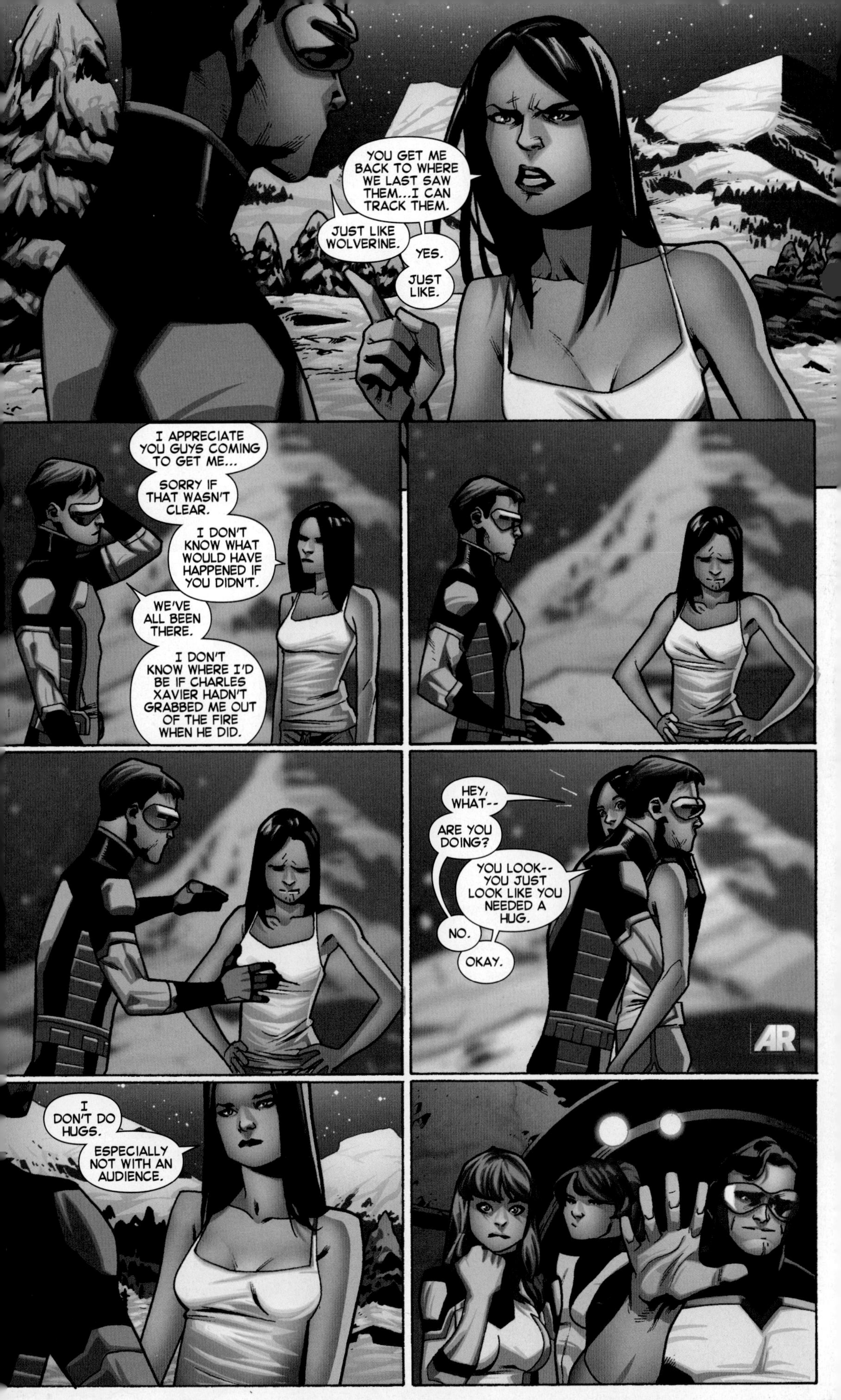

YOU GET ME BACK TO WHERE WE LAST SAW THEM...I CAN TRACK THEM.
JUST LIKE WOLVERINE.
YES.
JUST LIKE.
I APPRECIATE YOU GUYS COMING TO GET ME...
SORRY IF THAT WASN'T CLEAR.
I DON'T KNOW WHAT WOULD HAVE HAPPENED IF YOU DIDN'T.
WE'VE ALL BEEN THERE.
I DON'T KNOW WHERE I'D BE IF CHARLES XAVIER HADN'T GRABBED ME OUT OF THE FIRE WHEN HE DID.
HEY, WHAT--
ARE YOU DOING?
YOU LOOK--YOU JUST LOOK LIKE YOU NEEDED A HUG.
NO.
OKAY.
I DON'T DO HUGS.
ESPECIALLY NOT WITH AN AUDIENCE.

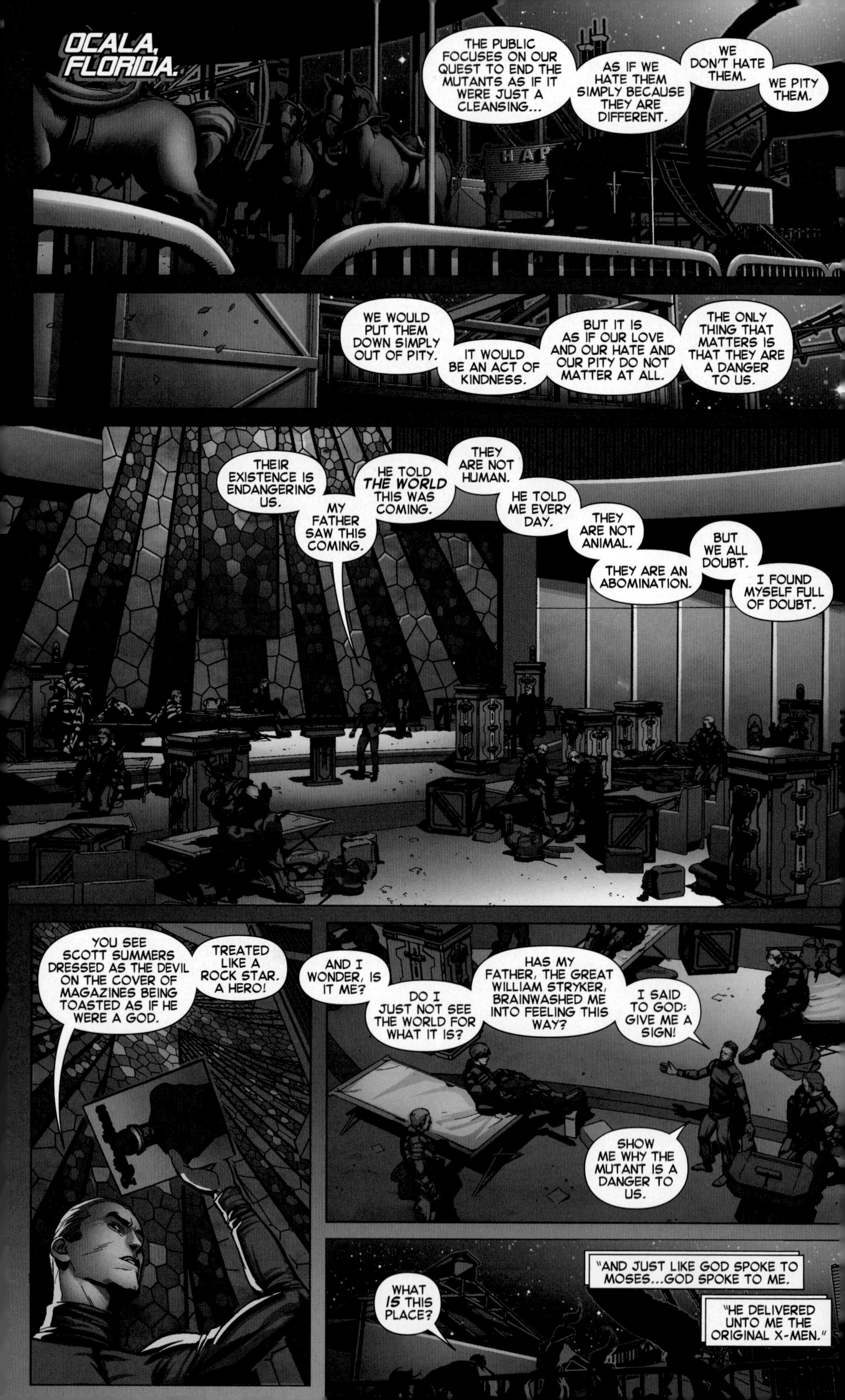
OCALA, FLORIDA.
THE PUBLIC FOCUSES ON OUR QUEST TO END THE MUTANTS AS IF IT WERE JUST A CLEANSING...
AS IF WE HATE THEM SIMPLY BECAUSE THEY ARE DIFFERENT.
WE DON'T HATE THEM.
WE PITY THEM.
WE WOULD PUT THEM DOWN SIMPLY OUT OF PITY.
IT WOULD BE AN ACT OF KINDNESS.
BUT IT IS AS IF OUR LOVE AND OUR HATE AND OUR PITY DO NOT MATTER AT ALL.
THE ONLY THING THAT MATTERS IS THAT THEY ARE A DANGER TO US.
THEIR EXISTENCE IS ENDANGERING US.
MY FATHER SAW THIS COMING.
HE TOLD THE WORLD THIS WAS COMING.
THEY ARE NOT HUMAN.
HE TOLD ME EVERY DAY.
THEY ARE NOT ANIMAL.
THEY ARE AN ABOMINATION.
BUT WE ALL DOUBT.
I FOUND MYSELF FULL OF DOUBT.
YOU SEE SCOTT SUMMERS DRESSED AS THE DEVIL ON THE COVER OF MAGAZINES BEING TOASTED AS IF HE WERE A GOD.
TREATED LIKE A ROCK STAR. A HERO!
AND I WONDER, IS IT ME?
DO I JUST NOT SEE THE WORLD FOR WHAT IT IS?
HAS MY FATHER, THE GREAT WILLIAM STRYKER, BRAINWASHED ME INTO FEELING THIS WAY?
I SAID TO GOD: GIVE ME A SIGN!
SHOW ME WHY THE MUTANT IS A DANGER TO US.
"AND JUST LIKE GOD SPOKE TO MOSES...GOD SPOKE TO ME.
"HE DELIVERED UNTO ME THE ORIGINAL X-MEN."
WHAT IS THIS PLACE?

"THAT MEANS THEY ARE BREAKING THE RULES OF TIME AND SPACE AS IF THESE RULES DON'T APPLY TO THEM.

"AS IF THEIR NEEDS ARE MORE IMPORTANT THAN OURS.

FOR THEY ARE OUR BURNING BUSH.

THE ORIGINAL X-MEN, WHO LAST NIGHT FELLED *MANY* OF OUR PURIFIER BROTHERS, ARE LIVING IN THE NOW?! WHAT ARE THEY *DOING* HERE?

"YOU DON'T HAVE TO BE A SCIENTIST TO KNOW THAT IF THEY ARE HERE INSTEAD OF WHERE THEY *BELONG*, THEN OUR FUTURE, THE FUTURE OF OUR CHILDREN, IS IN *DANGER.*

"WE COULD VERY WELL CEASE TO EXIST BECAUSE OF THEIR SELFISH ACTIONS."

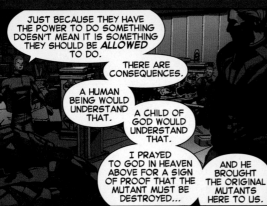

JUST BECAUSE THEY HAVE THE POWER TO DO SOMETHING DOESN'T MEAN IT IS SOMETHING THEY SHOULD BE *ALLOWED* TO DO.

THERE ARE CONSEQUENCES.

A HUMAN BEING WOULD UNDERSTAND THAT.

A CHILD OF GOD WOULD UNDERSTAND THAT.

I PRAYED TO GOD IN HEAVEN ABOVE FOR A SIGN OF PROOF THAT THE MUTANT MUST BE DESTROYED...

AND HE BROUGHT THE ORIGINAL MUTANTS HERE TO US.

HE GAVE US A--

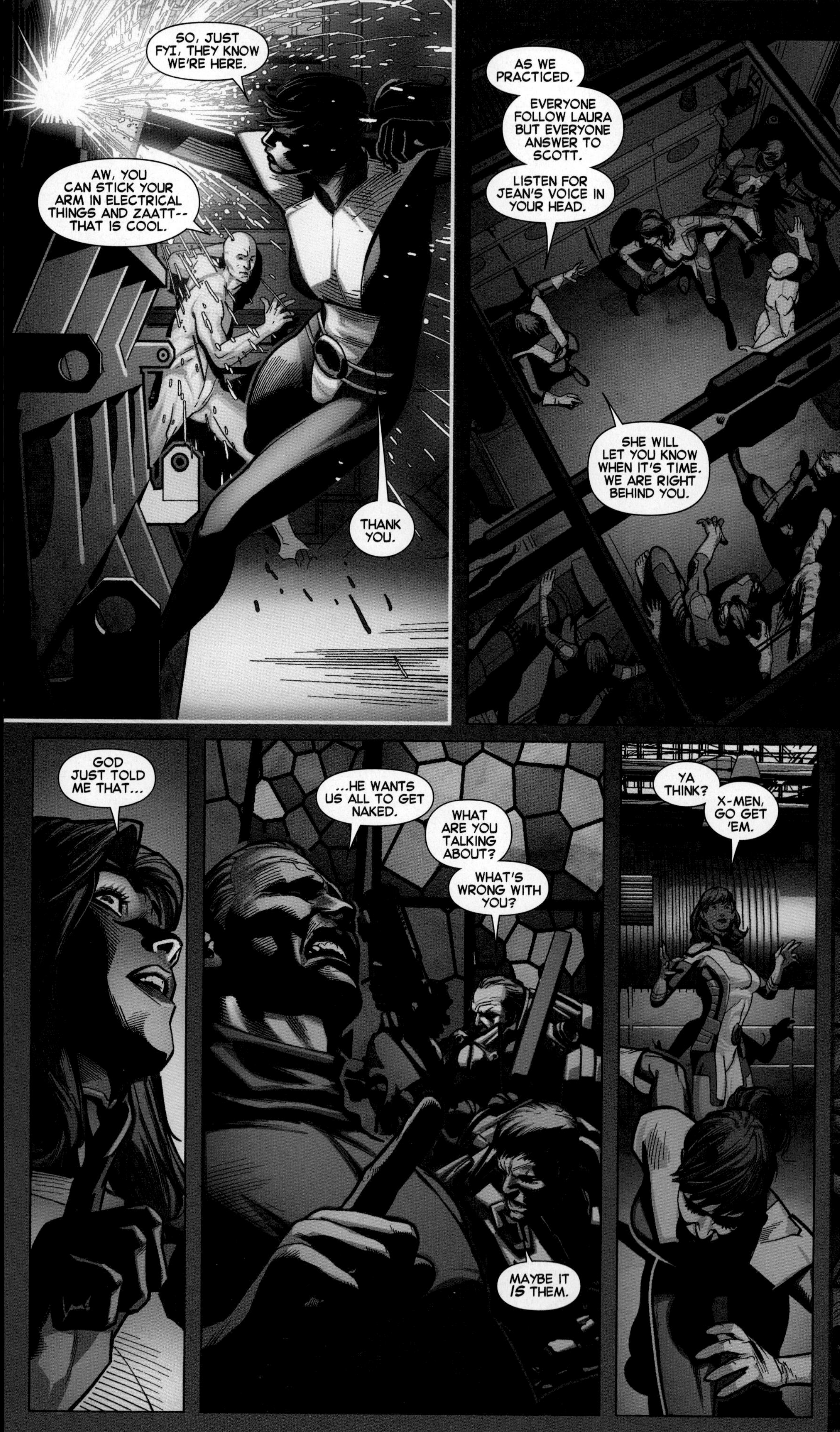
SO, JUST FYI, THEY KNOW WE'RE HERE.
AW, YOU CAN STICK YOUR ARM IN ELECTRICAL THINGS AND ZAATT-- THAT IS COOL.
THANK YOU.
AS WE PRACTICED.
EVERYONE FOLLOW LAURA BUT EVERYONE ANSWER TO SCOTT.
LISTEN FOR JEAN'S VOICE IN YOUR HEAD.
SHE WILL LET YOU KNOW WHEN IT'S TIME. WE ARE RIGHT BEHIND YOU.
GOD JUST TOLD ME THAT...
...HE WANTS US ALL TO GET NAKED.
WHAT ARE YOU TALKING ABOUT?
WHAT'S WRONG WITH YOU?
MAYBE IT *IS* THEM.
YA THINK?
X-MEN, GO GET 'EM.

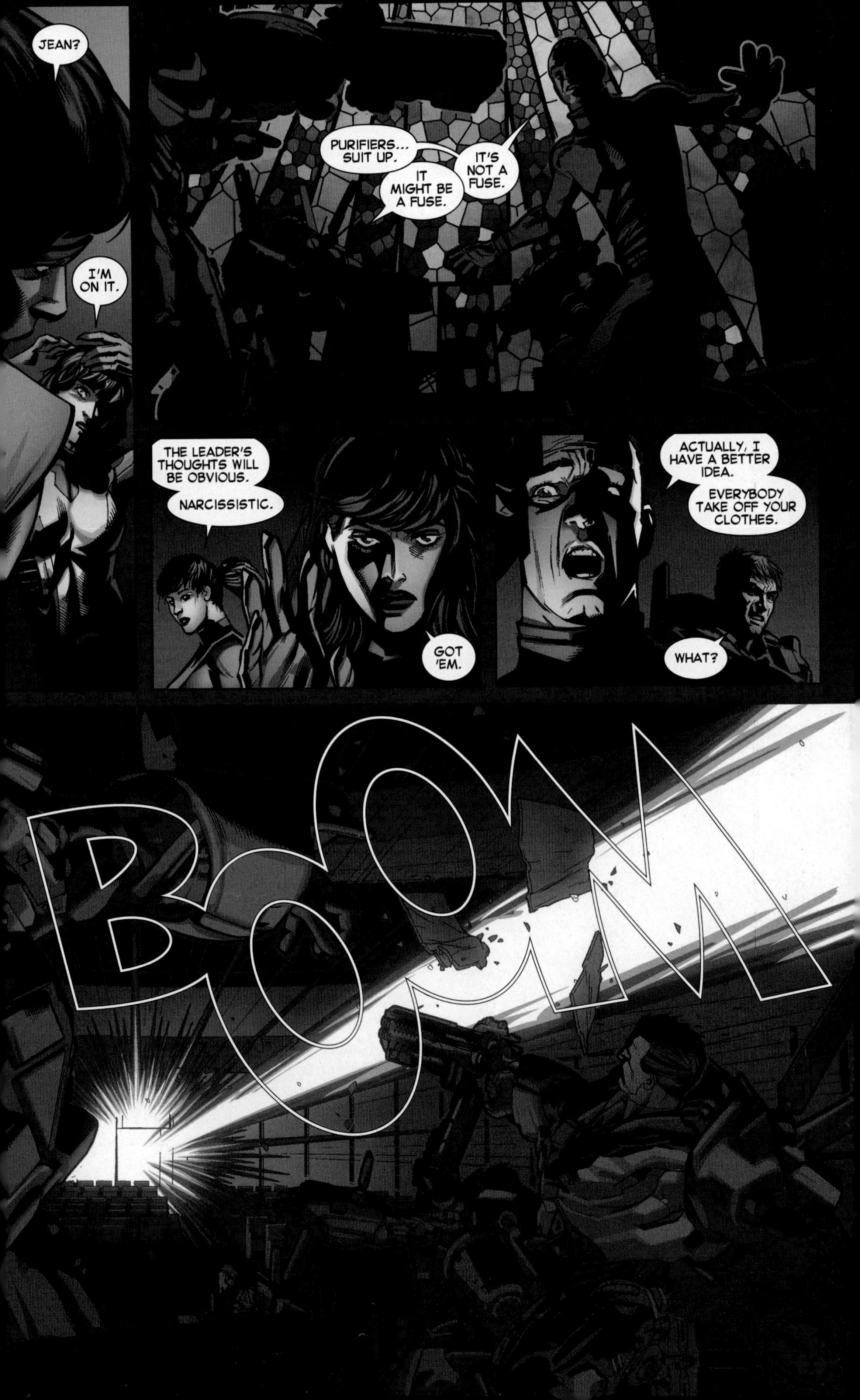
JEAN?
PURIFIERS... SUIT UP.
IT MIGHT BE A FUSE.
IT'S NOT A FUSE.
I'M ON IT.
THE LEADER'S THOUGHTS WILL BE OBVIOUS.
NARCISSISTIC.
GOT 'EM.
ACTUALLY, I HAVE A BETTER IDEA.
EVERYBODY TAKE OFF YOUR CLOTHES.
WHAT?
BOOM

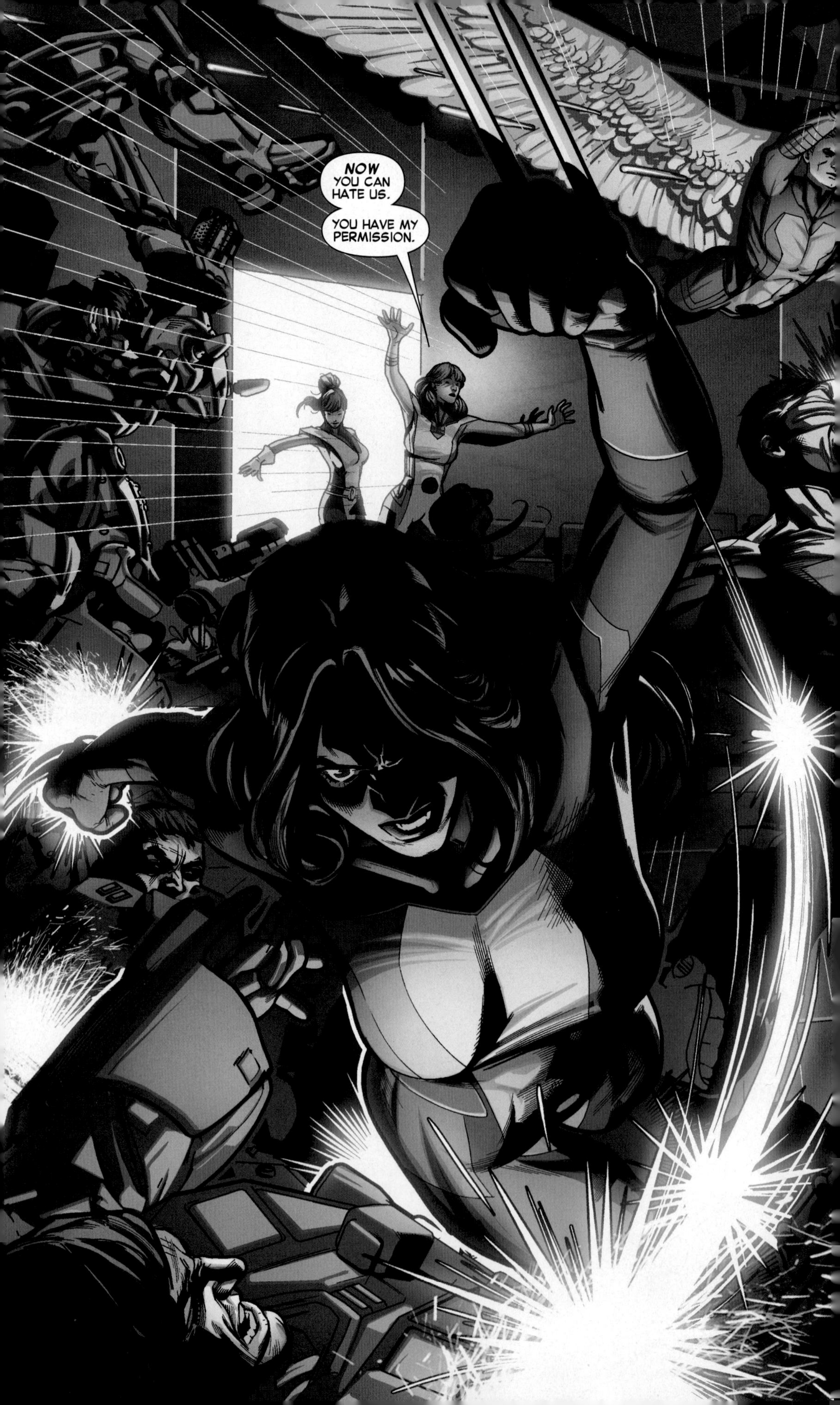
NOW YOU CAN HATE US.
YOU HAVE MY PERMISSION.

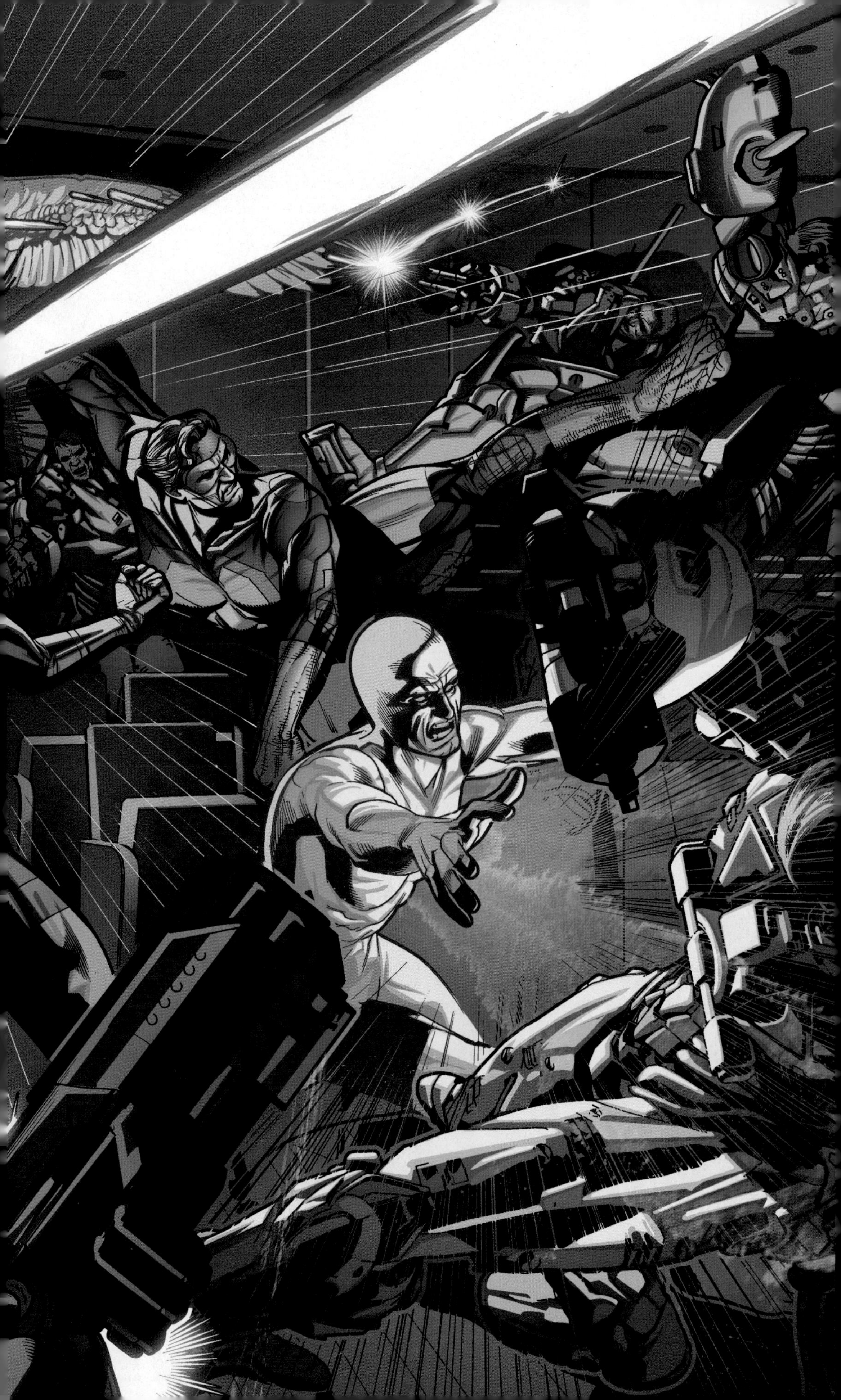

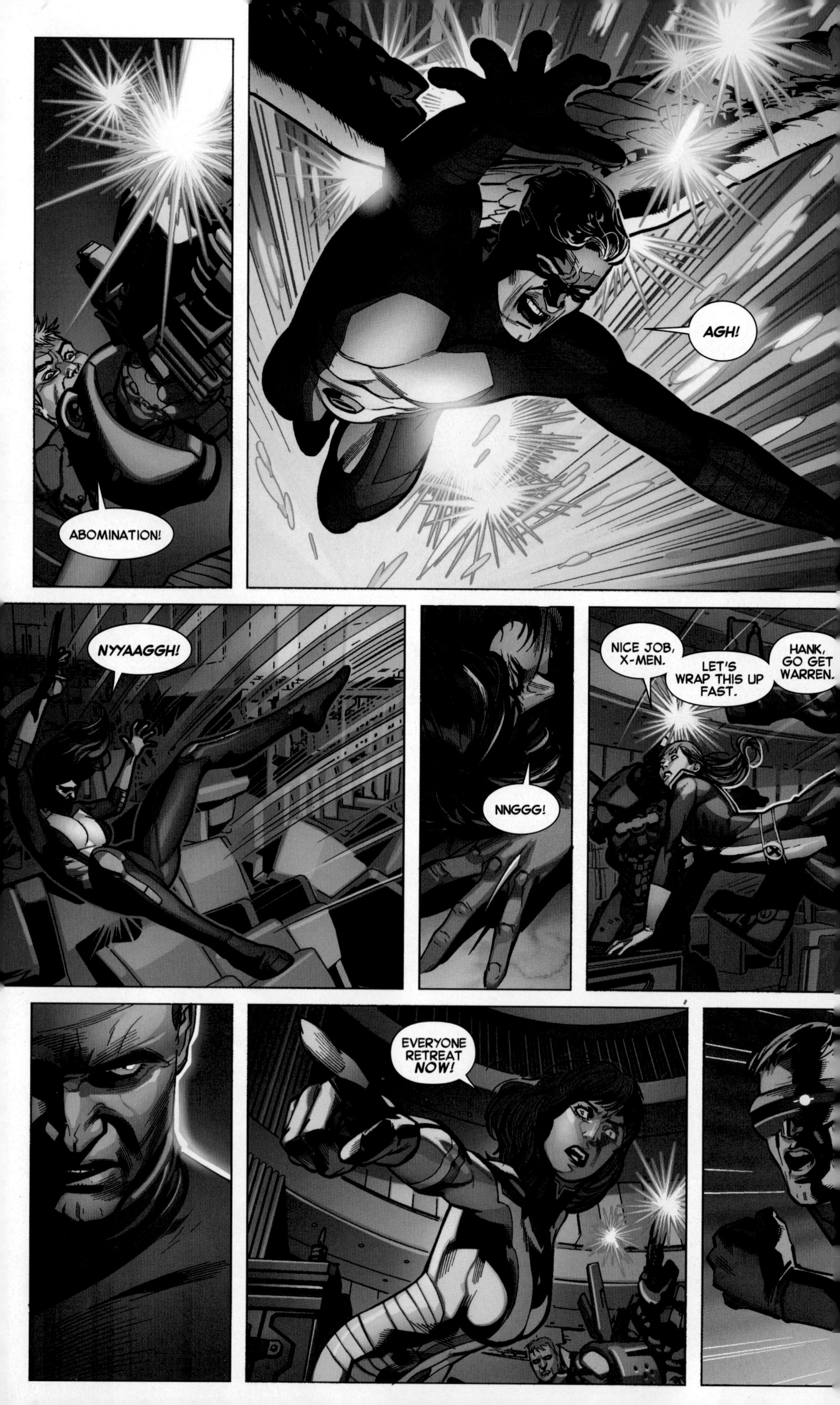
ABOMINATION!
AGH!
NYYAAGGH!
NNGGG!
NICE JOB, X-MEN.
LET'S WRAP THIS UP FAST.
HANK, GO GET WARREN.
EVERYONE RETREAT NOW!

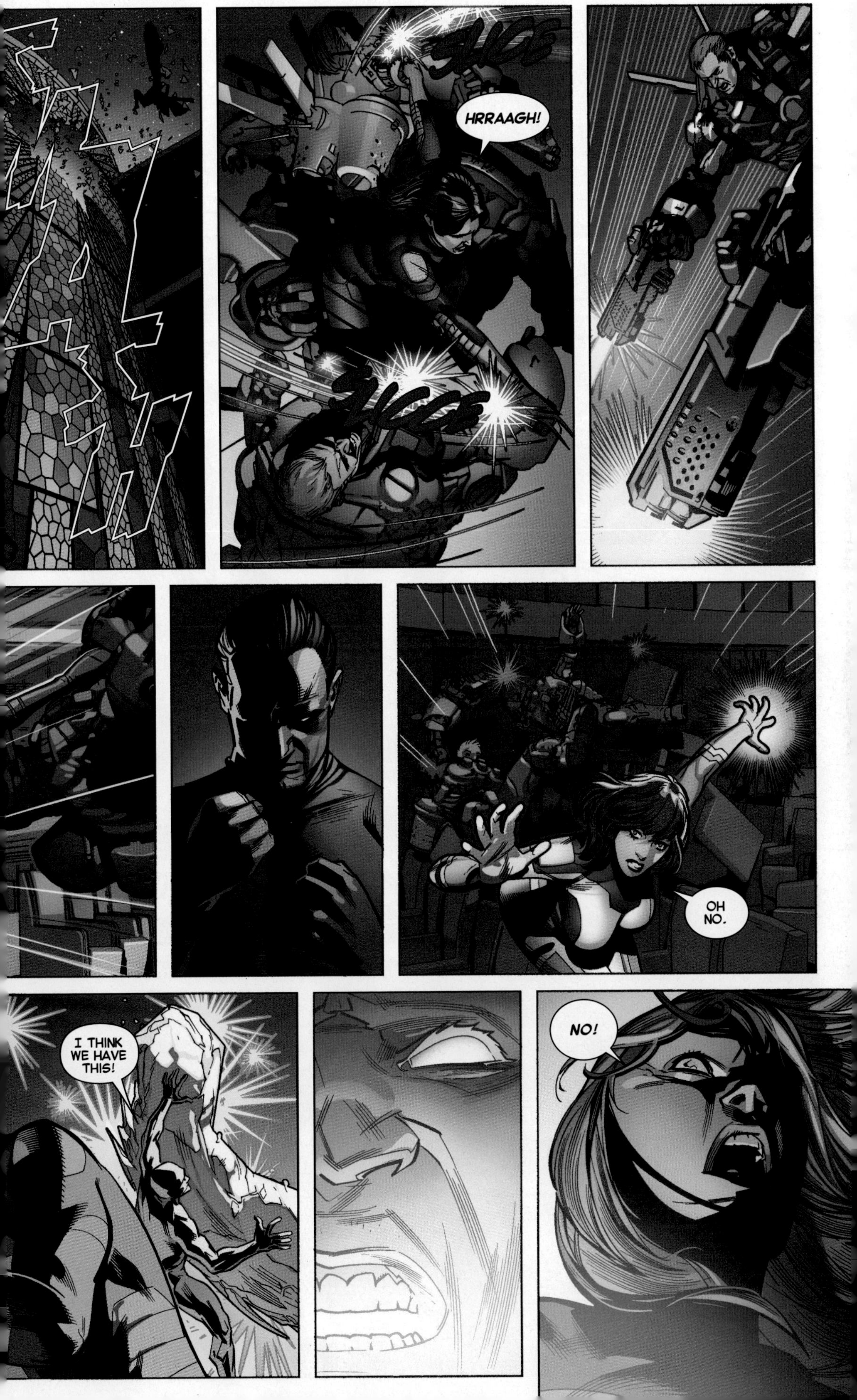

HRRAAGH!
OH NO.
I THINK WE HAVE THIS!
NO!

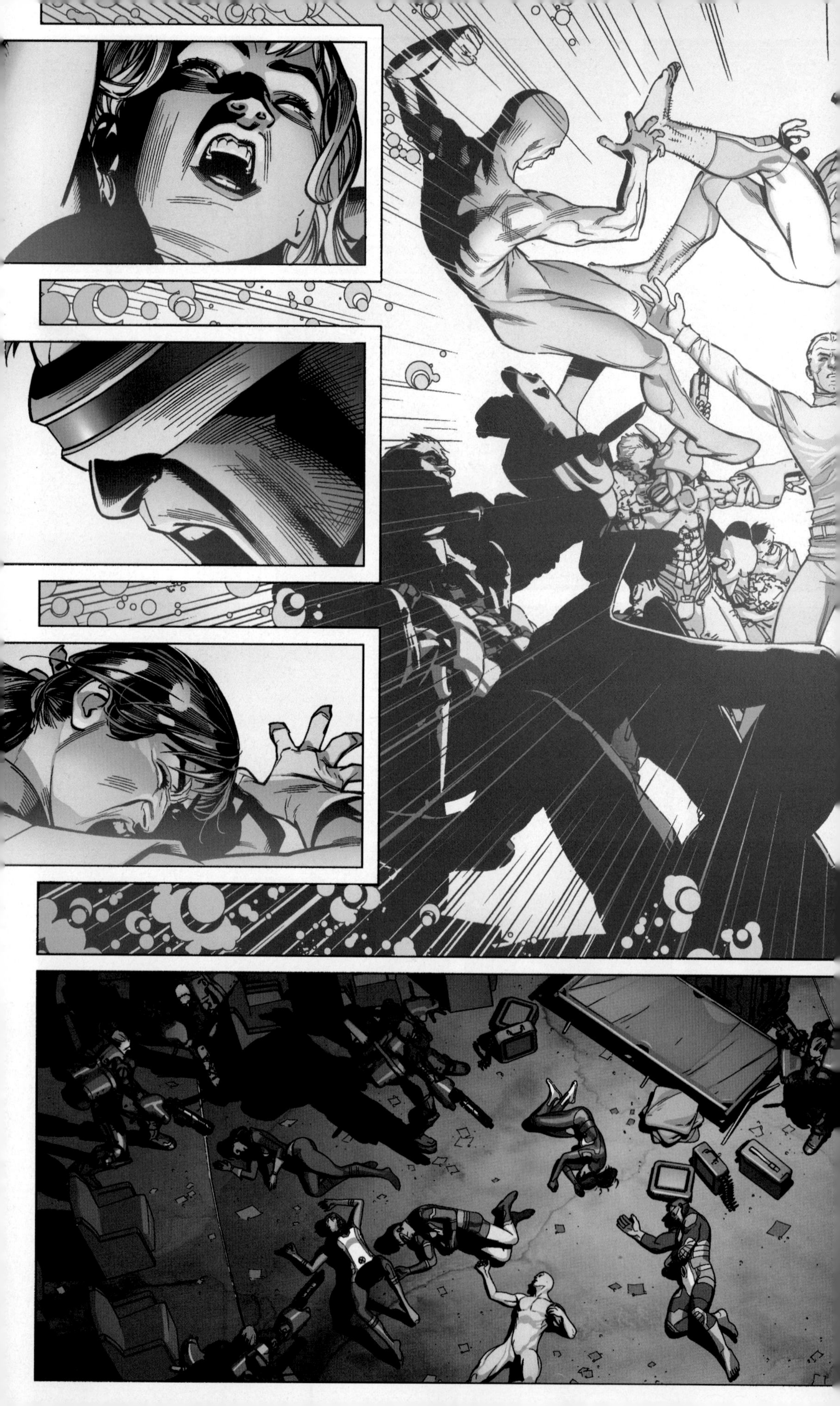

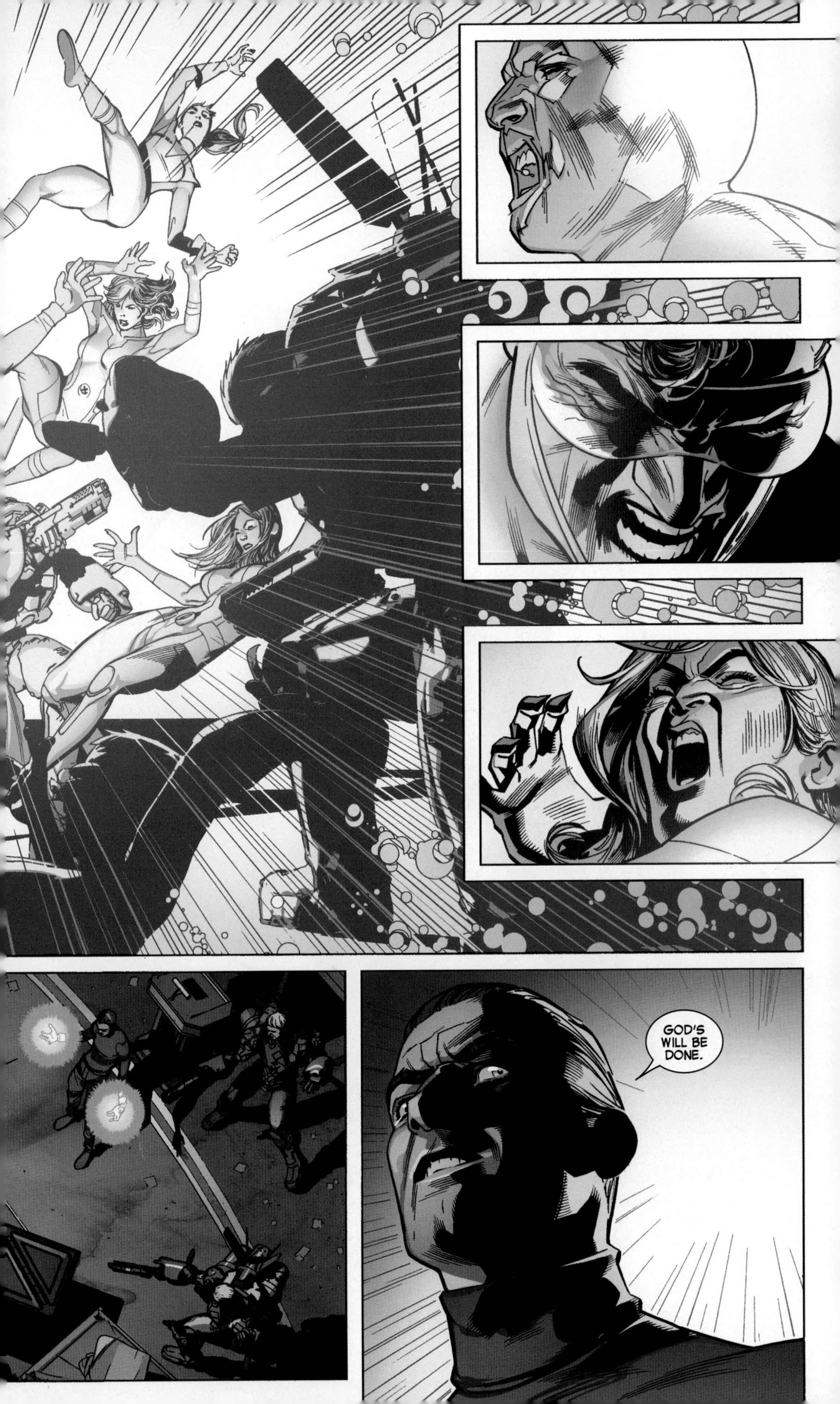
GOD'S WILL BE DONE.

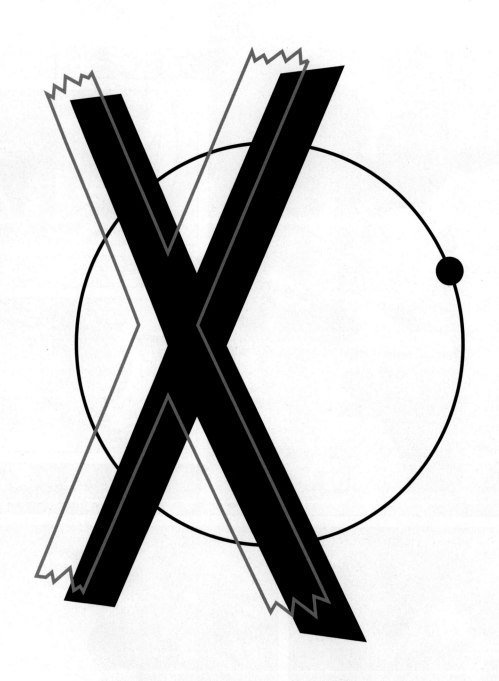

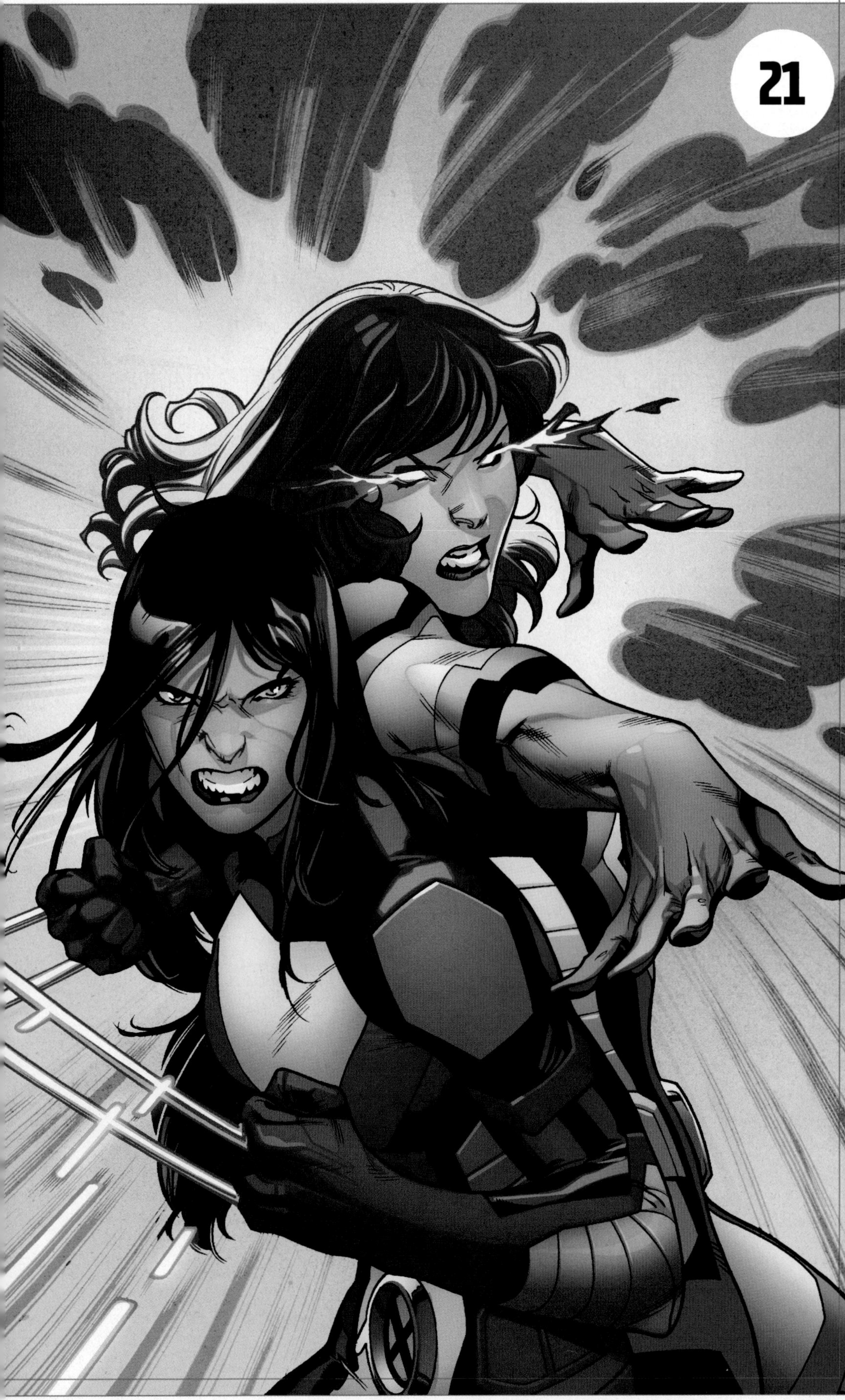
21

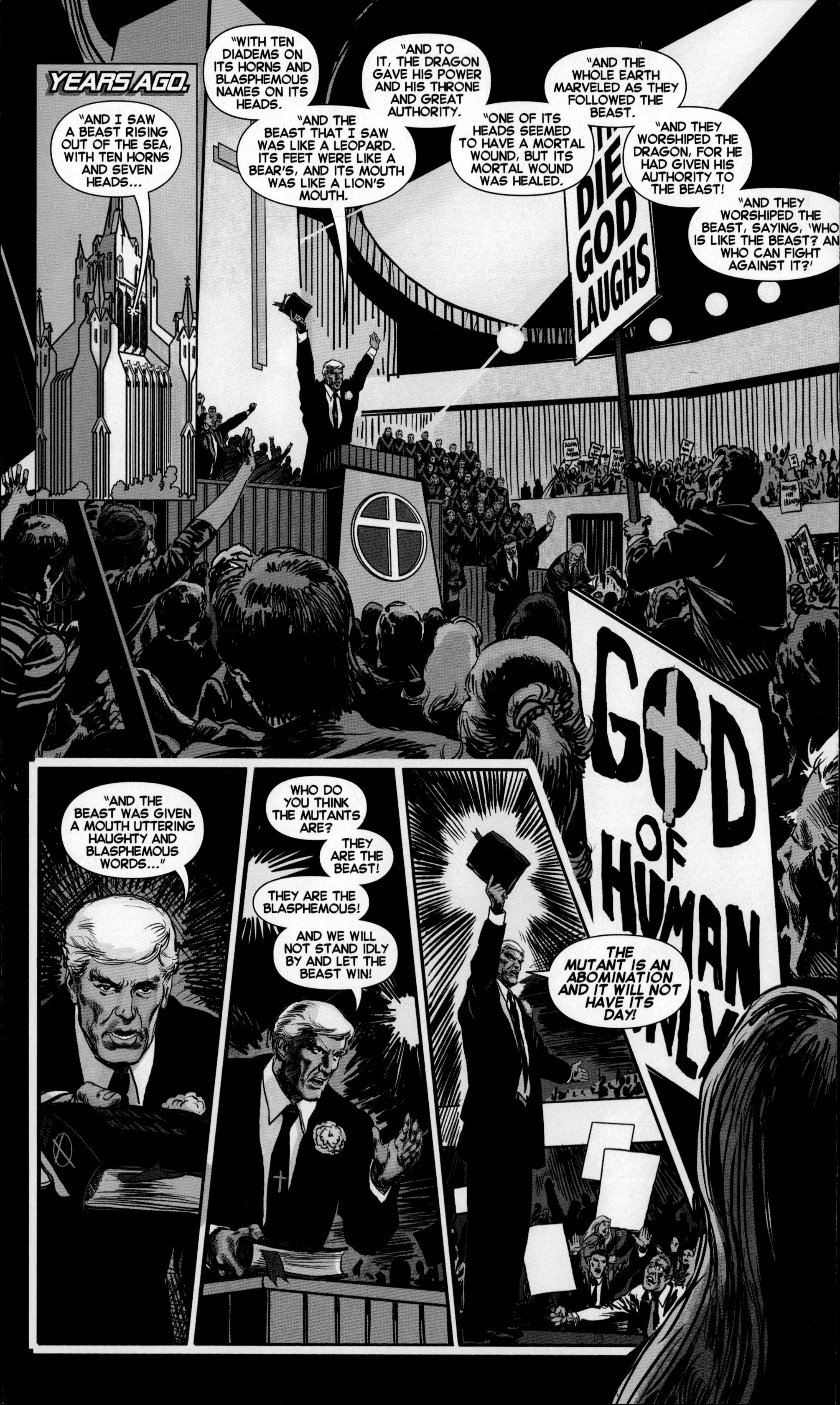
YEARS AGO.
"AND I SAW A BEAST RISING OUT OF THE SEA, WITH TEN HORNS AND SEVEN HEADS...
"WITH TEN DIADEMS ON ITS HORNS AND BLASPHEMOUS NAMES ON ITS HEADS.
"AND THE BEAST THAT I SAW WAS LIKE A LEOPARD. ITS FEET WERE LIKE A BEAR'S, AND ITS MOUTH WAS LIKE A LION'S MOUTH.
"AND TO IT, THE DRAGON GAVE HIS POWER AND HIS THRONE AND GREAT AUTHORITY.
"ONE OF ITS HEADS SEEMED TO HAVE A MORTAL WOUND, BUT ITS MORTAL WOUND WAS HEALED.
"AND THE WHOLE EARTH MARVELED AS THEY FOLLOWED THE BEAST.
"AND THEY WORSHIPED THE DRAGON, FOR HE HAD GIVEN HIS AUTHORITY TO THE BEAST!
"AND THEY WORSHIPED THE BEAST, SAYING, 'WHO IS LIKE THE BEAST? AN WHO CAN FIGHT AGAINST IT?'
DIE GOD LAUGHS
GOD OF HUMAN
"AND THE BEAST WAS GIVEN A MOUTH UTTERING HAUGHTY AND BLASPHEMOUS WORDS..."
WHO DO YOU THINK THE MUTANTS ARE?
THEY ARE THE BEAST!
THEY ARE THE BLASPHEMOUS!
AND WE WILL NOT STAND IDLY BY AND LET THE BEAST WIN!
THE MUTANT IS AN ABOMINATION AND IT WILL NOT HAVE ITS DAY!

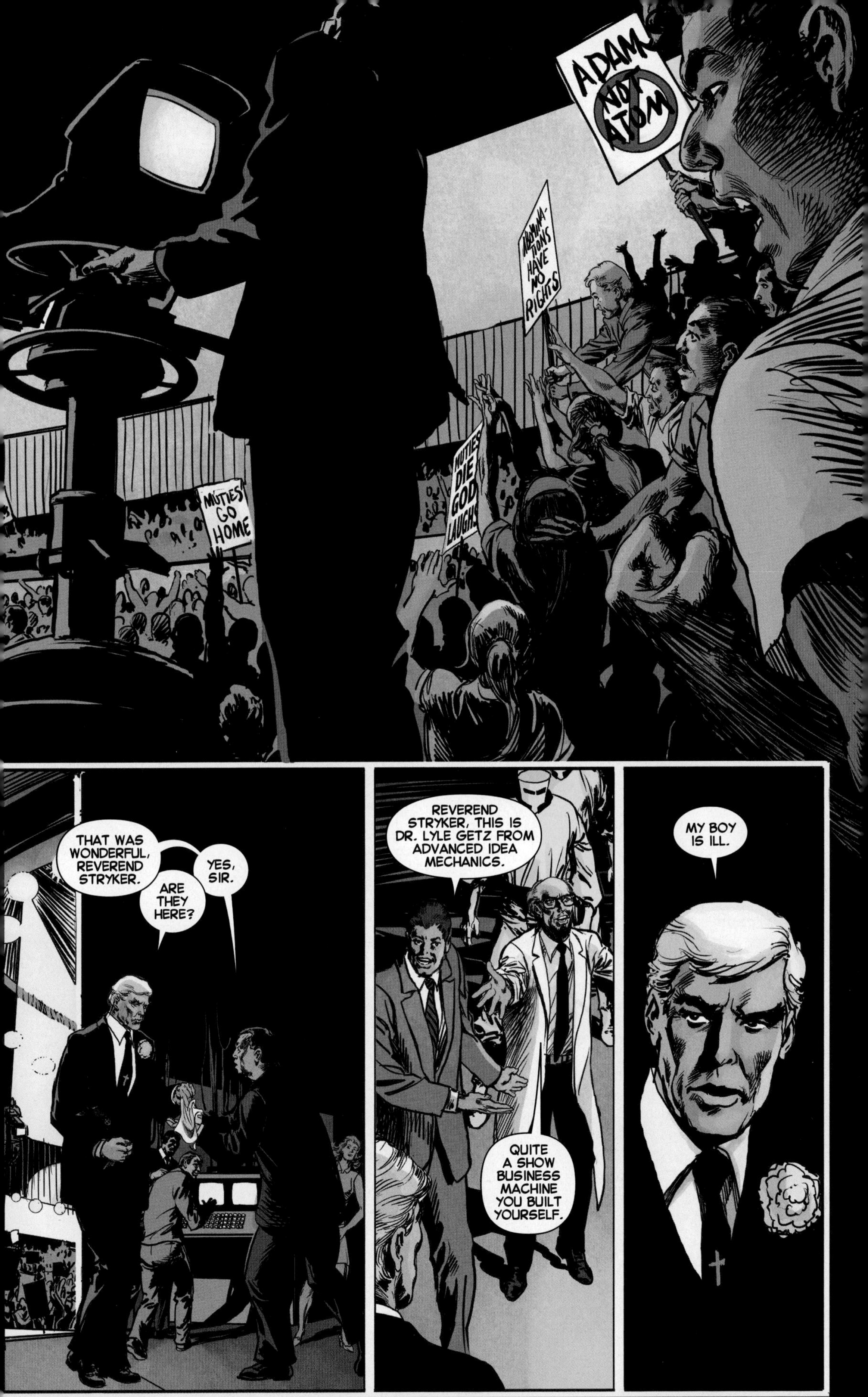

ADAM NOT ATOM
ABOMINA-TIONS HAVE NO RIGHTS
MUTIES GO HOME
MUTIES DIE GOD LAUGHS
THAT WAS WONDERFUL, REVEREND STRYKER.
YES, SIR.
ARE THEY HERE?
REVEREND STRYKER, THIS IS DR. LYLE GETZ FROM ADVANCED IDEA MECHANICS.
QUITE A SHOW BUSINESS MACHINE YOU BUILT YOURSELF.
MY BOY IS ILL.

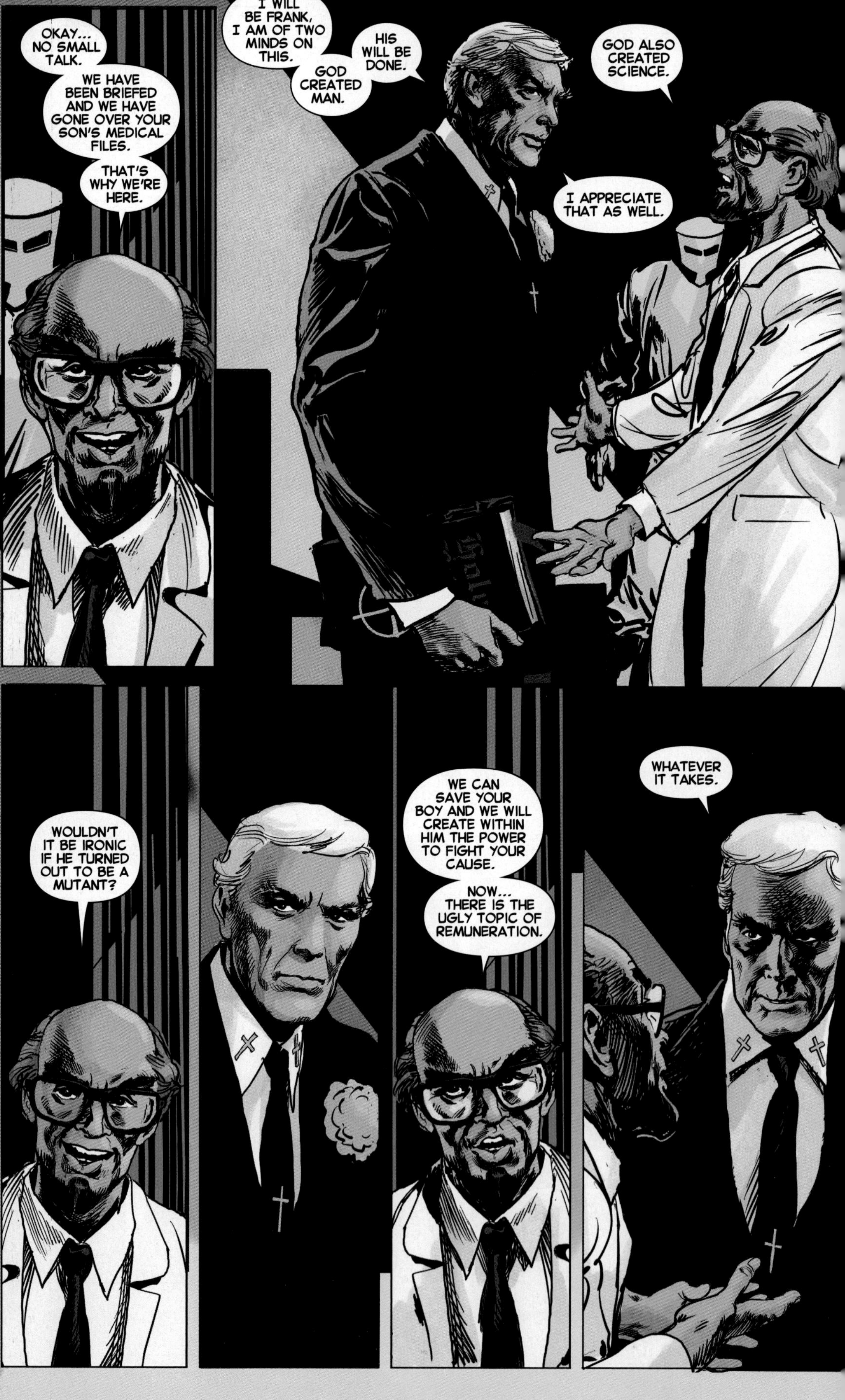
OKAY... NO SMALL TALK.
WE HAVE BEEN BRIEFED AND WE HAVE GONE OVER YOUR SON'S MEDICAL FILES.
THAT'S WHY WE'RE HERE.
I WILL BE FRANK, I AM OF TWO MINDS ON THIS.
GOD CREATED MAN.
HIS WILL BE DONE.
GOD ALSO CREATED SCIENCE.
I APPRECIATE THAT AS WELL.
WOULDN'T IT BE IRONIC IF HE TURNED OUT TO BE A MUTANT?
WE CAN SAVE YOUR BOY AND WE WILL CREATE WITHIN HIM THE POWER TO FIGHT YOUR CAUSE.
NOW... THERE IS THE UGLY TOPIC OF REMUNERATION.
WHATEVER IT TAKES.

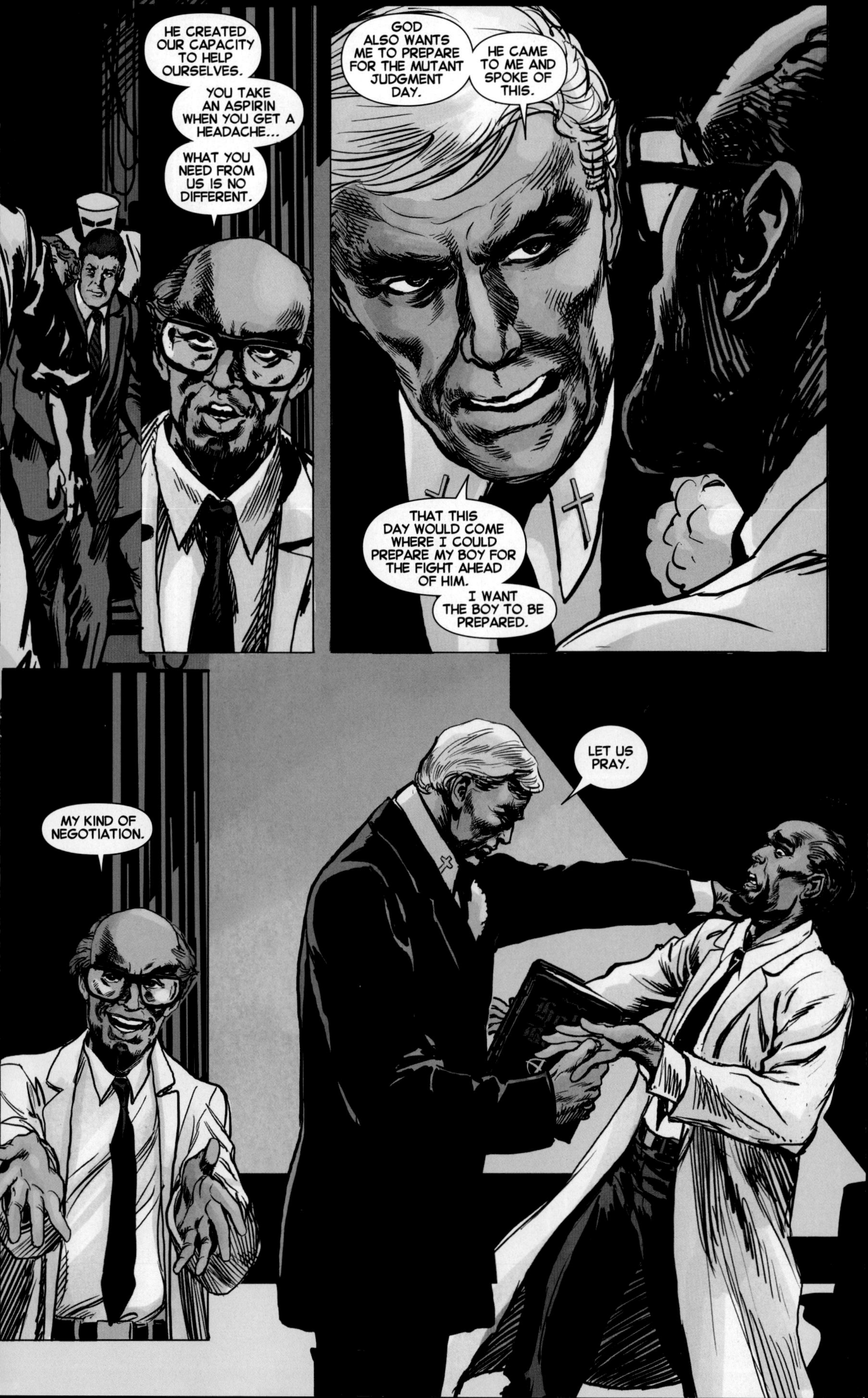
HE CREATED OUR CAPACITY TO HELP OURSELVES.
YOU TAKE AN ASPIRIN WHEN YOU GET A HEADACHE...
WHAT YOU NEED FROM US IS NO DIFFERENT.
GOD ALSO WANTS ME TO PREPARE FOR THE MUTANT JUDGMENT DAY.
HE CAME TO ME AND SPOKE OF THIS.
THAT THIS DAY WOULD COME WHERE I COULD PREPARE MY BOY FOR THE FIGHT AHEAD OF HIM.
I WANT THE BOY TO BE PREPARED.
MY KIND OF NEGOTIATION.
LET US PRAY.

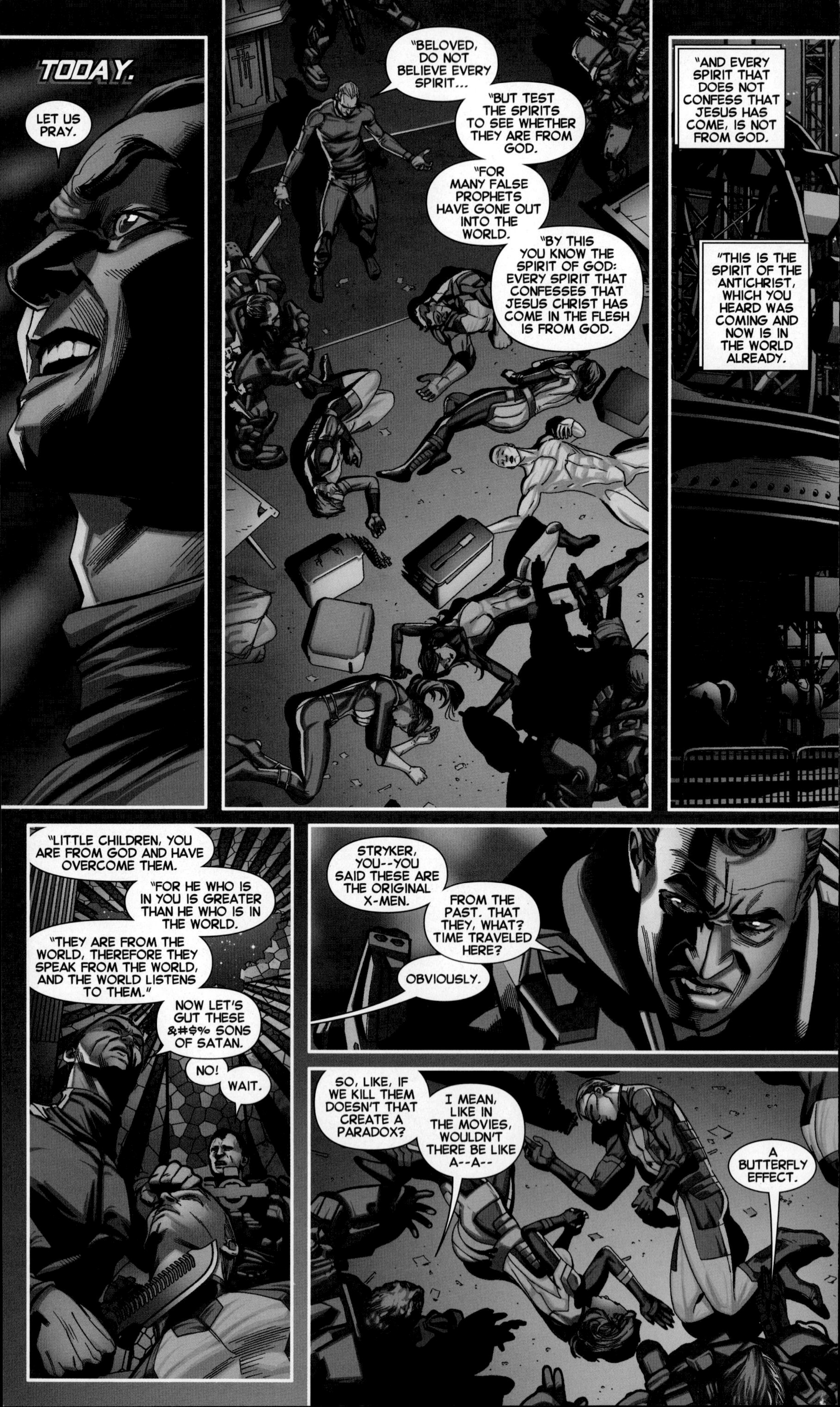
TODAY.
LET US PRAY.
"BELOVED, DO NOT BELIEVE EVERY SPIRIT...
"BUT TEST THE SPIRITS TO SEE WHETHER THEY ARE FROM GOD.
"FOR MANY FALSE PROPHETS HAVE GONE OUT INTO THE WORLD.
"BY THIS YOU KNOW THE SPIRIT OF GOD: EVERY SPIRIT THAT CONFESSES THAT JESUS CHRIST HAS COME IN THE FLESH IS FROM GOD.
"AND EVERY SPIRIT THAT DOES NOT CONFESS THAT JESUS HAS COME, IS NOT FROM GOD.
"THIS IS THE SPIRIT OF THE ANTICHRIST, WHICH YOU HEARD WAS COMING AND NOW IS IN THE WORLD ALREADY.
"LITTLE CHILDREN, YOU ARE FROM GOD AND HAVE OVERCOME THEM.
"FOR HE WHO IS IN YOU IS GREATER THAN HE WHO IS IN THE WORLD.
"THEY ARE FROM THE WORLD, THEREFORE THEY SPEAK FROM THE WORLD, AND THE WORLD LISTENS TO THEM."
NOW LET'S GUT THESE &#$% SONS OF SATAN.
NO!
WAIT.
STRYKER, YOU--YOU SAID THESE ARE THE ORIGINAL X-MEN.
FROM THE PAST. THAT THEY, WHAT? TIME TRAVELED HERE?
OBVIOUSLY.
SO, LIKE, IF WE KILL THEM DOESN'T THAT CREATE A PARADOX?
I MEAN, LIKE IN THE MOVIES, WOULDN'T THERE BE LIKE A--A--
A BUTTERFLY EFFECT.

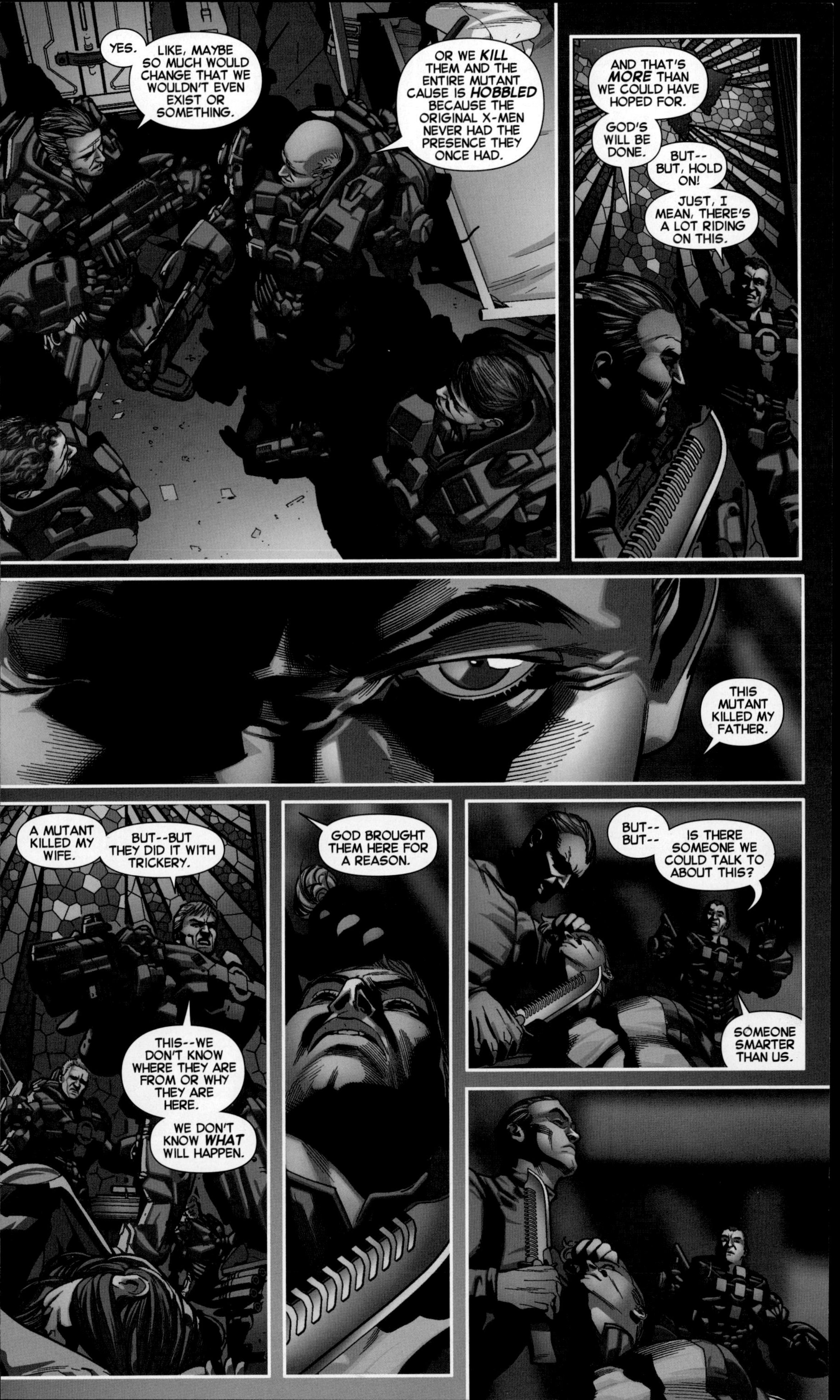
YES.
LIKE, MAYBE SO MUCH WOULD CHANGE THAT WE WOULDN'T EVEN EXIST OR SOMETHING.
OR WE **KILL** THEM AND THE ENTIRE MUTANT CAUSE IS ***HOBBLED*** BECAUSE THE ORIGINAL X-MEN NEVER HAD THE PRESENCE THEY ONCE HAD.
AND THAT'S ***MORE*** THAN WE COULD HAVE HOPED FOR.
GOD'S WILL BE DONE.
BUT--
BUT, HOLD ON!
JUST, I MEAN, THERE'S A LOT RIDING ON THIS.
THIS MUTANT KILLED MY FATHER.
A MUTANT KILLED MY WIFE.
BUT--BUT THEY DID IT WITH TRICKERY.
THIS--WE DON'T KNOW WHERE THEY ARE FROM OR WHY THEY ARE HERE.
WE DON'T KNOW ***WHAT*** WILL HAPPEN.
GOD BROUGHT THEM HERE FOR A REASON.
BUT-- BUT--
IS THERE SOMEONE WE COULD TALK TO ABOUT THIS?
SOMEONE SMARTER THAN US.

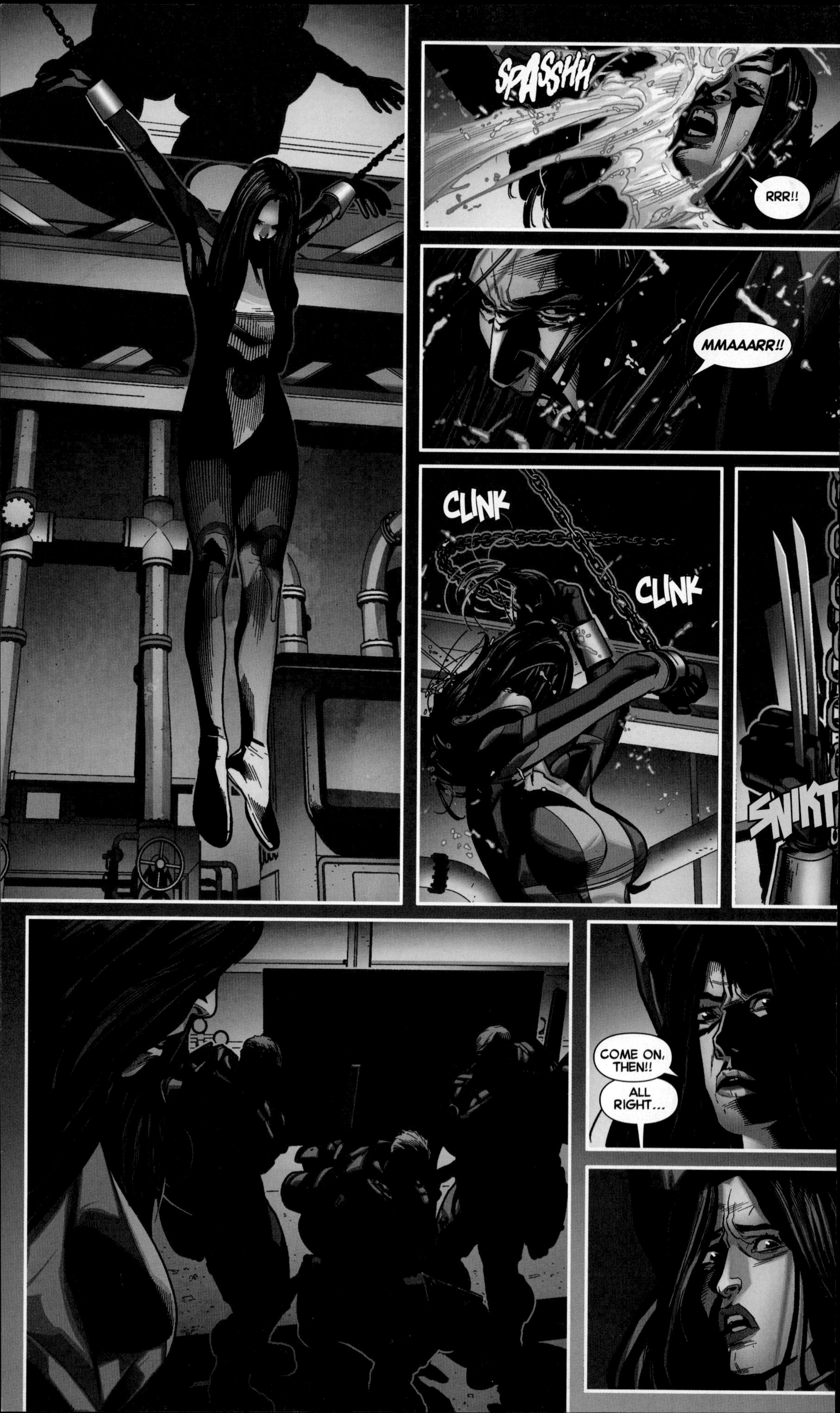
SPASSHH
RRR!!
MMAAARR!!
CLINK
CLINK
SNIKT
COME ON, THEN!!
ALL RIGHT...

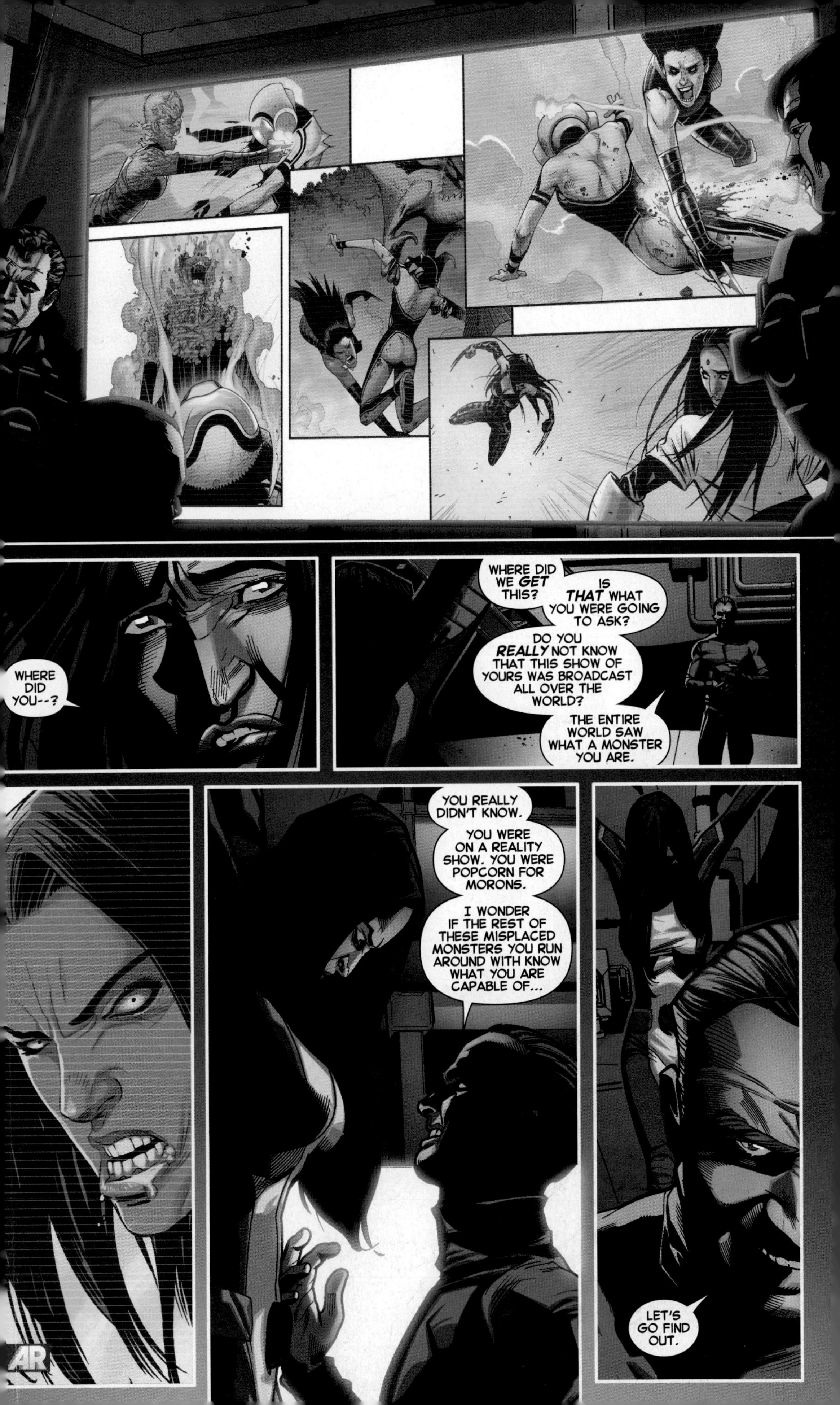
WHERE DID YOU--?
WHERE DID WE GET THIS?
IS THAT WHAT YOU WERE GOING TO ASK?
DO YOU REALLY NOT KNOW THAT THIS SHOW OF YOURS WAS BROADCAST ALL OVER THE WORLD?
THE ENTIRE WORLD SAW WHAT A MONSTER YOU ARE.
YOU REALLY DIDN'T KNOW.
YOU WERE ON A REALITY SHOW. YOU WERE POPCORN FOR MORONS.
I WONDER IF THE REST OF THESE MISPLACED MONSTERS YOU RUN AROUND WITH KNOW WHAT YOU ARE CAPABLE OF...
LET'S GO FIND OUT.

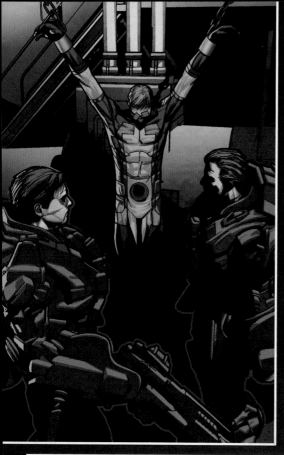

IS HE AWAKE?

I'M AWAKE.

WHY ARE YOU HERE, SCOTT SUMMERS?

I'M HAPPY TO LEAVE.

WHY ARE YOU HERE IN THIS TIME?

I'D LIKE TO TALK TO MY LAWYER.

NYYAAGGH!

HELP HIM REMEMBER.

DR. STRYKER, A.I.M. IS HERE.

I'M DR. MONICA RAPPACCINI, OF A.I.M.

YOU CALLED?

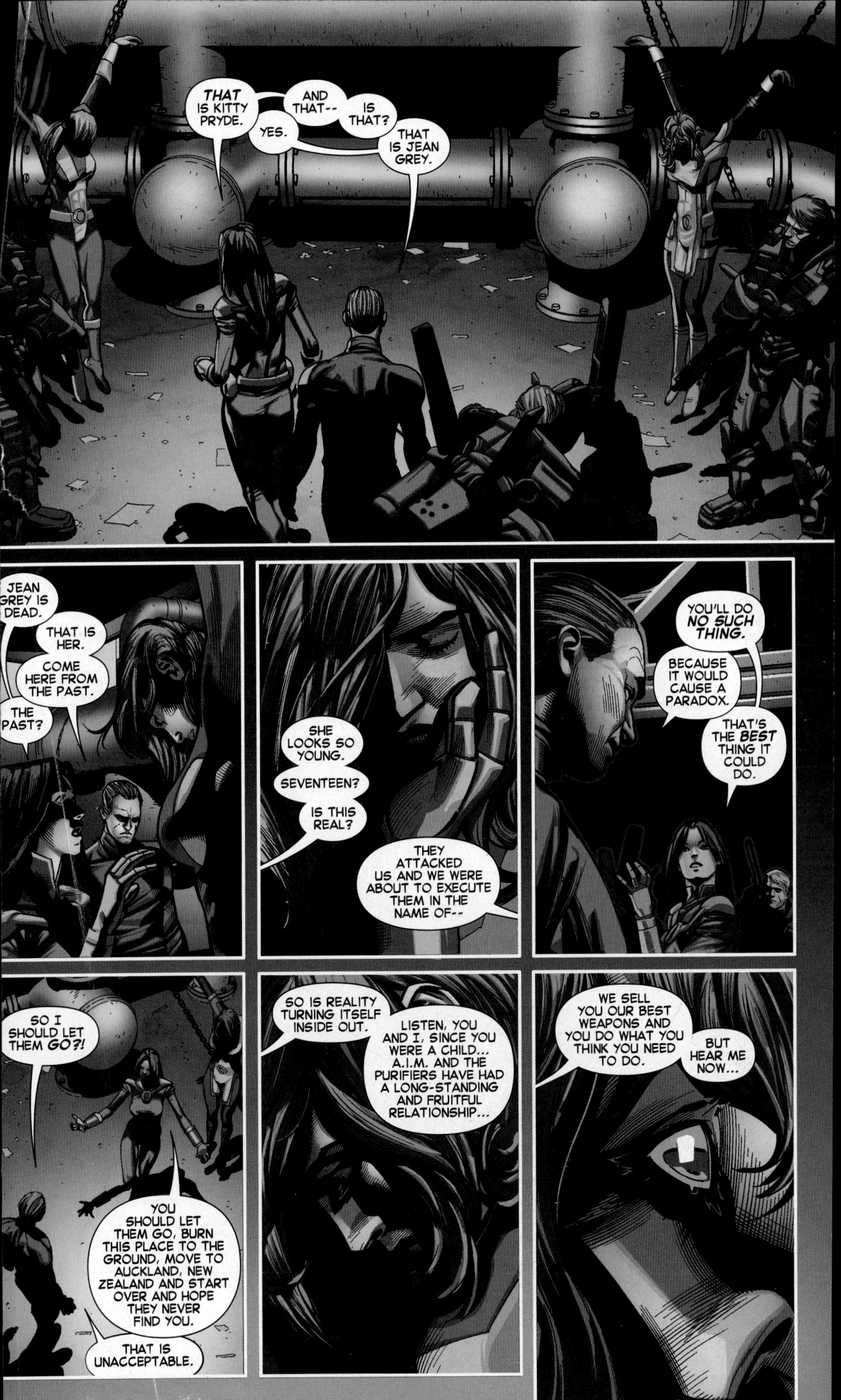

THAT IS KITTY PRYDE.
AND THAT--
IS THAT?
YES.
THAT IS JEAN GREY.
JEAN GREY IS DEAD.
THAT IS HER.
COME HERE FROM THE PAST.
THE PAST?
SHE LOOKS SO YOUNG.
SEVENTEEN?
IS THIS REAL?
THEY ATTACKED US AND WE WERE ABOUT TO EXECUTE THEM IN THE NAME OF--
YOU'LL DO NO SUCH THING.
BECAUSE IT WOULD CAUSE A PARADOX.
THAT'S THE BEST THING IT COULD DO.
SO I SHOULD LET THEM GO?!
YOU SHOULD LET THEM GO, BURN THIS PLACE TO THE GROUND, MOVE TO AUCKLAND, NEW ZEALAND AND START OVER AND HOPE THEY NEVER FIND YOU.
THAT IS UNACCEPTABLE.
SO IS REALITY TURNING ITSELF INSIDE OUT.
LISTEN, YOU AND I, SINCE YOU WERE A CHILD... A.I.M. AND THE PURIFIERS HAVE HAD A LONG-STANDING AND FRUITFUL RELATIONSHIP...
WE SELL YOU OUR BEST WEAPONS AND YOU DO WHAT YOU THINK YOU NEED TO DO.
BUT HEAR ME NOW...

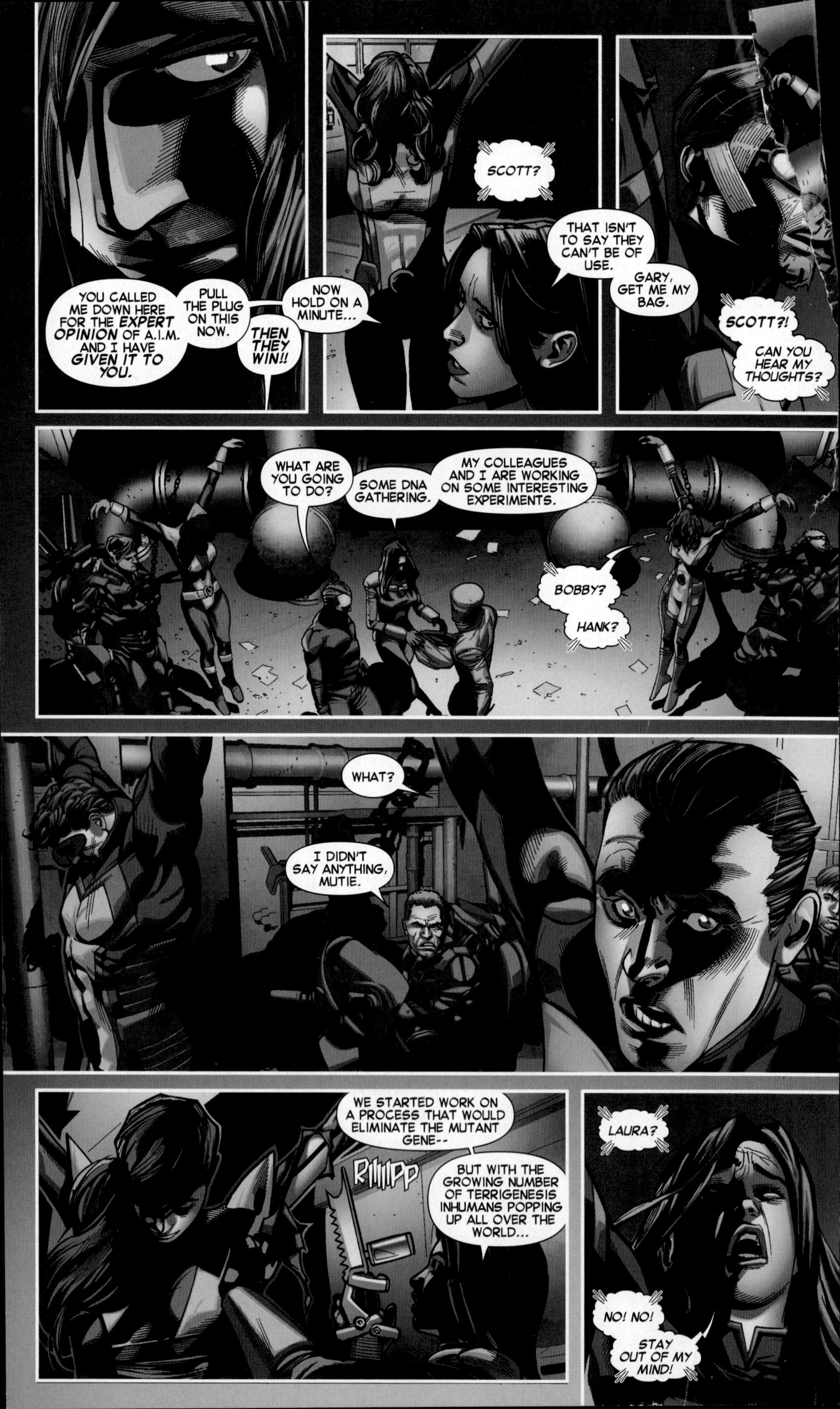
YOU CALLED ME DOWN HERE FOR THE EXPERT OPINION OF A.I.M. AND I HAVE GIVEN IT TO YOU.
PULL THE PLUG ON THIS NOW.
THEN THEY WIN!!
NOW HOLD ON A MINUTE...
SCOTT?
THAT ISN'T TO SAY THEY CAN'T BE OF USE.
GARY, GET ME MY BAG.
SCOTT?!
CAN YOU HEAR MY THOUGHTS?
WHAT ARE YOU GOING TO DO?
SOME DNA GATHERING.
MY COLLEAGUES AND I ARE WORKING ON SOME INTERESTING EXPERIMENTS.
BOBBY?
HANK?
WHAT?
I DIDN'T SAY ANYTHING, MUTIE.
WE STARTED WORK ON A PROCESS THAT WOULD ELIMINATE THE MUTANT GENE--
RIIIIPP
BUT WITH THE GROWING NUMBER OF TERRIGENESIS INHUMANS POPPING UP ALL OVER THE WORLD...
LAURA?
NO! NO!
STAY OUT OF MY MIND!

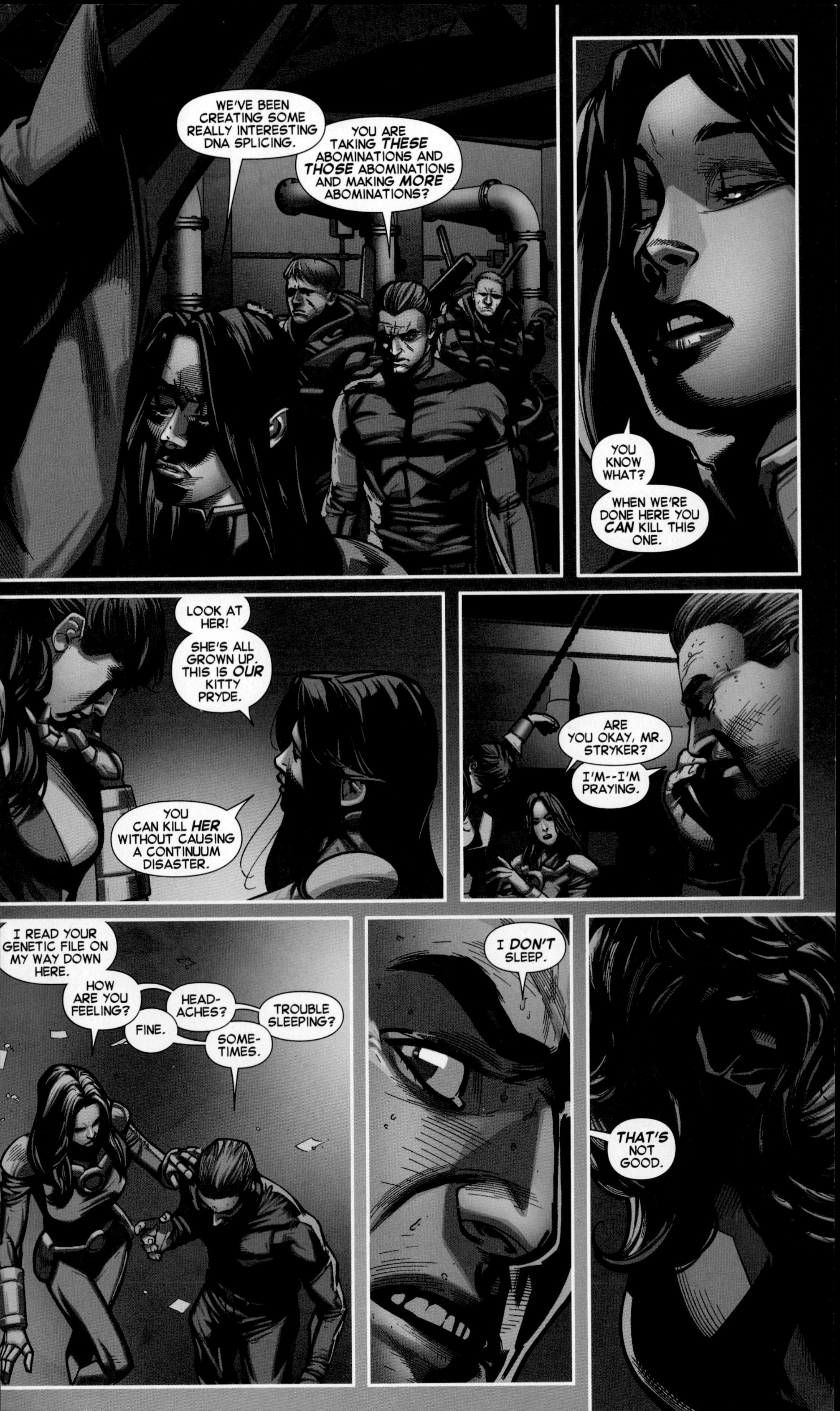
WE'VE BEEN CREATING SOME REALLY INTERESTING DNA SPLICING.
YOU ARE TAKING *THESE* ABOMINATIONS AND *THOSE* ABOMINATIONS AND MAKING *MORE* ABOMINATIONS?
YOU KNOW WHAT?
WHEN WE'RE DONE HERE YOU *CAN* KILL THIS ONE.
LOOK AT HER!
SHE'S ALL GROWN UP. THIS IS *OUR* KITTY PRYDE.
YOU CAN KILL *HER* WITHOUT CAUSING A CONTINUUM DISASTER.
ARE YOU OKAY, MR. STRYKER?
I'M--I'M PRAYING.
I READ YOUR GENETIC FILE ON MY WAY DOWN HERE.
HOW ARE YOU FEELING?
FINE.
HEAD-ACHES?
SOME-TIMES.
TROUBLE SLEEPING?
I *DON'T* SLEEP.
THAT'S NOT GOOD.

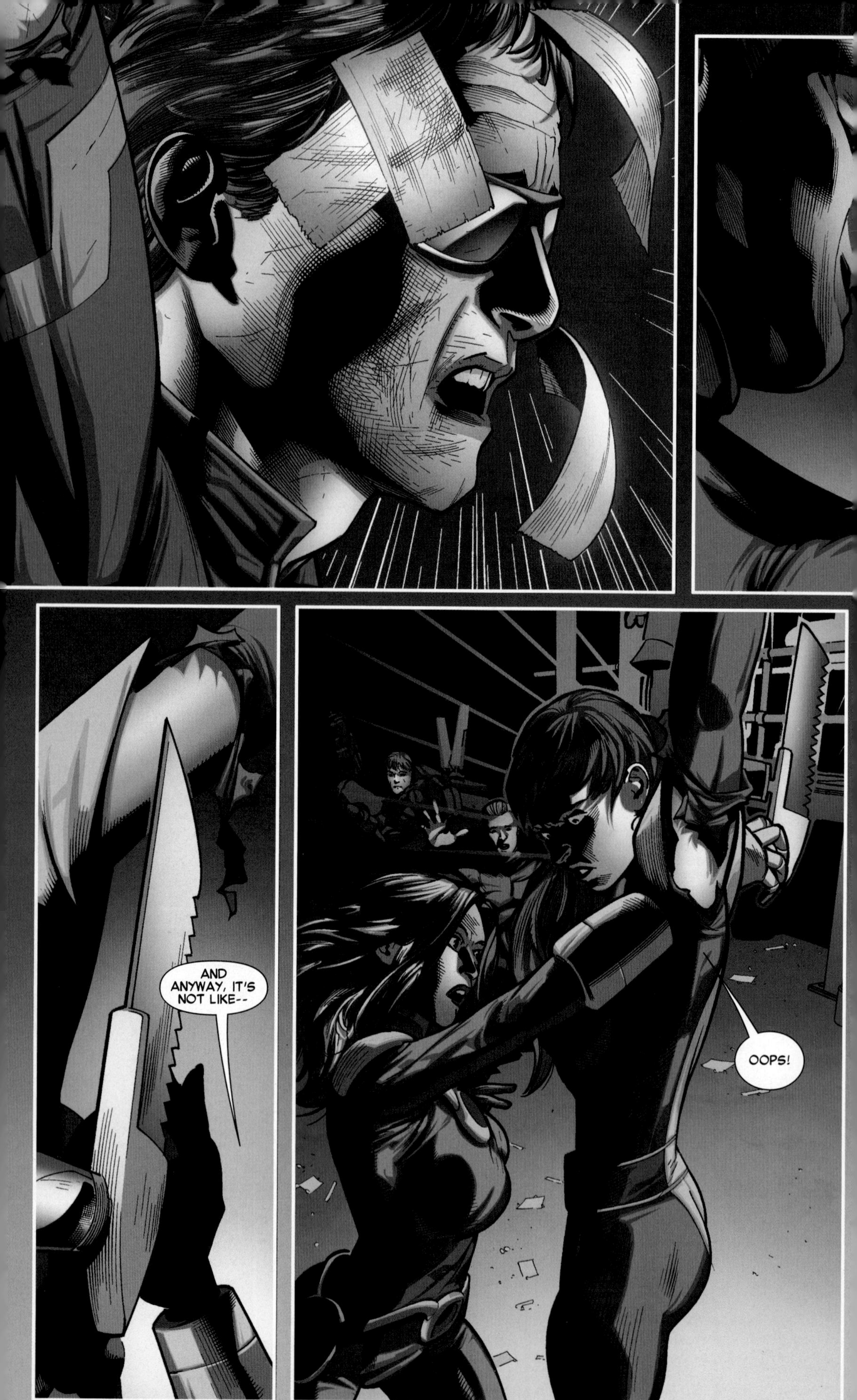
AND ANYWAY, IT'S NOT LIKE--
OOPS!

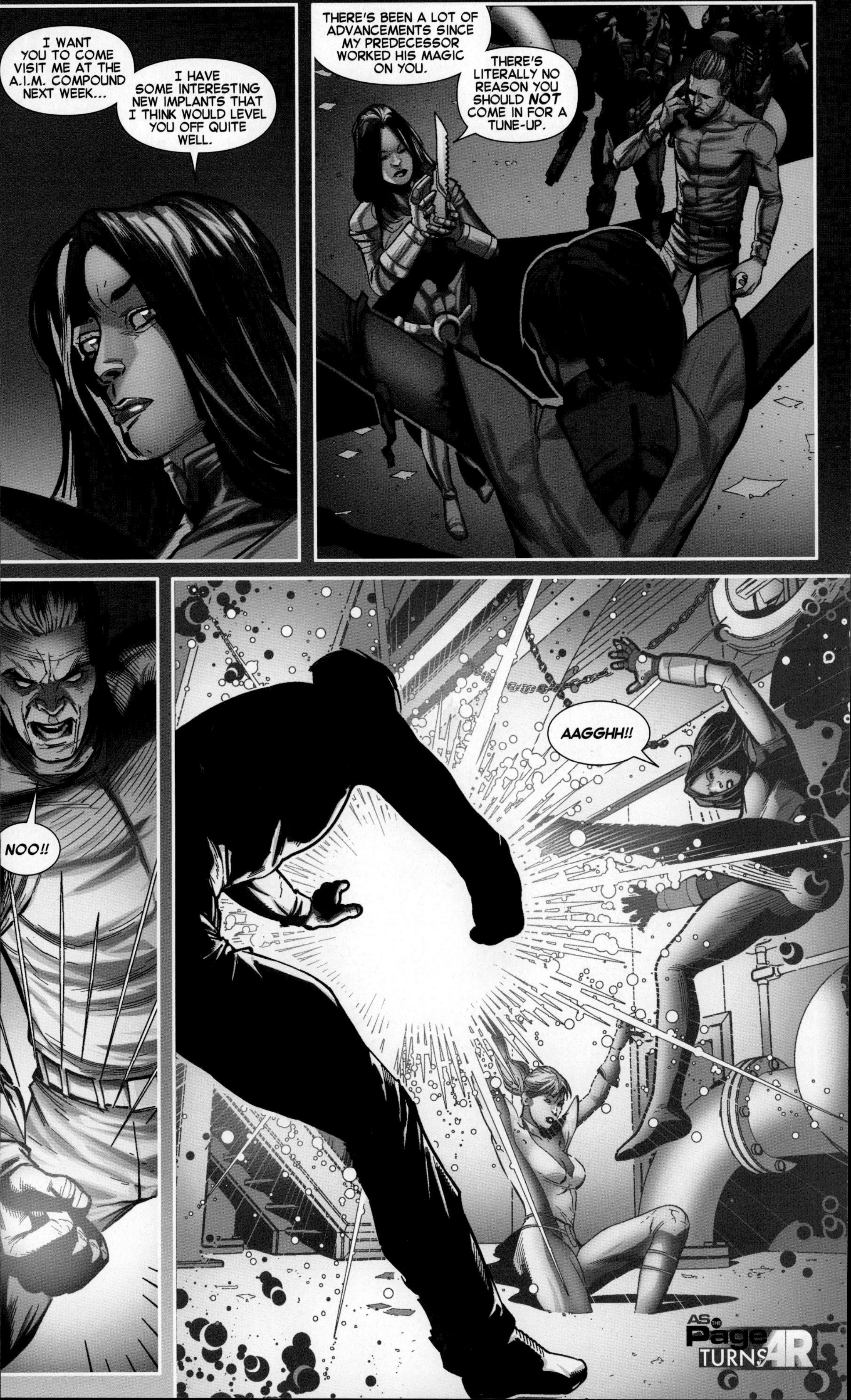
I WANT YOU TO COME VISIT ME AT THE A.I.M. COMPOUND NEXT WEEK...
I HAVE SOME INTERESTING NEW IMPLANTS THAT I THINK WOULD LEVEL YOU OFF QUITE WELL.
THERE'S BEEN A LOT OF ADVANCEMENTS SINCE MY PREDECESSOR WORKED HIS MAGIC ON YOU.
THERE'S LITERALLY NO REASON YOU SHOULD NOT COME IN FOR A TUNE-UP.
NOO!!
AAGGHH!!

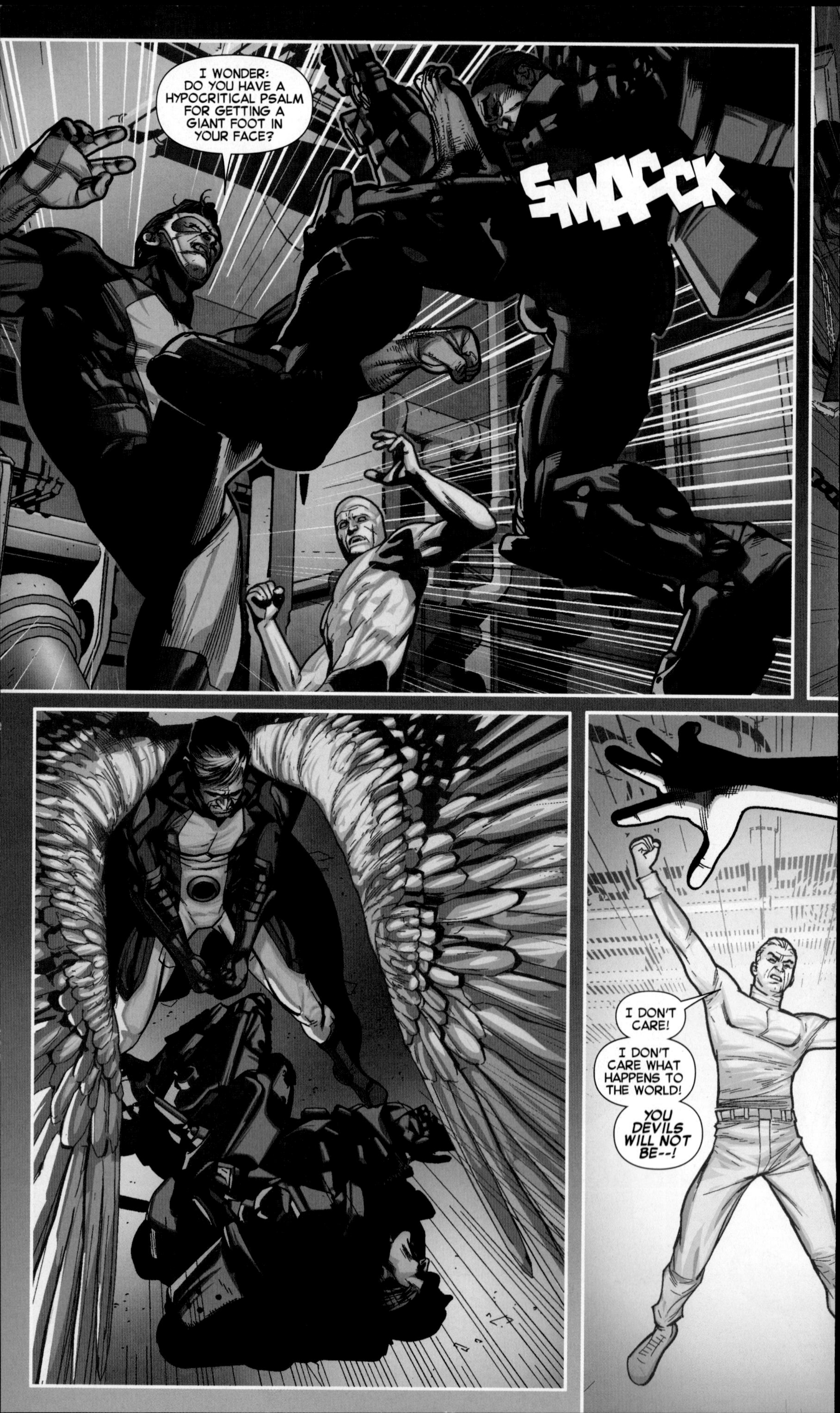
I WONDER: DO YOU HAVE A HYPOCRITICAL PSALM FOR GETTING A GIANT FOOT IN YOUR FACE?
SMACCK
I DON'T CARE!
I DON'T CARE WHAT HAPPENS TO THE WORLD!
YOU DEVILS WILL NOT BE--!

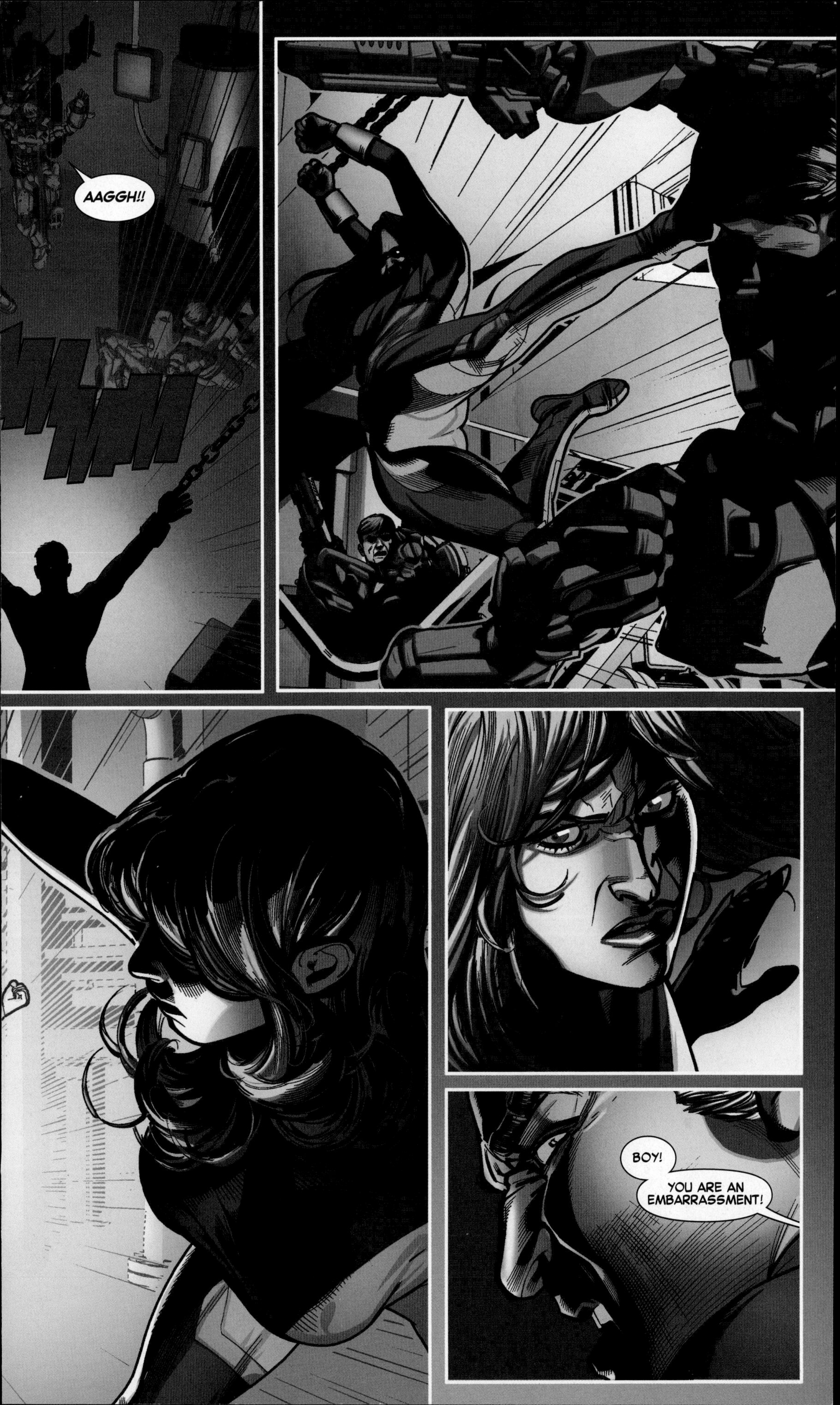
AAGGH!!
BOY!
YOU ARE AN EMBARRASSMENT!

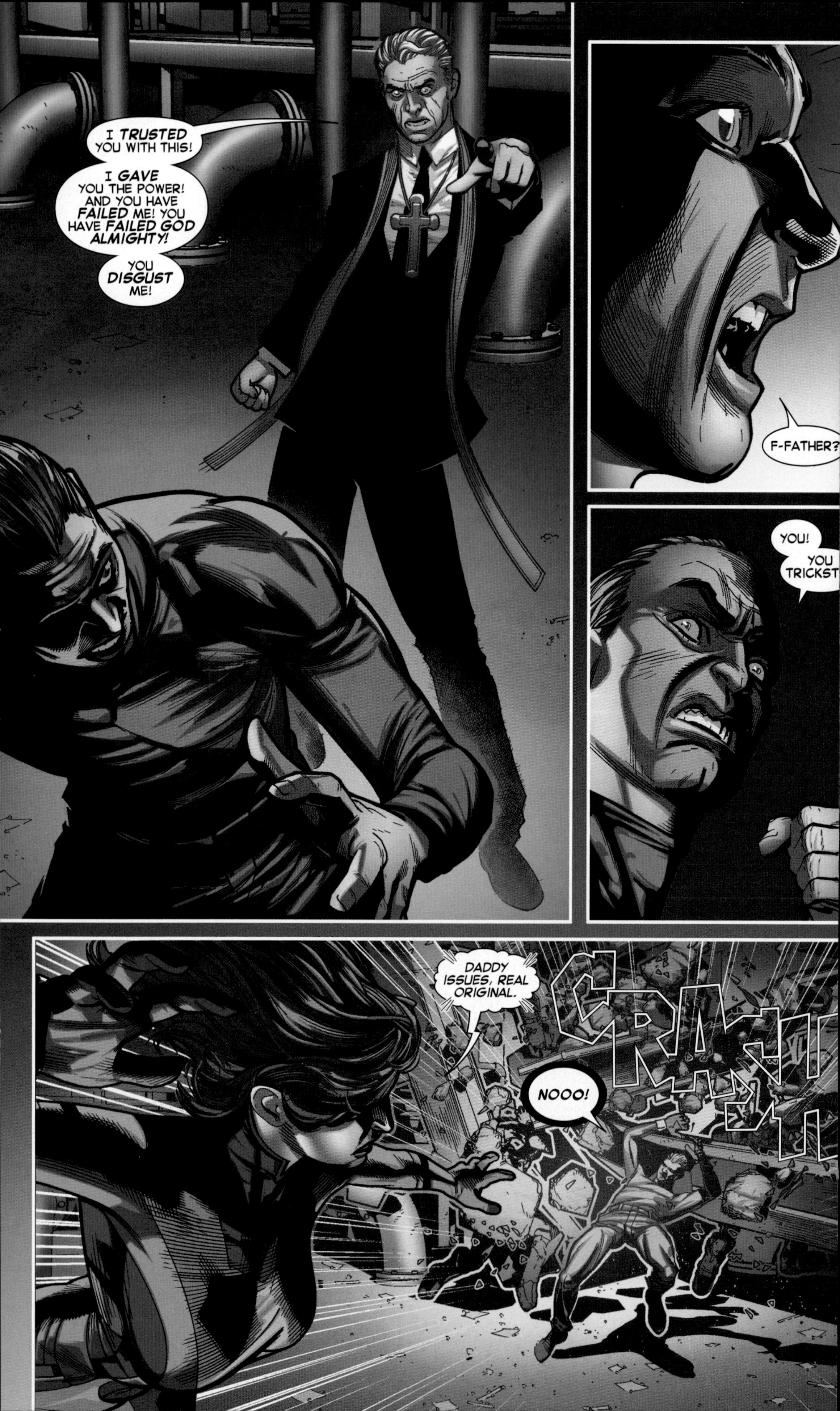

I TRUSTED YOU WITH THIS!
I GAVE YOU THE POWER! AND YOU HAVE FAILED ME! YOU HAVE FAILED GOD ALMIGHTY!
YOU DISGUST ME!
F-FATHER?
YOU!
YOU TRICKST
DADDY ISSUES. REAL ORIGINAL.
NOOO!

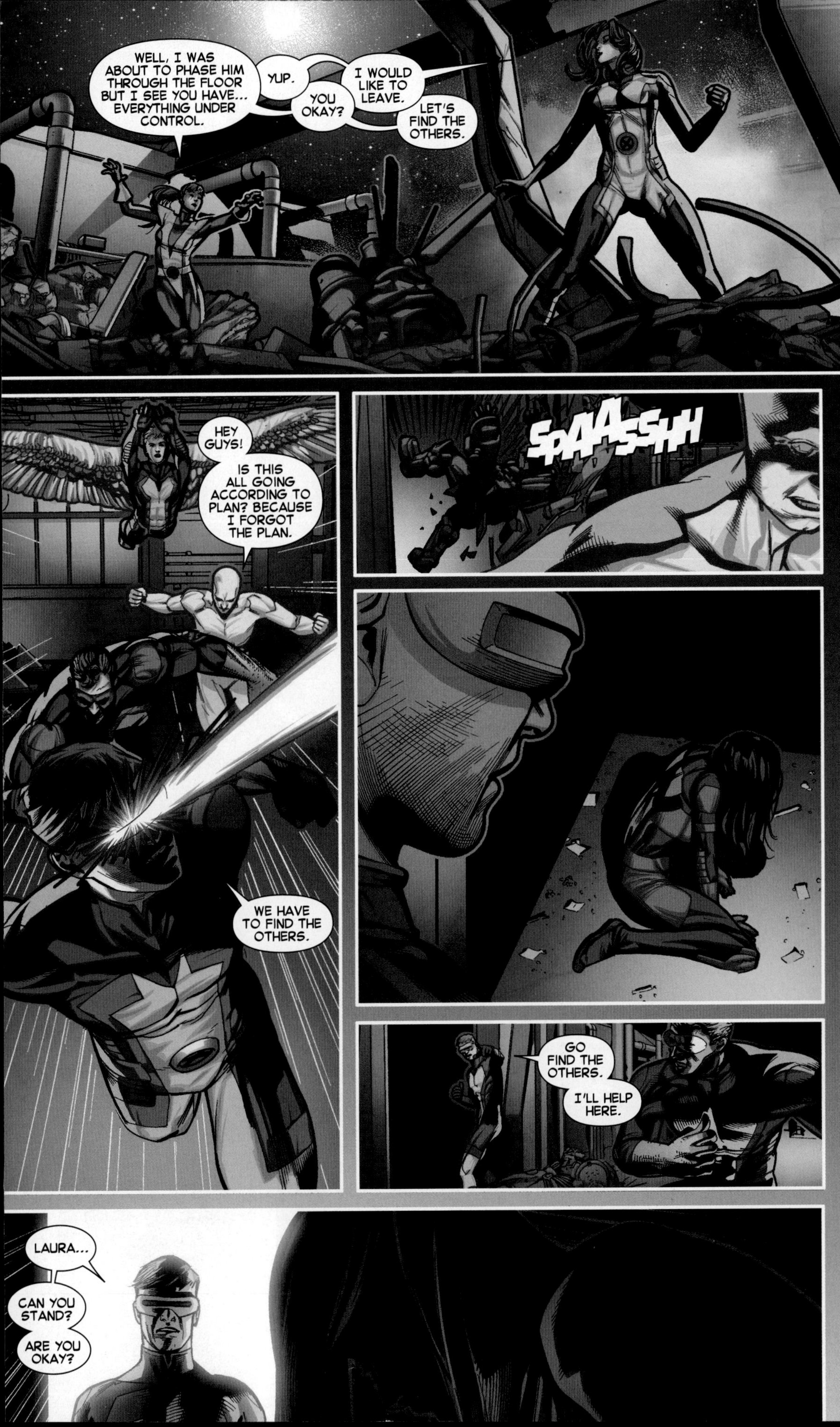

WELL, I WAS ABOUT TO PHASE HIM THROUGH THE FLOOR BUT I SEE YOU HAVE... EVERYTHING UNDER CONTROL.
YUP.
YOU OKAY?
I WOULD LIKE TO LEAVE.
LET'S FIND THE OTHERS.
HEY GUYS!
IS THIS ALL GOING ACCORDING TO PLAN? BECAUSE I FORGOT THE PLAN.
WE HAVE TO FIND THE OTHERS.
SPAASSHH
GO FIND THE OTHERS.
I'LL HELP HERE.
LAURA...
CAN YOU STAND?
ARE YOU OKAY?

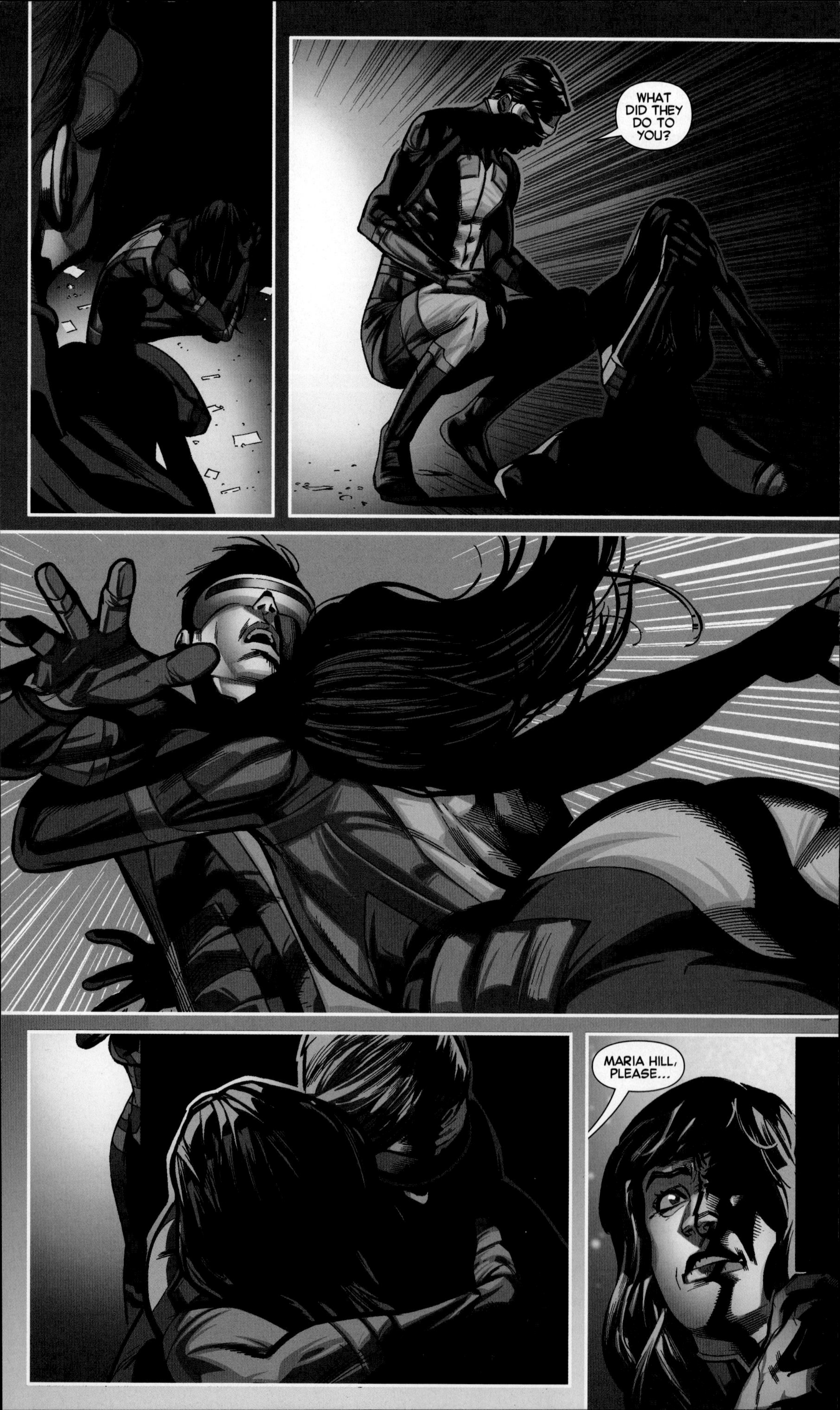
WHAT DID THEY DO TO YOU?
MARIA HILL, PLEASE...

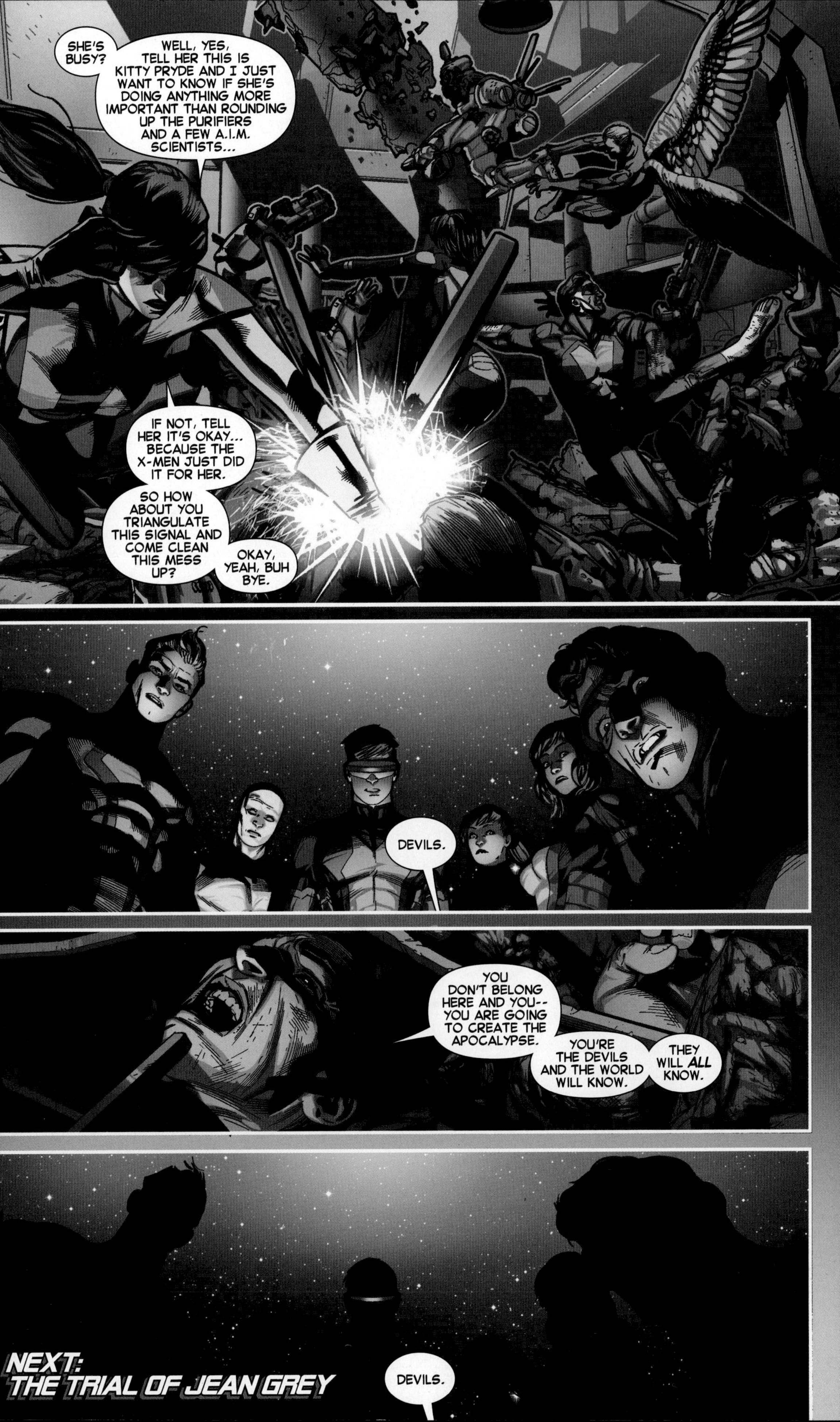
SHE'S BUSY?
WELL, YES, TELL HER THIS IS KITTY PRYDE AND I JUST WANT TO KNOW IF SHE'S DOING ANYTHING MORE IMPORTANT THAN ROUNDING UP THE PURIFIERS AND A FEW A.I.M. SCIENTISTS...
IF NOT, TELL HER IT'S OKAY... BECAUSE THE X-MEN JUST DID IT FOR HER.
SO HOW ABOUT YOU TRIANGULATE THIS SIGNAL AND COME CLEAN THIS MESS UP?
OKAY, YEAH, BUH BYE.
DEVILS.
YOU DON'T BELONG HERE AND YOU-- YOU ARE GOING TO CREATE THE APOCALYPSE.
YOU'RE THE DEVILS AND THE WORLD WILL KNOW.
THEY WILL ALL KNOW.
NEXT: THE TRIAL OF JEAN GREY
DEVILS.

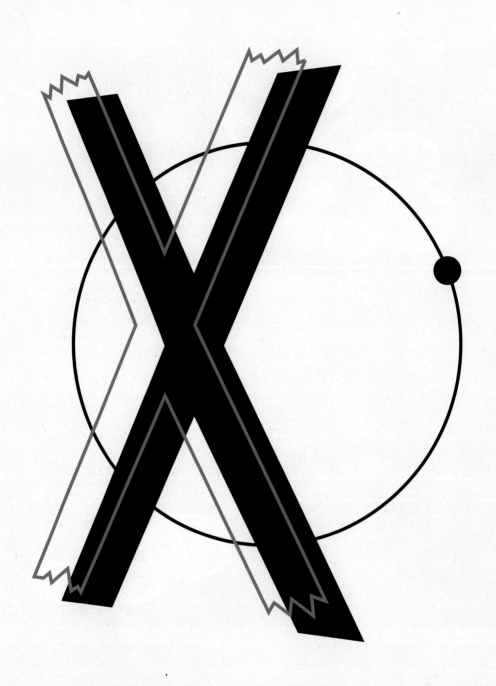

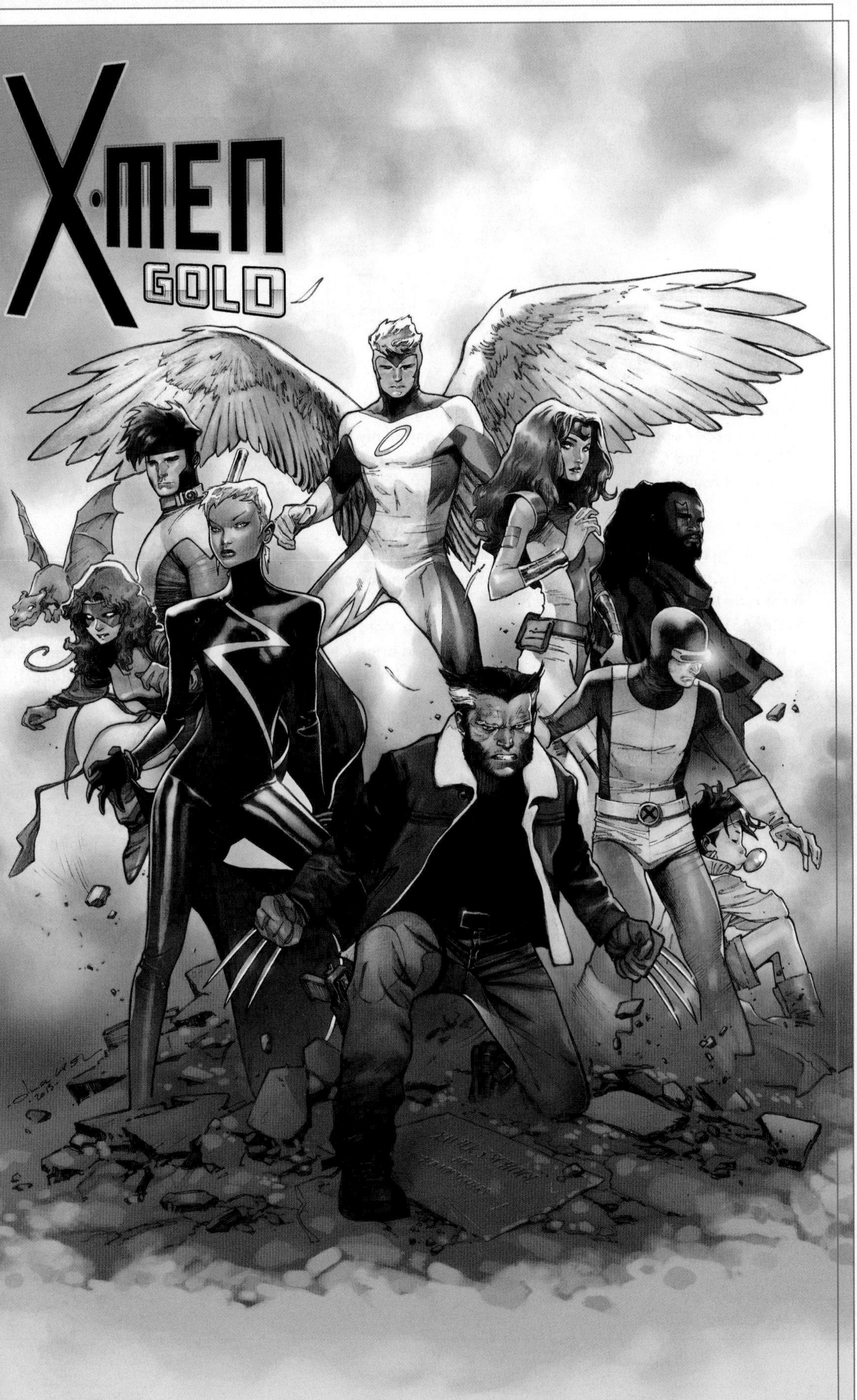
X-MEN
GOLD

X-MEN GOLD

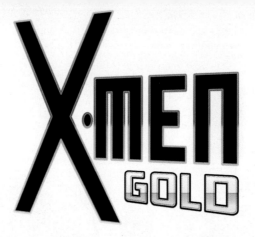

Welcome X-Fans,

When I was 12 years old, sitting in a hospital bed after breaking my arm, my brother Matt brought me a brown paper bag full of X-Men comics and changed my life. While I waited for my arm to heal, I read X-MEN #13 and CLASSIC X-MEN #14 and my mind was blown. A nerdy choirboy on the west side of Cleveland found solace in the strangest heroes of all and the X-Men have been a part of my life ever since.

It is with great pride that I welcome you to this very special issue commemorating 50 years of the X-Men. It is truly an honor that so many of the most important creators in the X-Men's publishing history were able to join in on this. First of all, the grand poo-bah of the Marvel Universe and co-creator of the X-Men, STAN LEE, was gracious enough to script a story starring the original five X-Men! Joining him are LOUISE and WALTER SIMONSON, who helped bring Cyclops, Marvel Girl, Iceman, Angel and the Beast back together in X-FACTOR many years later (in addition to Louise's long run as X-Men Editor!).

There's also a story by former Marvel Editor-In-Chief and second man ever to write the X-Men, ROY THOMAS. Roy is joined by PAT OLLIFFE for an off-beat story staring BANSHEE and SUNFIRE before they joined the X-Men!

Every X-Fan knows that the comic that started a second life for the X-Men was 1975's GIANT-SIZE X-MEN. The writer of that landmark issue and the co-creator of Wolverine, LEN WEIN is joined here by artist-extraordinaire JORGE MOLINA for a story that takes place right in the middle of GSXM!

FABIAN NICIEZA wrote some of the most popular X-Men stories in the 1990's (including much of the "X-Cutioner's Song" story that made the X-Men an addiction for this X-Editor). Joining him is SALVADOR LARROCA whose runs on X-TREME X-MEN and X-MEN cement him as one of X-Fandom's favorite artists.

But the first story and centerpiece of this volume is by one of the men most responsible for turning the X-Men into the biggest comics franchise of all time--CHRIS CLAREMONT. Chris, alongside some of the greatest artists and story-tellers to ever draw comics, took a book that had been cancelled years before and made it the must-read book that dominated the comic book marketplace for more than a decade. Joining Chris for this story is classic X-Men artist and NEW MUTANTS co-creator BOB MCLEOD!

Lastly, following these classic stories are samples of some current X-Men books that we think readers who may have stopped reading the exploits of the Children of the Atom might enjoy!

Here's to 50 more years!

Nick Lowe
X-Men Senior Editor

50th ANNIVERSARY

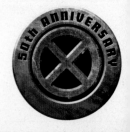

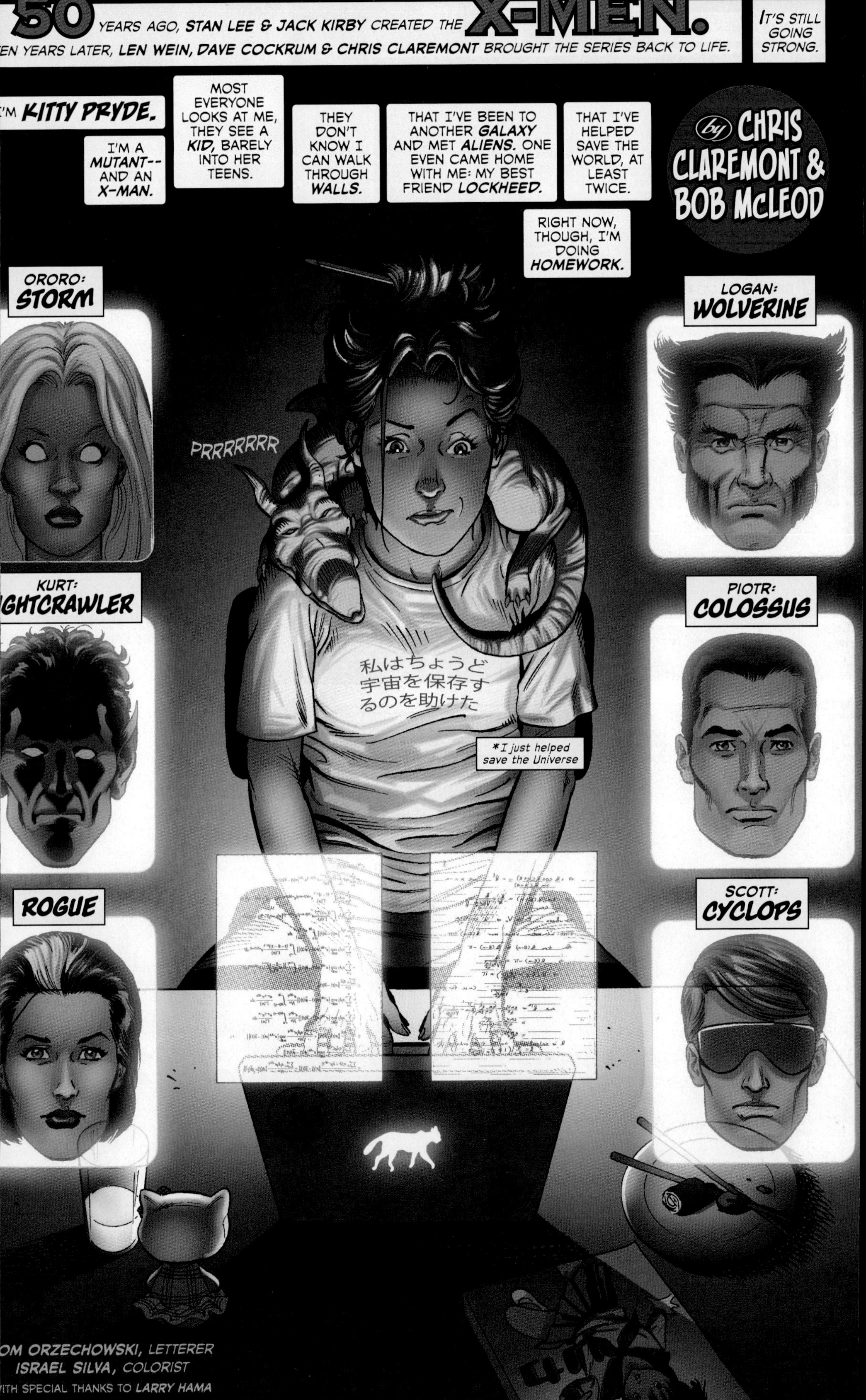

50 YEARS AGO, STAN LEE & JACK KIRBY CREATED THE X-MEN.
EN YEARS LATER, LEN WEIN, DAVE COCKRUM & CHRIS CLAREMONT BROUGHT THE SERIES BACK TO LIFE.
IT'S STILL GOING STRONG.
'M KITTY PRYDE.
I'M A MUTANT-- AND AN X-MAN.
MOST EVERYONE LOOKS AT ME, THEY SEE A KID, BARELY INTO HER TEENS.
THEY DON'T KNOW I CAN WALK THROUGH WALLS.
THAT I'VE BEEN TO ANOTHER GALAXY AND MET ALIENS. ONE EVEN CAME HOME WITH ME: MY BEST FRIEND LOCKHEED.
THAT I'VE HELPED SAVE THE WORLD, AT LEAST TWICE.
RIGHT NOW, THOUGH, I'M DOING HOMEWORK.
by CHRIS CLAREMONT & BOB McLEOD
ORORO: STORM
LOGAN: WOLVERINE
PRRRRRRR
KURT: IGHTCRAWLER
PIOTR: COLOSSUS
私はちょうど宇宙を保存するのを助けた
*I just helped save the Universe
ROGUE
SCOTT: CYCLOPS
OM ORZECHOWSKI, LETTERER
ISRAEL SILVA, COLORIST
ITH SPECIAL THANKS TO LARRY HAMA

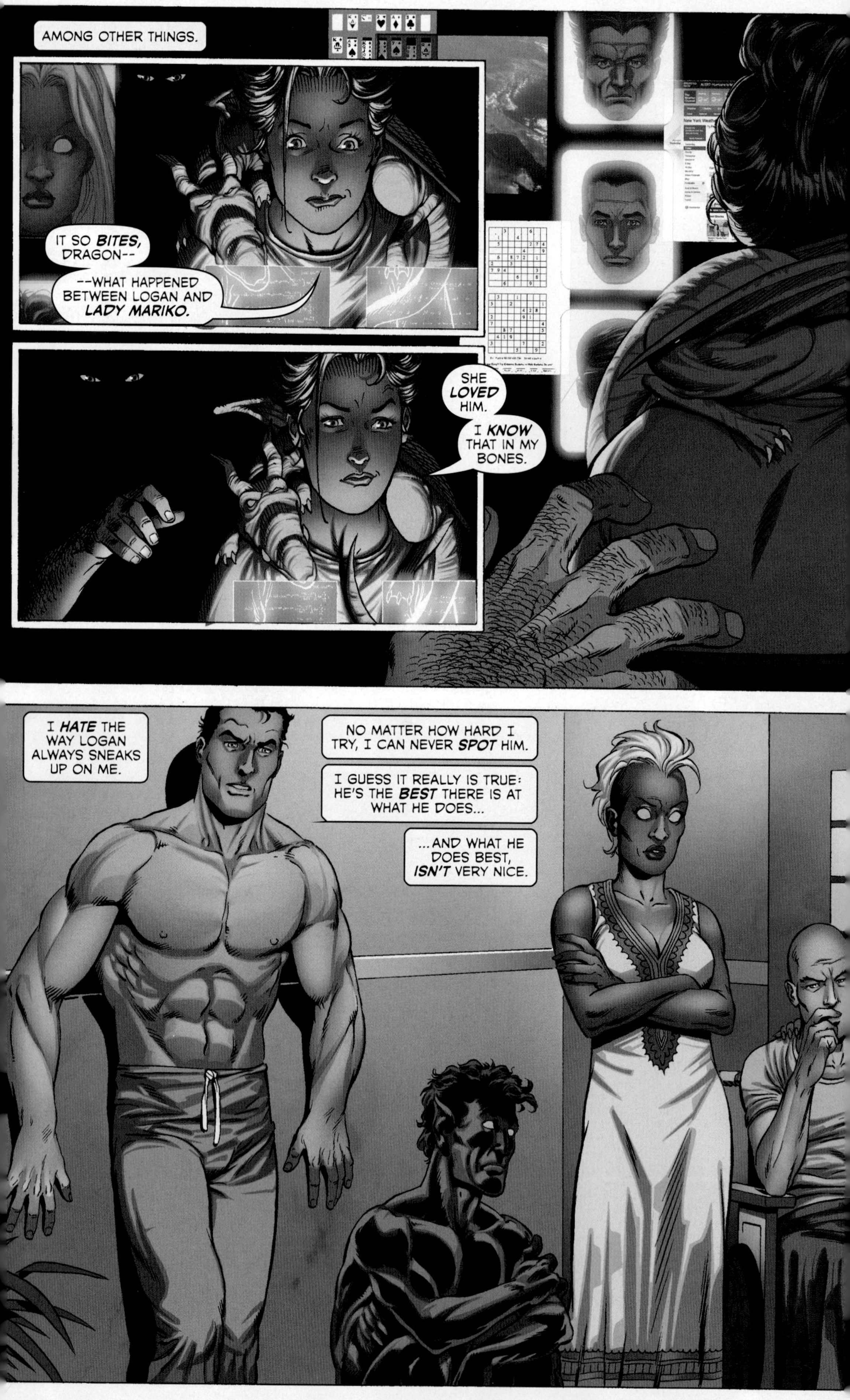
AMONG OTHER THINGS.
IT SO BITES, DRAGON--
--WHAT HAPPENED BETWEEN LOGAN AND LADY MARIKO.
SHE LOVED HIM.
I KNOW THAT IN MY BONES.
I HATE THE WAY LOGAN ALWAYS SNEAKS UP ON ME.
NO MATTER HOW HARD I TRY, I CAN NEVER SPOT HIM.
I GUESS IT REALLY IS TRUE: HE'S THE BEST THERE IS AT WHAT HE DOES...
...AND WHAT HE DOES BEST, ISN'T VERY NICE.

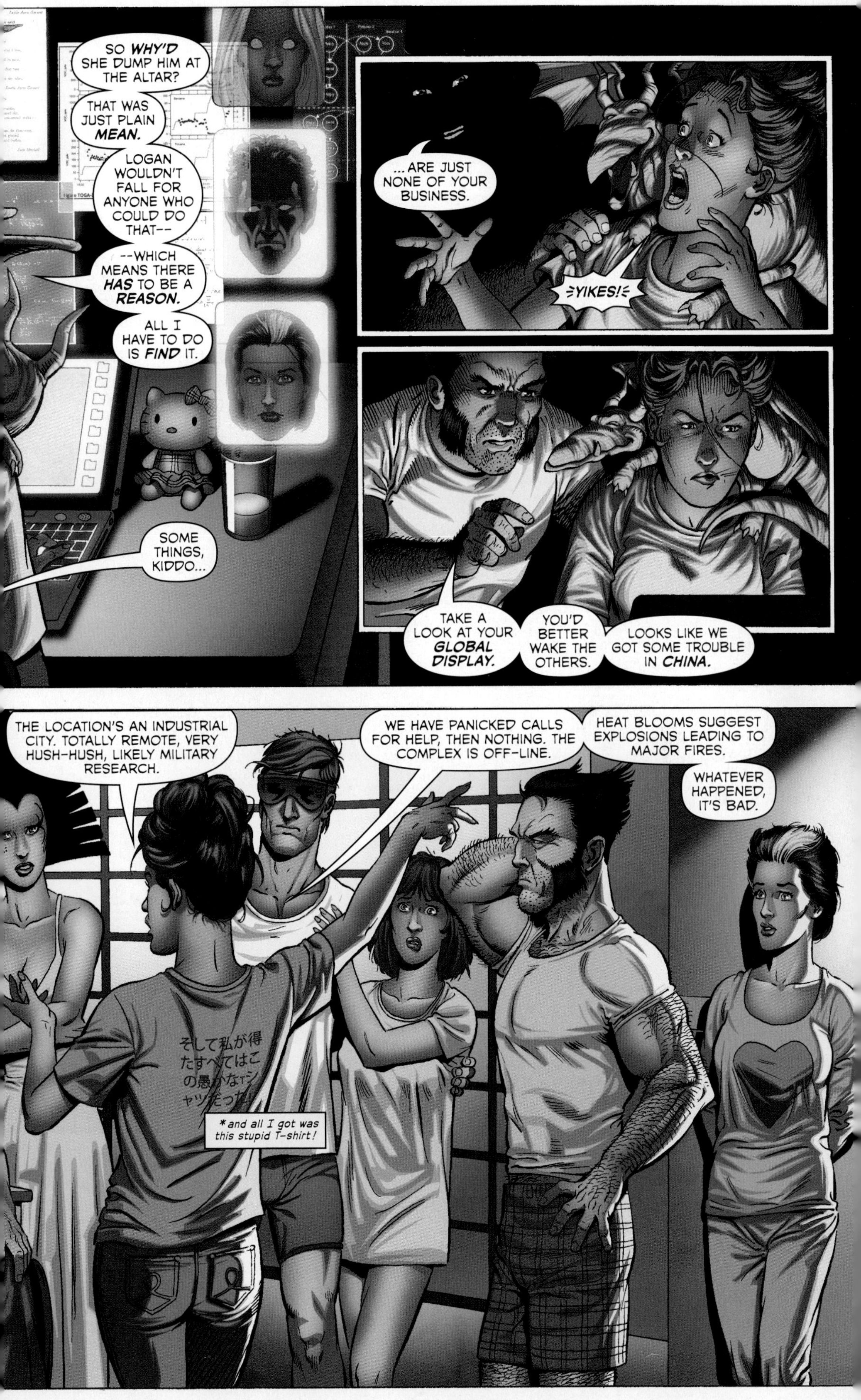
SO WHY'D SHE DUMP HIM AT THE ALTAR?
THAT WAS JUST PLAIN MEAN.
LOGAN WOULDN'T FALL FOR ANYONE WHO COULD DO THAT--
--WHICH MEANS THERE HAS TO BE A REASON.
ALL I HAVE TO DO IS FIND IT.
SOME THINGS, KIDDO...
...ARE JUST NONE OF YOUR BUSINESS.
YIKES!
TAKE A LOOK AT YOUR GLOBAL DISPLAY.
YOU'D BETTER WAKE THE OTHERS.
LOOKS LIKE WE GOT SOME TROUBLE IN CHINA.
THE LOCATION'S AN INDUSTRIAL CITY. TOTALLY REMOTE, VERY HUSH-HUSH, LIKELY MILITARY RESEARCH.
WE HAVE PANICKED CALLS FOR HELP, THEN NOTHING. THE COMPLEX IS OFF-LINE.
HEAT BLOOMS SUGGEST EXPLOSIONS LEADING TO MAJOR FIRES.
WHATEVER HAPPENED, IT'S BAD.
そして私が得
たすべてはこ
の愚かなTシ
*and all I got was this stupid T-shirt!

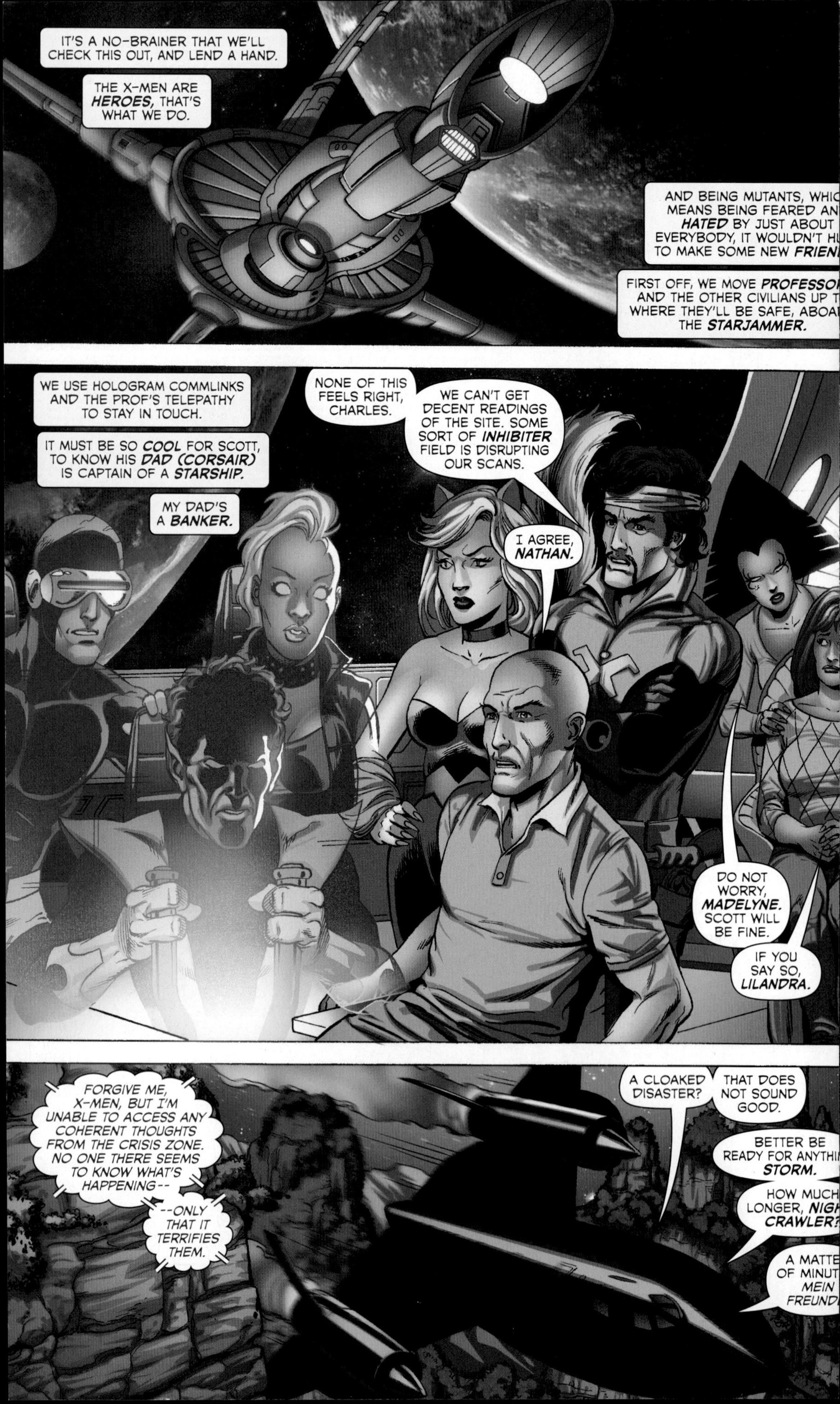

IT'S A NO-BRAINER THAT WE'LL CHECK THIS OUT, AND LEND A HAND.
THE X-MEN ARE HEROES, THAT'S WHAT WE DO.
AND BEING MUTANTS, WHIC MEANS BEING FEARED AN HATED BY JUST ABOUT EVERYBODY, IT WOULDN'T H TO MAKE SOME NEW FRIEN
FIRST OFF, WE MOVE PROFESSO AND THE OTHER CIVILIANS UP T WHERE THEY'LL BE SAFE, ABOA THE STARJAMMER.
WE USE HOLOGRAM COMMLINKS AND THE PROF'S TELEPATHY TO STAY IN TOUCH.
IT MUST BE SO COOL FOR SCOTT, TO KNOW HIS DAD (CORSAIR) IS CAPTAIN OF A STARSHIP.
MY DAD'S A BANKER.
NONE OF THIS FEELS RIGHT, CHARLES.
WE CAN'T GET DECENT READINGS OF THE SITE. SOME SORT OF INHIBITER FIELD IS DISRUPTING OUR SCANS.
I AGREE, NATHAN.
DO NOT WORRY, MADELYNE. SCOTT WILL BE FINE.
IF YOU SAY SO, LILANDRA.
FORGIVE ME, X-MEN, BUT I'M UNABLE TO ACCESS ANY COHERENT THOUGHTS FROM THE CRISIS ZONE. NO ONE THERE SEEMS TO KNOW WHAT'S HAPPENING--
--ONLY THAT IT TERRIFIES THEM.
A CLOAKED DISASTER?
THAT DOES NOT SOUND GOOD.
BETTER BE READY FOR ANYTHI STORM.
HOW MUCH LONGER, NIGH CRAWLER?
A MATTE OF MINUT MEIN FREUND

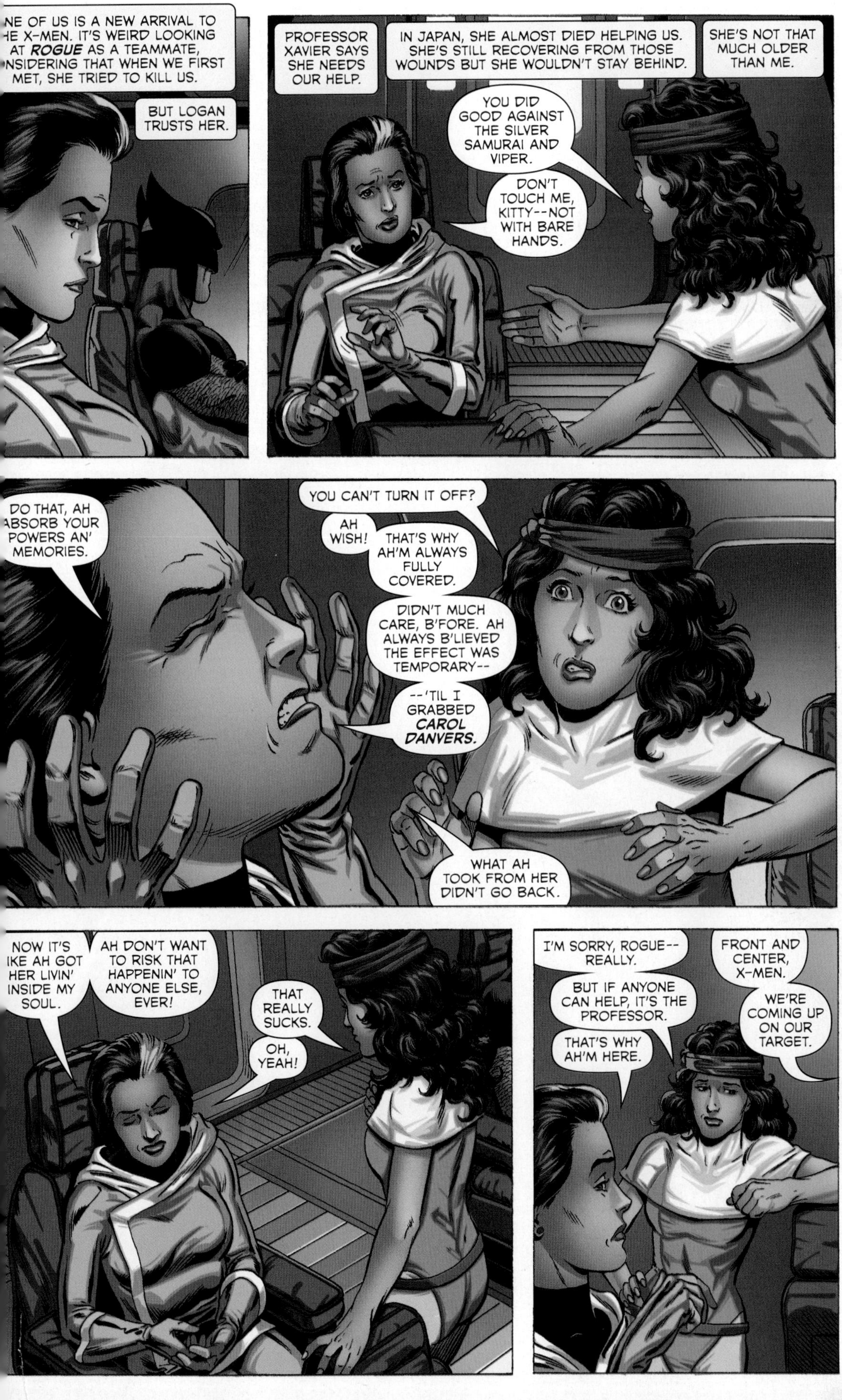
NE OF US IS A NEW ARRIVAL TO
HE X-MEN. IT'S WEIRD LOOKING
AT ROGUE AS A TEAMMATE,
NSIDERING THAT WHEN WE FIRST
MET, SHE TRIED TO KILL US.
BUT LOGAN TRUSTS HER.
PROFESSOR XAVIER SAYS SHE NEEDS OUR HELP.
IN JAPAN, SHE ALMOST DIED HELPING US. SHE'S STILL RECOVERING FROM THOSE WOUNDS BUT SHE WOULDN'T STAY BEHIND.
SHE'S NOT THAT MUCH OLDER THAN ME.
YOU DID GOOD AGAINST THE SILVER SAMURAI AND VIPER.
DON'T TOUCH ME, KITTY--NOT WITH BARE HANDS.
DO THAT, AH ABSORB YOUR POWERS AN' MEMORIES.
YOU CAN'T TURN IT OFF?
AH WISH!
THAT'S WHY AH'M ALWAYS FULLY COVERED.
DIDN'T MUCH CARE, B'FORE. AH ALWAYS B'LIEVED THE EFFECT WAS TEMPORARY--
--'TIL I GRABBED CAROL DANVERS.
WHAT AH TOOK FROM HER DIDN'T GO BACK.
NOW IT'S IKE AH GOT HER LIVIN' INSIDE MY SOUL.
AH DON'T WANT TO RISK THAT HAPPENIN' TO ANYONE ELSE, EVER!
THAT REALLY SUCKS.
OH, YEAH!
I'M SORRY, ROGUE--REALLY.
BUT IF ANYONE CAN HELP, IT'S THE PROFESSOR.
THAT'S WHY AH'M HERE.
FRONT AND CENTER, X-MEN.
WE'RE COMING UP ON OUR TARGET.

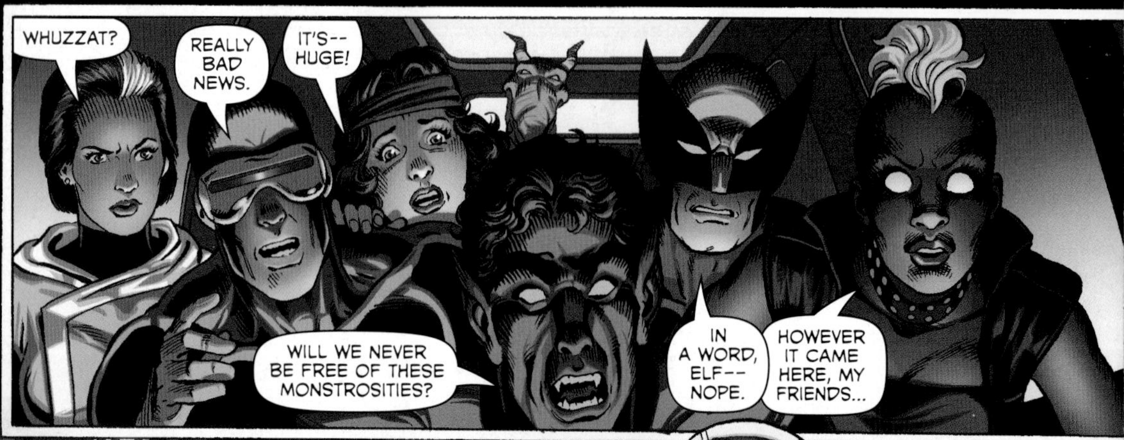
WHUZZAT?
REALLY BAD NEWS.
IT'S-- HUGE!
WILL WE NEVER BE FREE OF THESE MONSTROSITIES?
IN A WORD, ELF-- NOPE.
HOWEVER IT CAME HERE, MY FRIENDS...

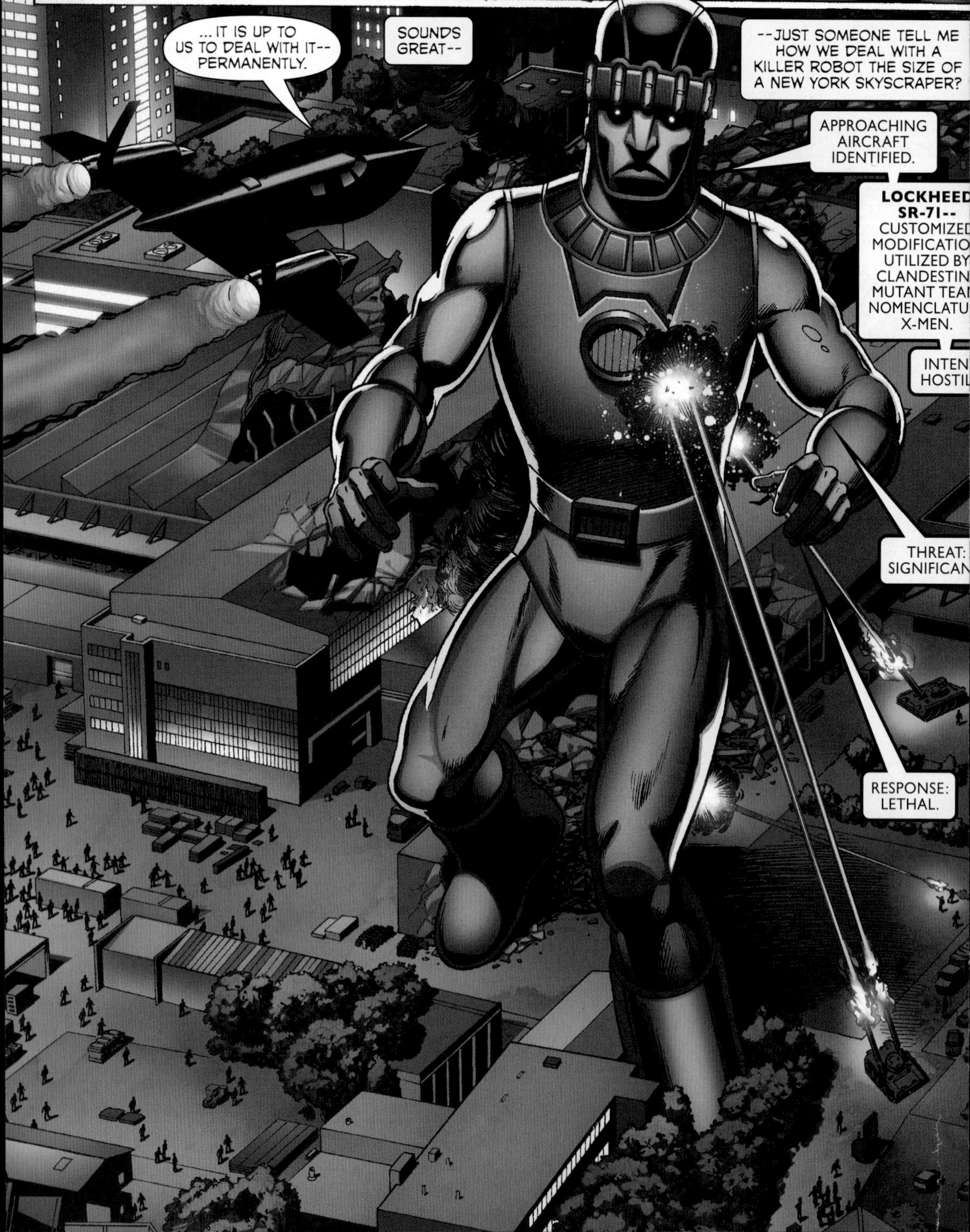
...IT IS UP TO US TO DEAL WITH IT-- PERMANENTLY.
SOUNDS GREAT--
--JUST SOMEONE TELL ME HOW WE DEAL WITH A KILLER ROBOT THE SIZE OF A NEW YORK SKYSCRAPER?
APPROACHING AIRCRAFT IDENTIFIED.
LOCKHEED SR-71-- CUSTOMIZED MODIFICATIO UTILIZED BY CLANDESTIN MUTANT TEAM NOMENCLATU X-MEN.
INTEN HOSTIL
THREAT: SIGNIFICAN
RESPONSE: LETHAL.

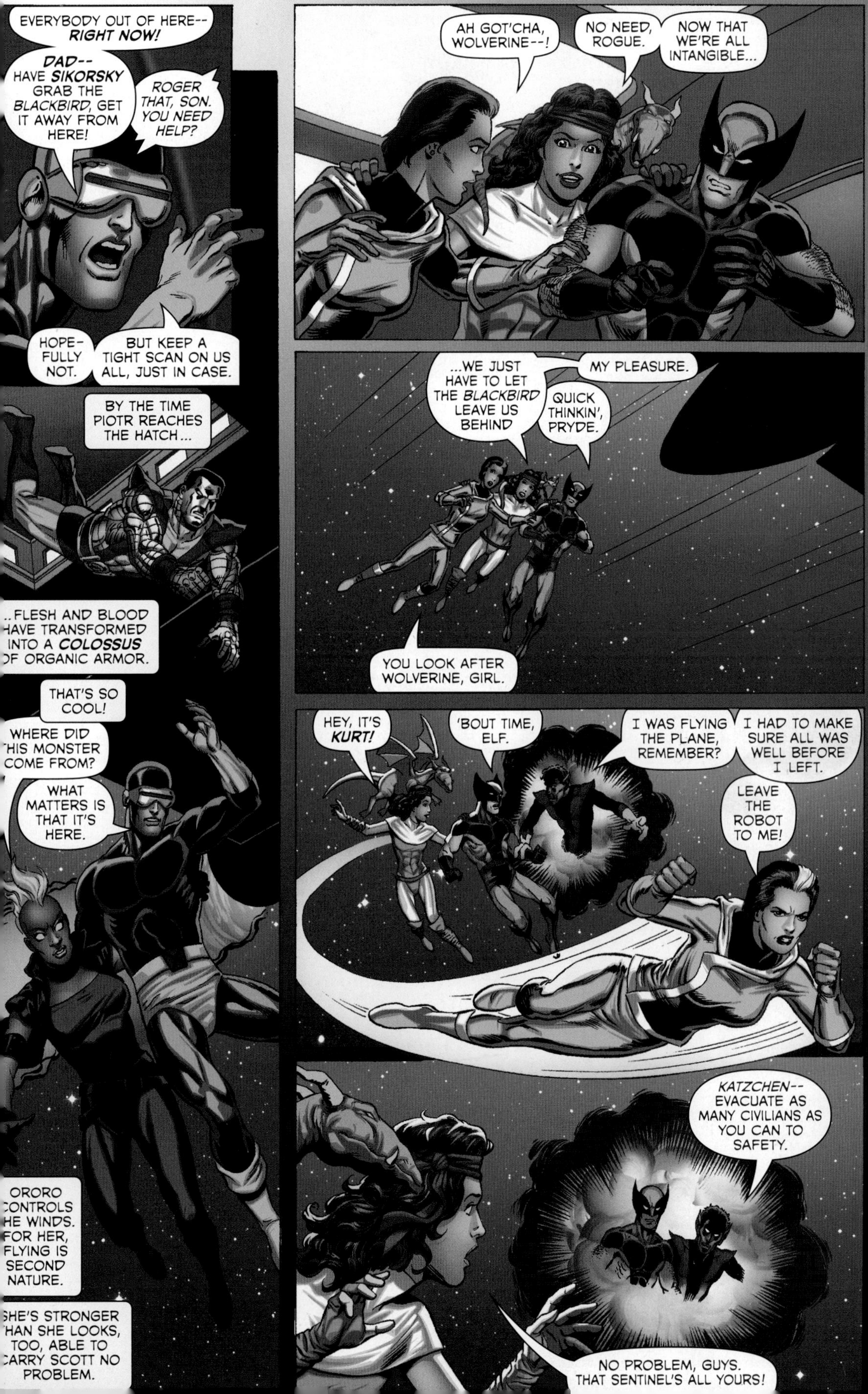
EVERYBODY OUT OF HERE-- RIGHT NOW!
DAD-- HAVE SIKORSKY GRAB THE BLACKBIRD, GET IT AWAY FROM HERE!
ROGER THAT, SON. YOU NEED HELP?
HOPE-FULLY NOT.
BUT KEEP A TIGHT SCAN ON US ALL, JUST IN CASE.
BY THE TIME PIOTR REACHES THE HATCH...
..FLESH AND BLOOD HAVE TRANSFORMED INTO A COLOSSUS OF ORGANIC ARMOR.
THAT'S SO COOL!
WHERE DID THIS MONSTER COME FROM?
WHAT MATTERS IS THAT IT'S HERE.
ORORO CONTROLS THE WINDS. FOR HER, FLYING IS SECOND NATURE.
SHE'S STRONGER THAN SHE LOOKS, TOO, ABLE TO CARRY SCOTT NO PROBLEM.
AH GOT'CHA, WOLVERINE--!
NO NEED, ROGUE.
NOW THAT WE'RE ALL INTANGIBLE...
...WE JUST HAVE TO LET THE BLACKBIRD LEAVE US BEHIND
MY PLEASURE.
QUICK THINKIN', PRYDE.
YOU LOOK AFTER WOLVERINE, GIRL.
HEY, IT'S KURT!
'BOUT TIME, ELF.
I WAS FLYING THE PLANE, REMEMBER?
I HAD TO MAKE SURE ALL WAS WELL BEFORE I LEFT.
LEAVE THE ROBOT TO ME!
KATZCHEN-- EVACUATE AS MANY CIVILIANS AS YOU CAN TO SAFETY.
NO PROBLEM, GUYS. THAT SENTINEL'S ALL YOURS!

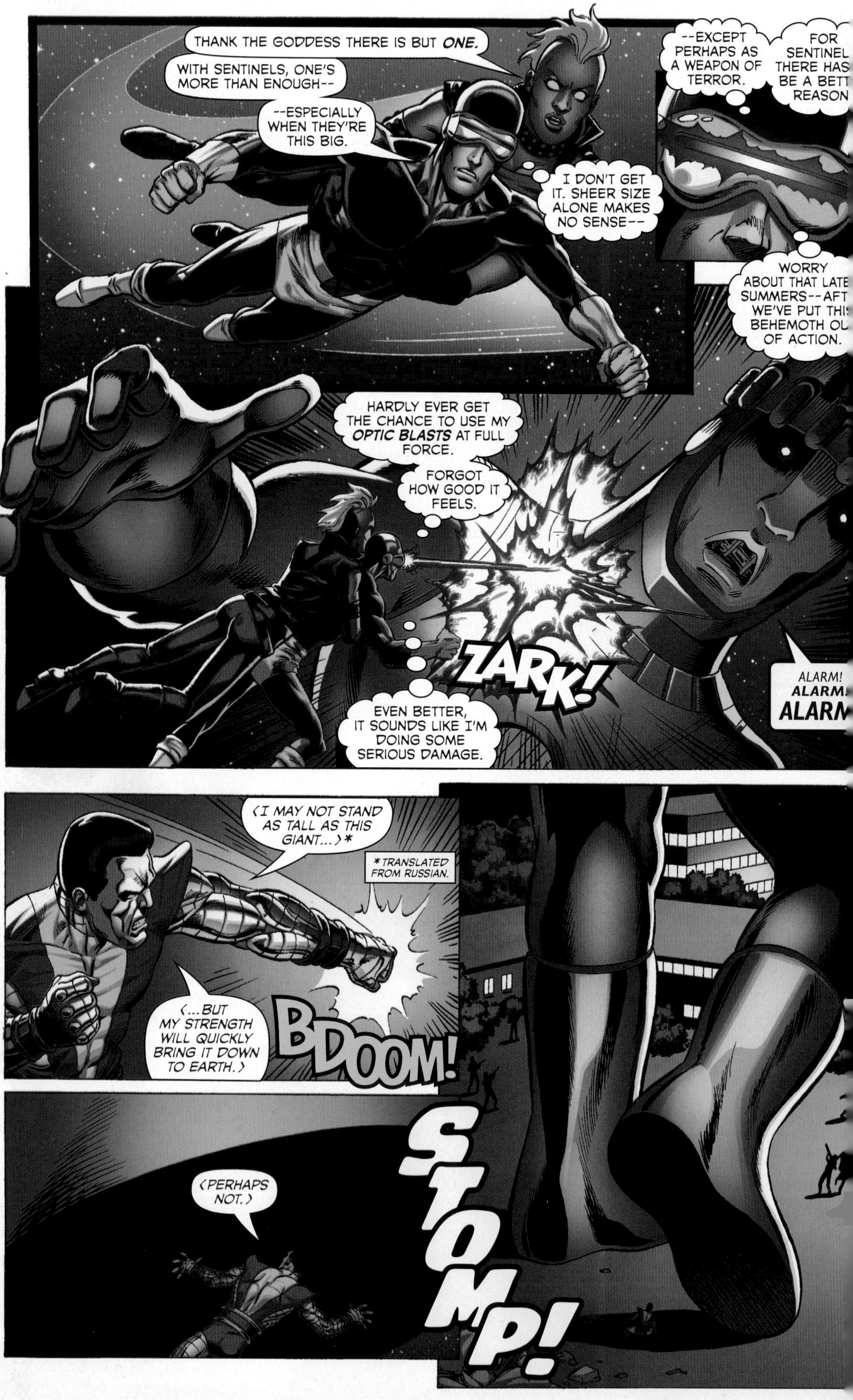
THANK THE GODDESS THERE IS BUT ONE.
WITH SENTINELS, ONE'S MORE THAN ENOUGH--
--ESPECIALLY WHEN THEY'RE THIS BIG.
I DON'T GET IT. SHEER SIZE ALONE MAKES NO SENSE--
--EXCEPT PERHAPS AS A WEAPON OF TERROR.
WORRY ABOUT THAT LATE
HARDLY EVER GET THE CHANCE TO USE MY OPTIC BLASTS AT FULL FORCE.
FORGOT HOW GOOD IT FEELS.
ZARK!
EVEN BETTER, IT SOUNDS LIKE I'M DOING SOME SERIOUS DAMAGE.
ALARM!
‹I MAY NOT STAND AS TALL AS THIS GIANT...›*
*TRANSLATED FROM RUSSIAN.
‹...BUT MY STRENGTH WILL QUICKLY BRING IT DOWN TO EARTH.›
BDOOM!
‹PERHAPS NOT.›
STOMP!

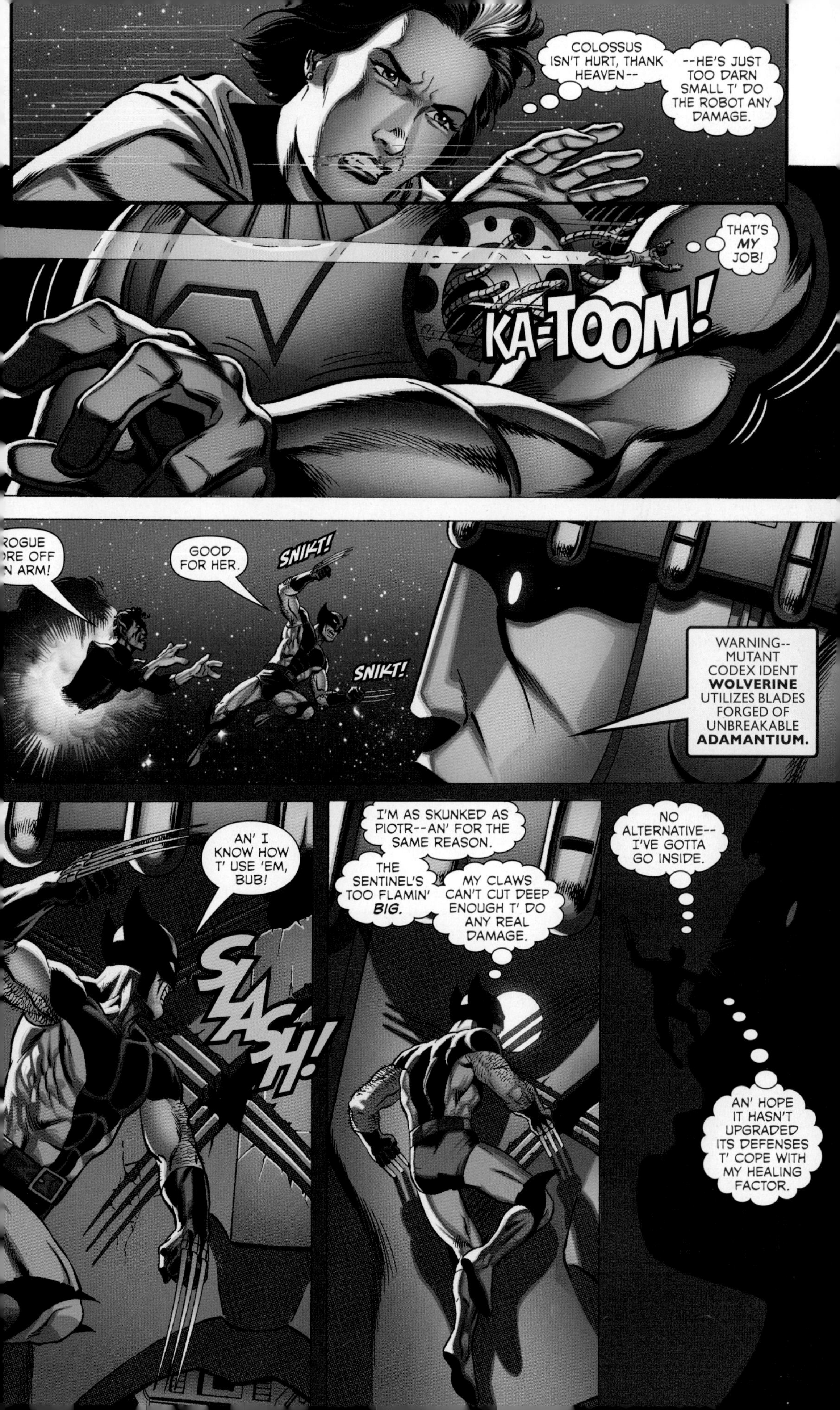
COLOSSUS ISN'T HURT, THANK HEAVEN--
--HE'S JUST TOO DARN SMALL T' DO THE ROBOT ANY DAMAGE.
THAT'S MY JOB!
KA-TOOM!
ROGUE ORE OFF N ARM!
GOOD FOR HER.
SNIKT!
SNIKT!
WARNING--MUTANT CODEX IDENT WOLVERINE UTILIZES BLADES FORGED OF UNBREAKABLE ADAMANTIUM.
AN' I KNOW HOW T' USE 'EM, BUB!
SLASH!
I'M AS SKUNKED AS PIOTR--AN' FOR THE SAME REASON.
THE SENTINEL'S TOO FLAMIN' BIG.
MY CLAWS CAN'T CUT DEEP ENOUGH T' DO ANY REAL DAMAGE.
NO ALTERNATIVE--I'VE GOTTA GO INSIDE.
AN' HOPE IT HASN'T UPGRADED ITS DEFENSES T' COPE WITH MY HEALING FACTOR.

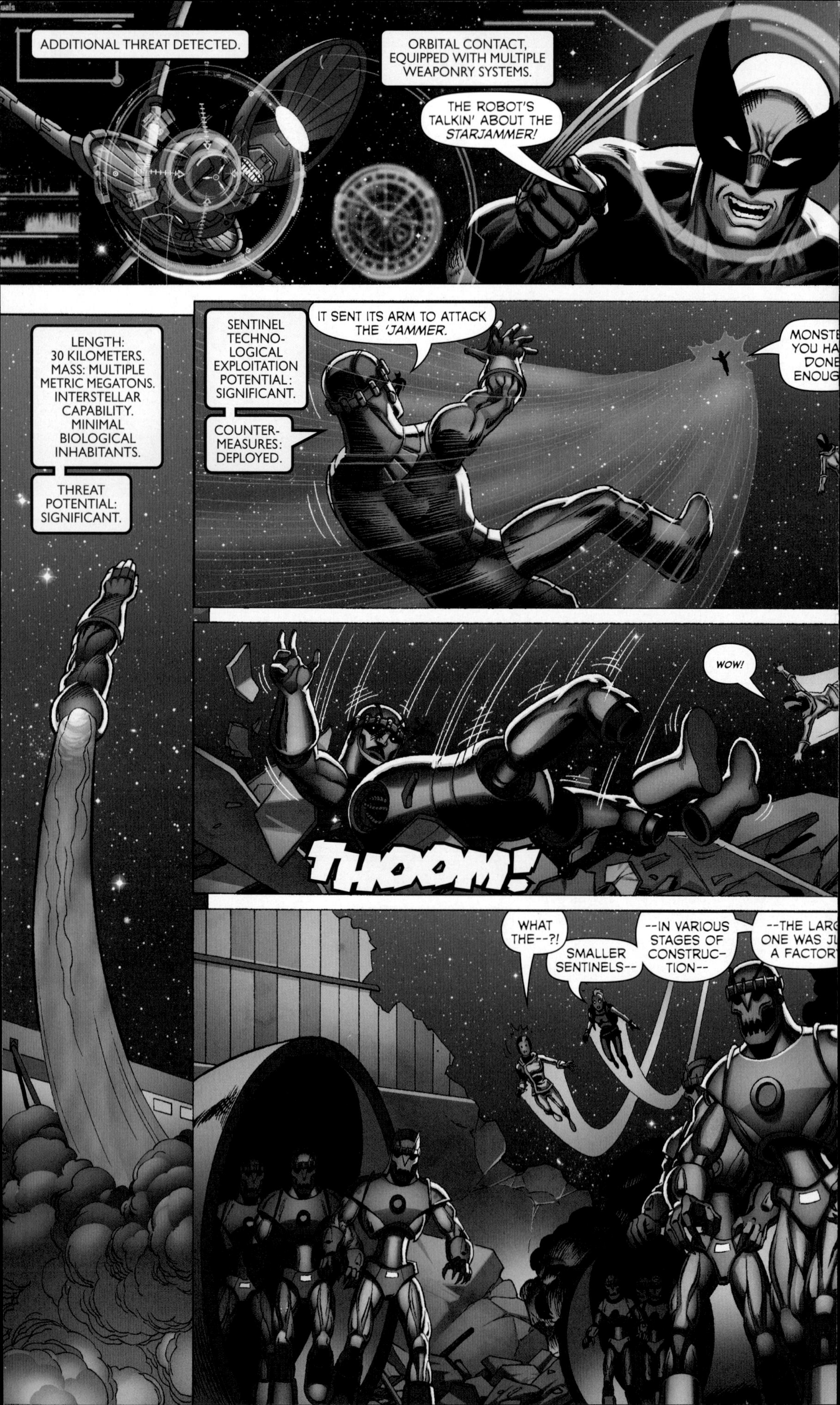

ADDITIONAL THREAT DETECTED.
ORBITAL CONTACT, EQUIPPED WITH MULTIPLE WEAPONRY SYSTEMS.
THE ROBOT'S TALKIN' ABOUT THE *STARJAMMER!*
LENGTH: 30 KILOMETERS. MASS: MULTIPLE METRIC MEGATONS. INTERSTELLAR CAPABILITY. MINIMAL BIOLOGICAL INHABITANTS.
THREAT POTENTIAL: SIGNIFICANT.
SENTINEL TECHNO-LOGICAL EXPLOITATION POTENTIAL: SIGNIFICANT.
COUNTER-MEASURES: DEPLOYED.
IT SENT ITS ARM TO ATTACK THE *'JAMMER.*
WOW!
THOOM!
WHAT THE--?!
SMALLER SENTINELS--
--IN VARIOUS STAGES OF CONSTRUC-TION--

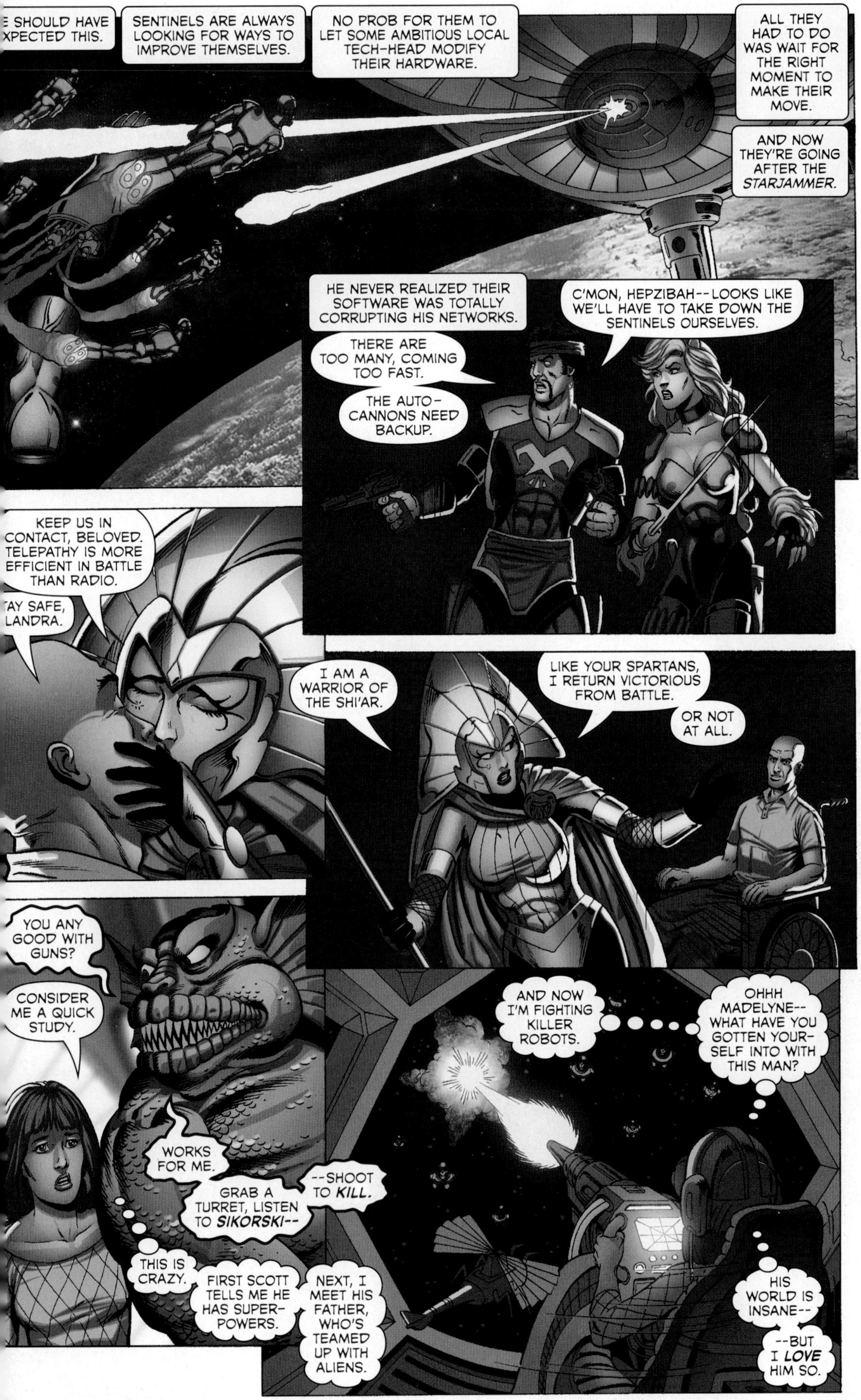

E SHOULD HAVE XPECTED THIS.
SENTINELS ARE ALWAYS LOOKING FOR WAYS TO IMPROVE THEMSELVES.
NO PROB FOR THEM TO LET SOME AMBITIOUS LOCAL TECH-HEAD MODIFY THEIR HARDWARE.
ALL THEY HAD TO DO WAS WAIT FOR THE RIGHT MOMENT TO MAKE THEIR MOVE.
AND NOW THEY'RE GOING AFTER THE *STARJAMMER.*
HE NEVER REALIZED THEIR SOFTWARE WAS TOTALLY CORRUPTING HIS NETWORKS.
THERE ARE TOO MANY, COMING TOO FAST.
THE AUTO-CANNONS NEED BACKUP.
C'MON, HEPZIBAH--LOOKS LIKE WE'LL HAVE TO TAKE DOWN THE SENTINELS OURSELVES.
KEEP US IN CONTACT, BELOVED. TELEPATHY IS MORE EFFICIENT IN BATTLE THAN RADIO.
TAY SAFE, LANDRA.
I AM A WARRIOR OF THE SHI'AR.
LIKE YOUR SPARTANS, I RETURN VICTORIOUS FROM BATTLE.
OR NOT AT ALL.
YOU ANY GOOD WITH GUNS?
CONSIDER ME A QUICK STUDY.
WORKS FOR ME.
GRAB A TURRET, LISTEN TO **SIKORSKI--**
--SHOOT TO **KILL.**
THIS IS CRAZY.
FIRST SCOTT TELLS ME HE HAS SUPER-POWERS.
NEXT, I MEET HIS FATHER, WHO'S TEAMED UP WITH ALIENS.
AND NOW I'M FIGHTING KILLER ROBOTS.
OHHH MADELYNE--WHAT HAVE YOU GOTTEN YOURSELF INTO WITH THIS MAN?
HIS WORLD IS INSANE--
--BUT I **LOVE** HIM SO.

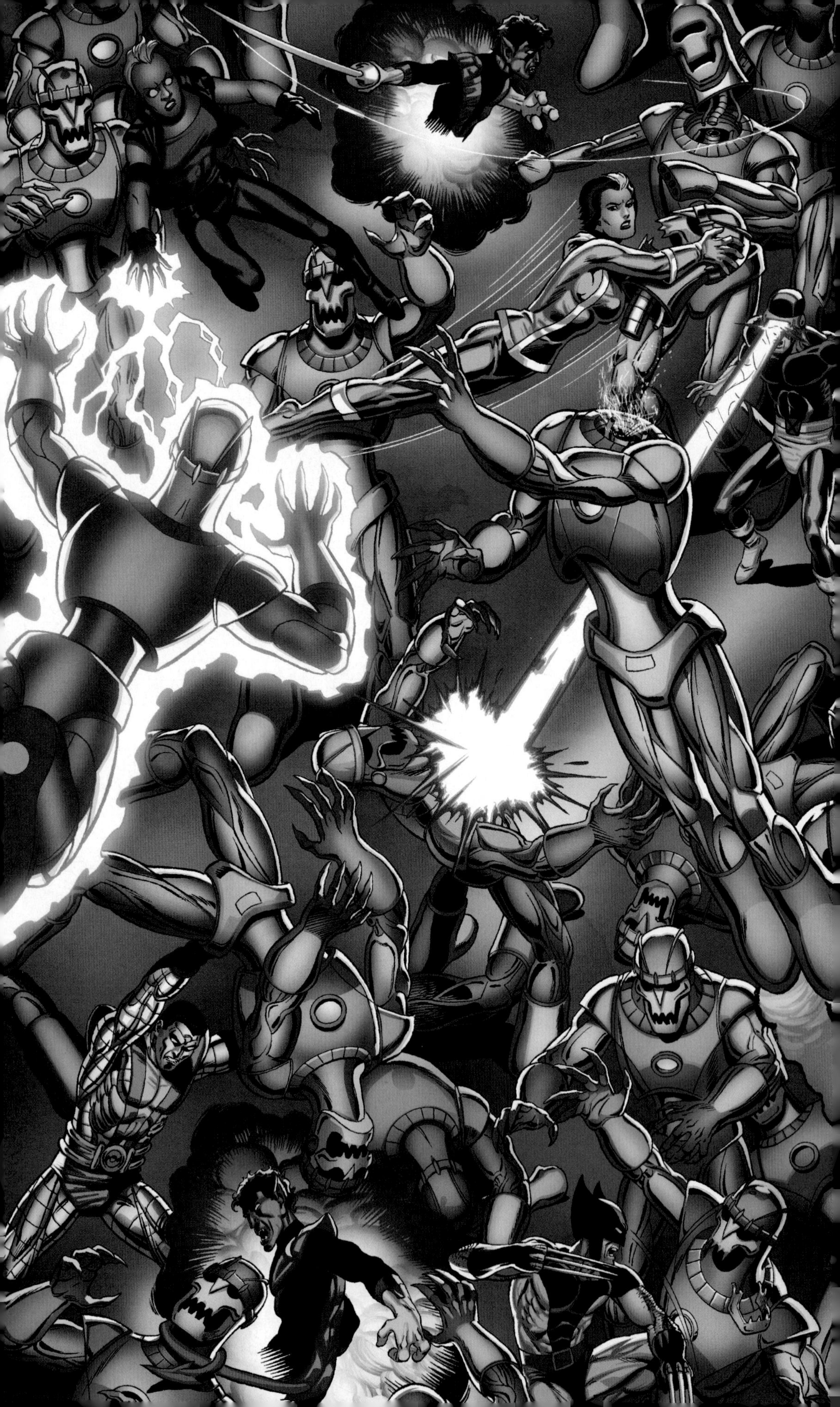

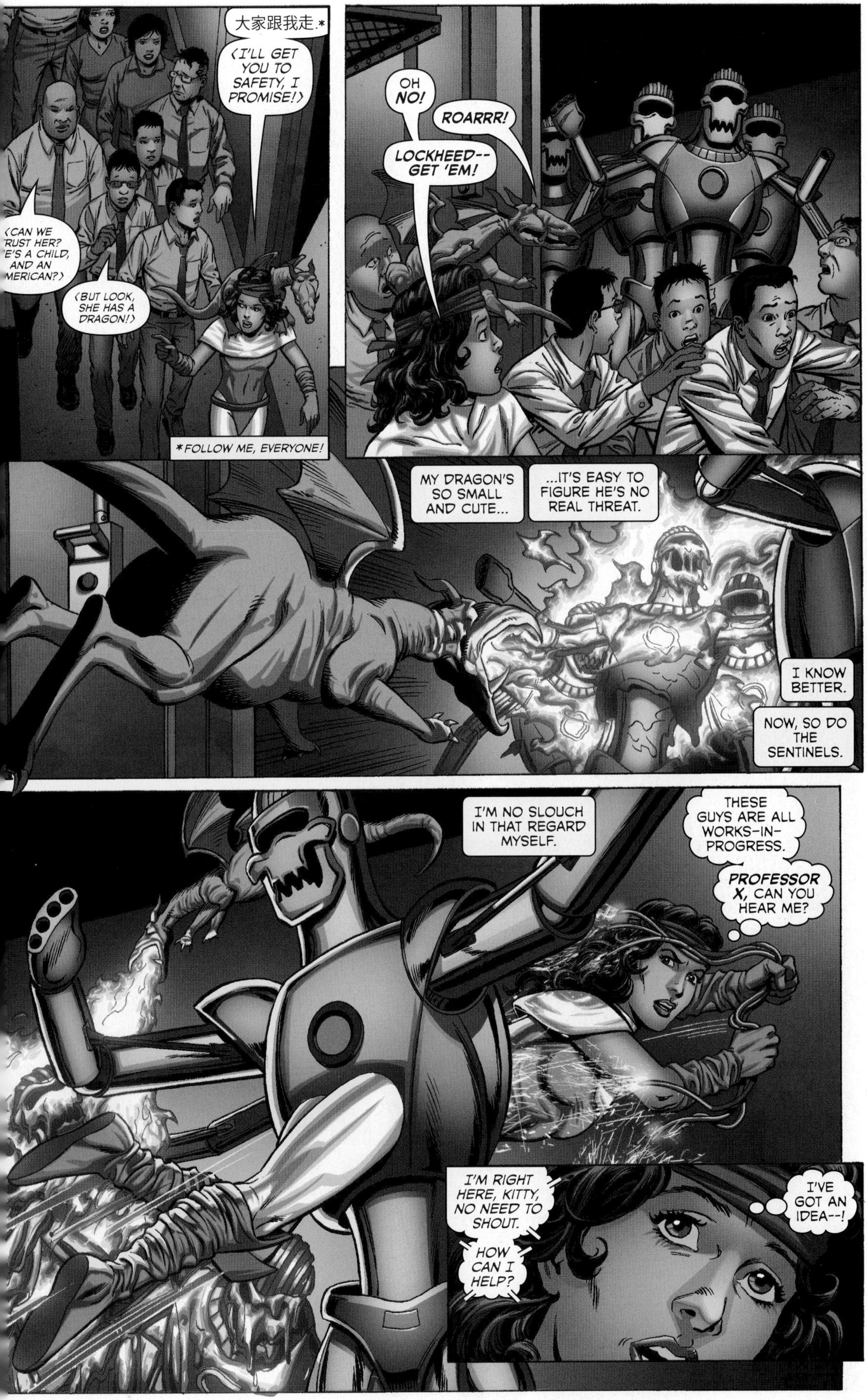

大家跟我走.*
‹I'LL GET YOU TO SAFETY, I PROMISE!›
‹CAN WE 'RUST HER? 'E'S A CHILD, AND AN MERICAN?›
‹BUT LOOK, SHE HAS A DRAGON!›
*FOLLOW ME, EVERYONE!
OH NO!
ROARRR!
LOCKHEED--GET 'EM!
MY DRAGON'S SO SMALL AND CUTE...
...IT'S EASY TO FIGURE HE'S NO REAL THREAT.
I KNOW BETTER.
NOW, SO DO THE SENTINELS.
I'M NO SLOUCH IN THAT REGARD MYSELF.
THESE GUYS ARE ALL WORKS-IN-PROGRESS.
PROFESSOR X, CAN YOU HEAR ME?
I'M RIGHT HERE, KITTY, NO NEED TO SHOUT.
HOW CAN I HELP?
I'VE GOT AN IDEA--!

YEARGKGH!

AH-- FELT THAT!

TOO MANY ROBOTS-- HITTIN' ME TOO FAST, TOO HARD-- --CAN'T TAKE MUCH MORE--!

SCHILDWACHTER--* --LEAVE MY FRIEND ALONE!

KZANG!

AS I FEARED, ROGUE STILL SUFFERS FROM THE WOUNDS SHE RECEIVED IN JAPAN.

I HAVE TO PROTECT HER.

* "SENTIN... IN GERM...

ANY IDEAS, CYCLOPS?

I-- I--!

I CAN'T CONCENTRATE.

I KEEP THINKING OF MADELYNE.

SHE'S UNDER ATTACK ABOARD THE STARJAMMER...

...AND THERE'S NOTHING I CAN DO TO HELP!

SCOTT, YOU HAVE TO FOCUS!

I KNOW YOU FEAR FOR THE WOMAN YOU LOVE-- --BUT RIGHT NOW, IT IS THE X-MEN WHO NEED YOU!

X-MEN-- STARJAMMER SENSORS REPORT THAT THESE NEO-SENTINELS ARE CONSTANTLY IMPROVING THEMSELVES!

IN SHORT ORDER, THEY WILL DEFEAT US.

WE HAVE TO STOP THE... NOW, WHILE W... STILL HAVE TH... CHANCE.

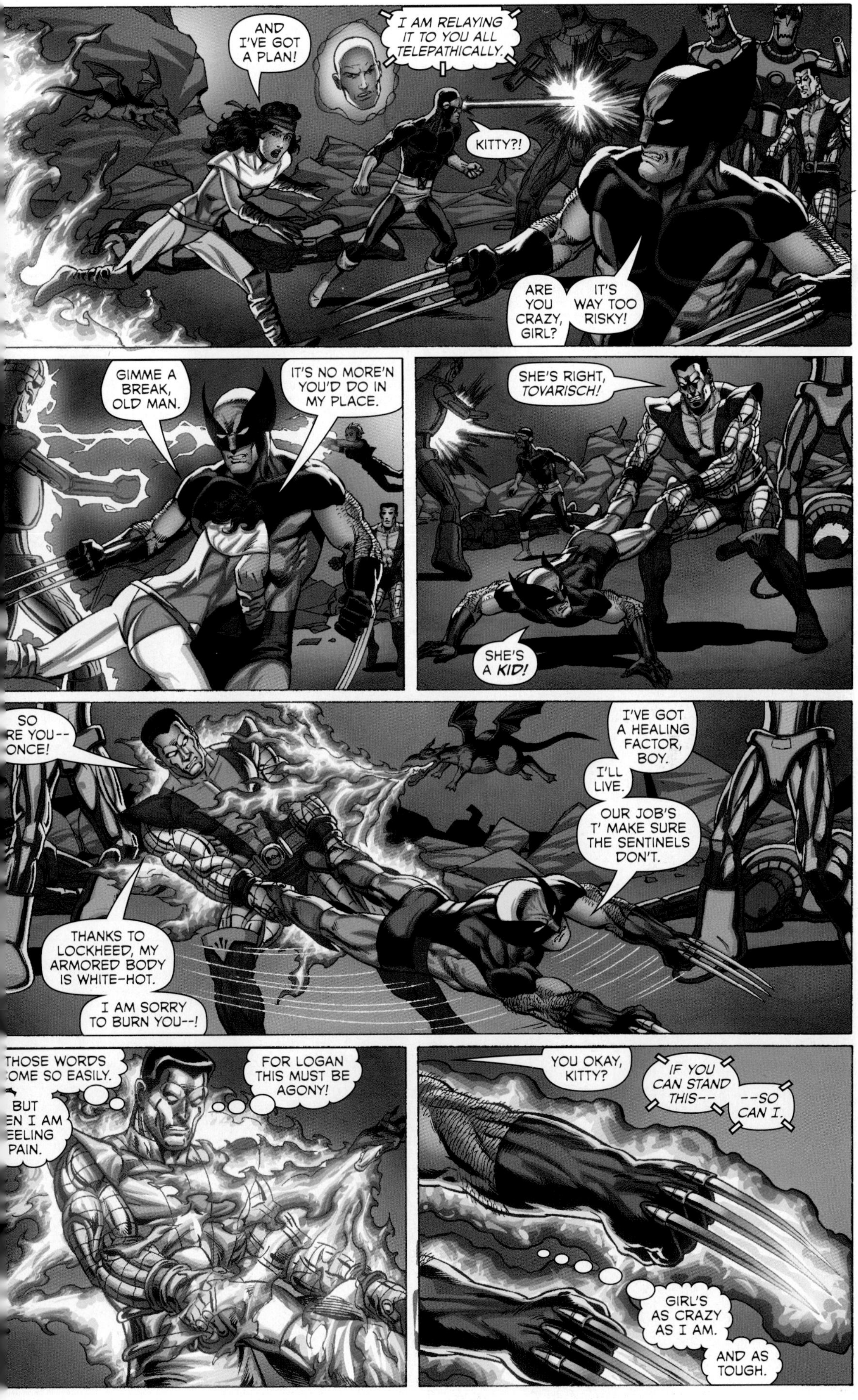
AND I'VE GOT A PLAN!
I AM RELAYING IT TO YOU ALL TELEPATHICALLY.
KITTY?!
ARE YOU CRAZY, GIRL?
IT'S WAY TOO RISKY!
GIMME A BREAK, OLD MAN.
IT'S NO MORE'N YOU'D DO IN MY PLACE.
SHE'S RIGHT, TOVARISCH!
SHE'S A KID!
SO RE YOU-- ONCE!
I'VE GOT A HEALING FACTOR, BOY.
I'LL LIVE.
OUR JOB'S T' MAKE SURE THE SENTINELS DON'T.
THANKS TO LOCKHEED, MY ARMORED BODY IS WHITE-HOT.
I AM SORRY TO BURN YOU--!
THOSE WORDS OME SO EASILY.
BUT EN I AM EELING PAIN.
FOR LOGAN THIS MUST BE AGONY!
YOU OKAY, KITTY?
IF YOU CAN STAND THIS--
--SO CAN I.
GIRL'S AS CRAZY AS I AM.
AND AS TOUGH.

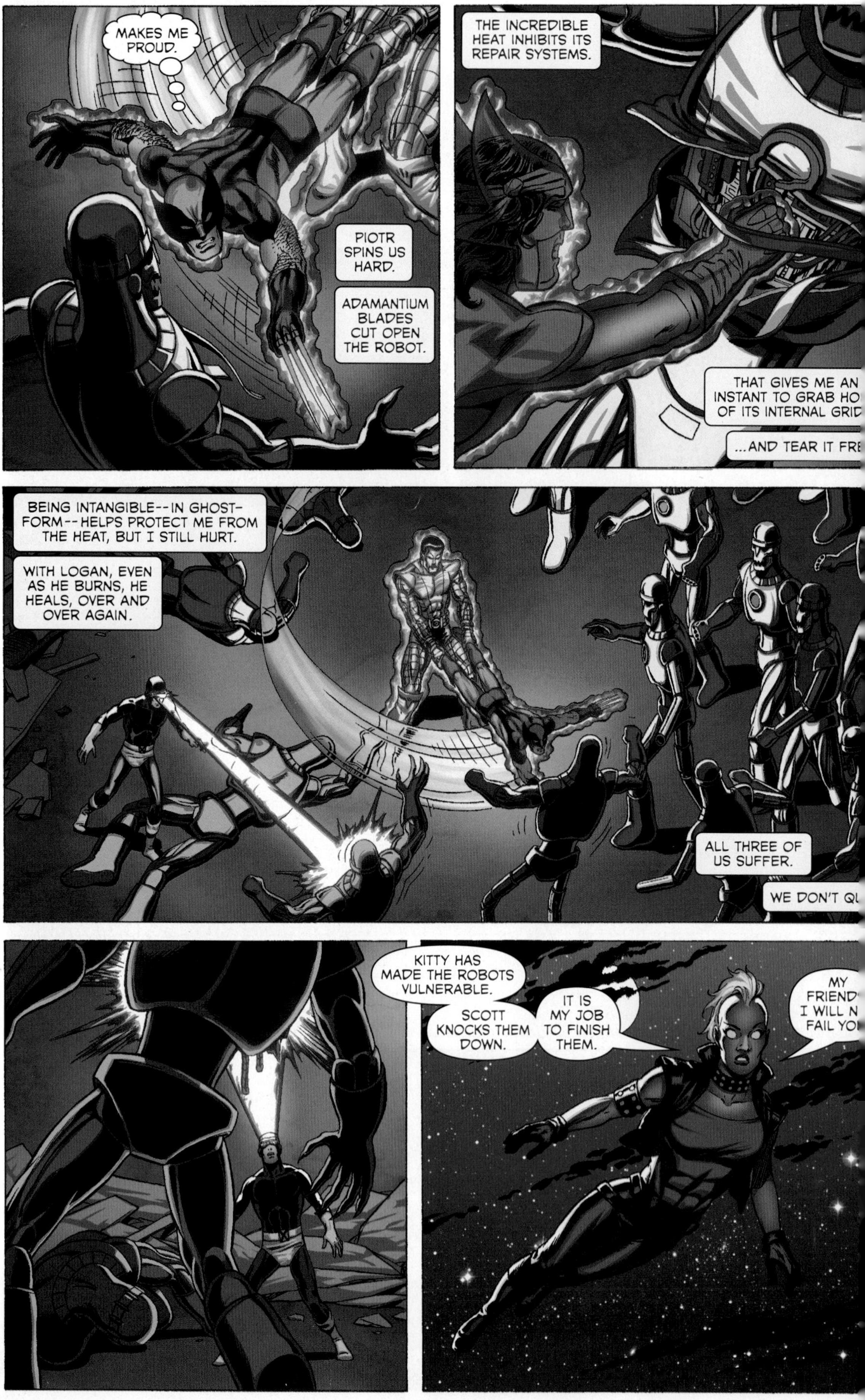
MAKES ME PROUD.
PIOTR SPINS US HARD.
ADAMANTIUM BLADES CUT OPEN THE ROBOT.
THE INCREDIBLE HEAT INHIBITS ITS REPAIR SYSTEMS.
THAT GIVES ME AN INSTANT TO GRAB HO
OF ITS INTERNAL GRID
...AND TEAR IT FRE
BEING INTANGIBLE--IN GHOST-FORM--HELPS PROTECT ME FROM THE HEAT, BUT I STILL HURT.
WITH LOGAN, EVEN AS HE BURNS, HE HEALS, OVER AND OVER AGAIN.
ALL THREE OF US SUFFER.
WE DON'T QU
KITTY HAS MADE THE ROBOTS VULNERABLE.
SCOTT KNOCKS THEM DOWN.
IT IS MY JOB TO FINISH THEM.
MY FRIEND
I WILL N
FAIL YO

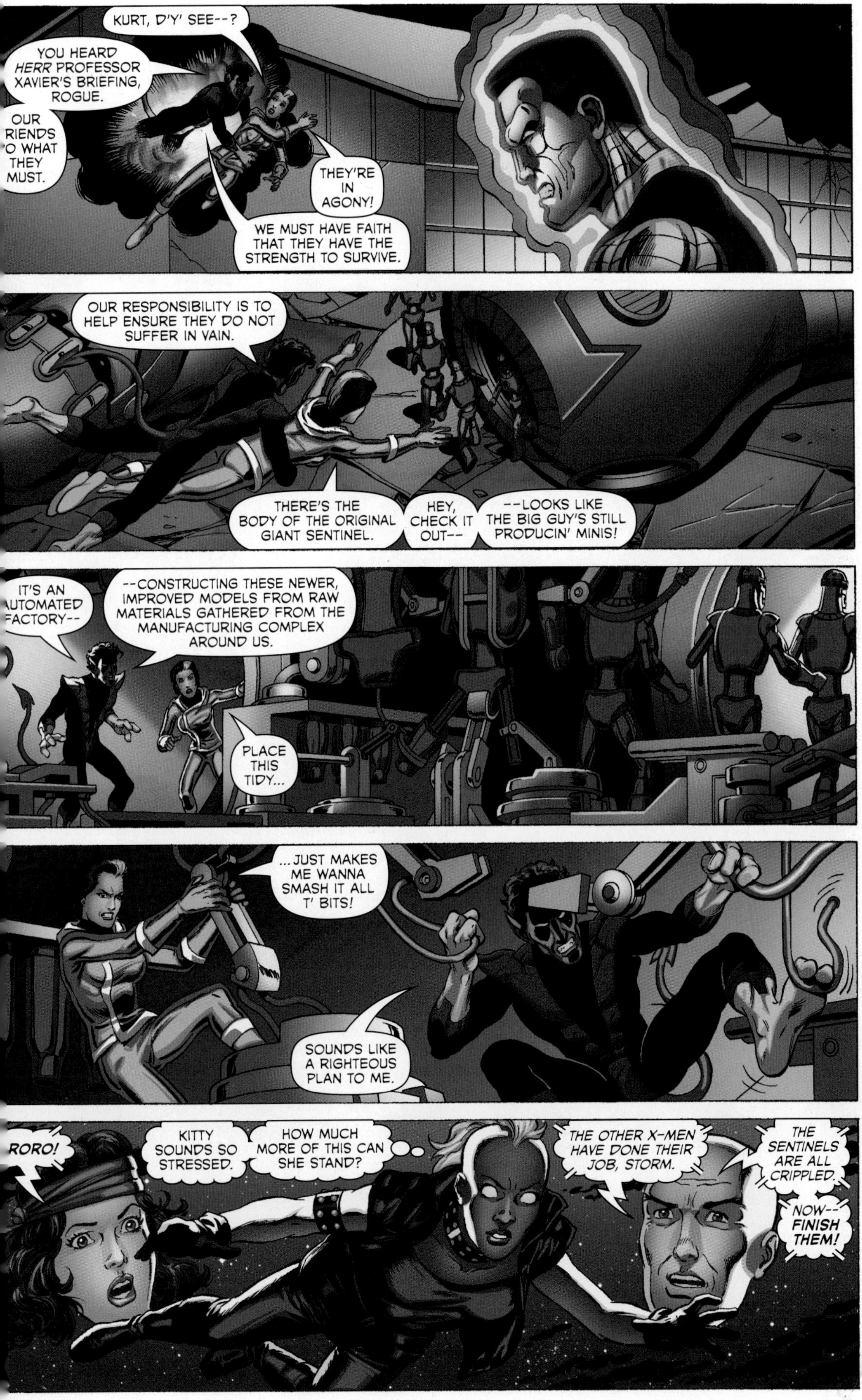

KURT, D'Y' SEE--?
YOU HEARD HERR PROFESSOR XAVIER'S BRIEFING, ROGUE.
OUR RIENDS O WHAT THEY MUST.
THEY'RE IN AGONY!
WE MUST HAVE FAITH THAT THEY HAVE THE STRENGTH TO SURVIVE.
OUR RESPONSIBILITY IS TO HELP ENSURE THEY DO NOT SUFFER IN VAIN.
THERE'S THE BODY OF THE ORIGINAL GIANT SENTINEL.
HEY, CHECK IT OUT--
--LOOKS LIKE THE BIG GUY'S STILL PRODUCIN' MINIS!
IT'S AN AUTOMATED FACTORY--
--CONSTRUCTING THESE NEWER, IMPROVED MODELS FROM RAW MATERIALS GATHERED FROM THE MANUFACTURING COMPLEX AROUND US.
PLACE THIS TIDY...
...JUST MAKES ME WANNA SMASH IT ALL T' BITS!
SOUNDS LIKE A RIGHTEOUS PLAN TO ME.
RORO!
KITTY SOUNDS SO STRESSED.
HOW MUCH MORE OF THIS CAN SHE STAND?
THE OTHER X-MEN HAVE DONE THEIR JOB, STORM.
THE SENTINELS ARE ALL CRIPPLED.
NOW--FINISH THEM!

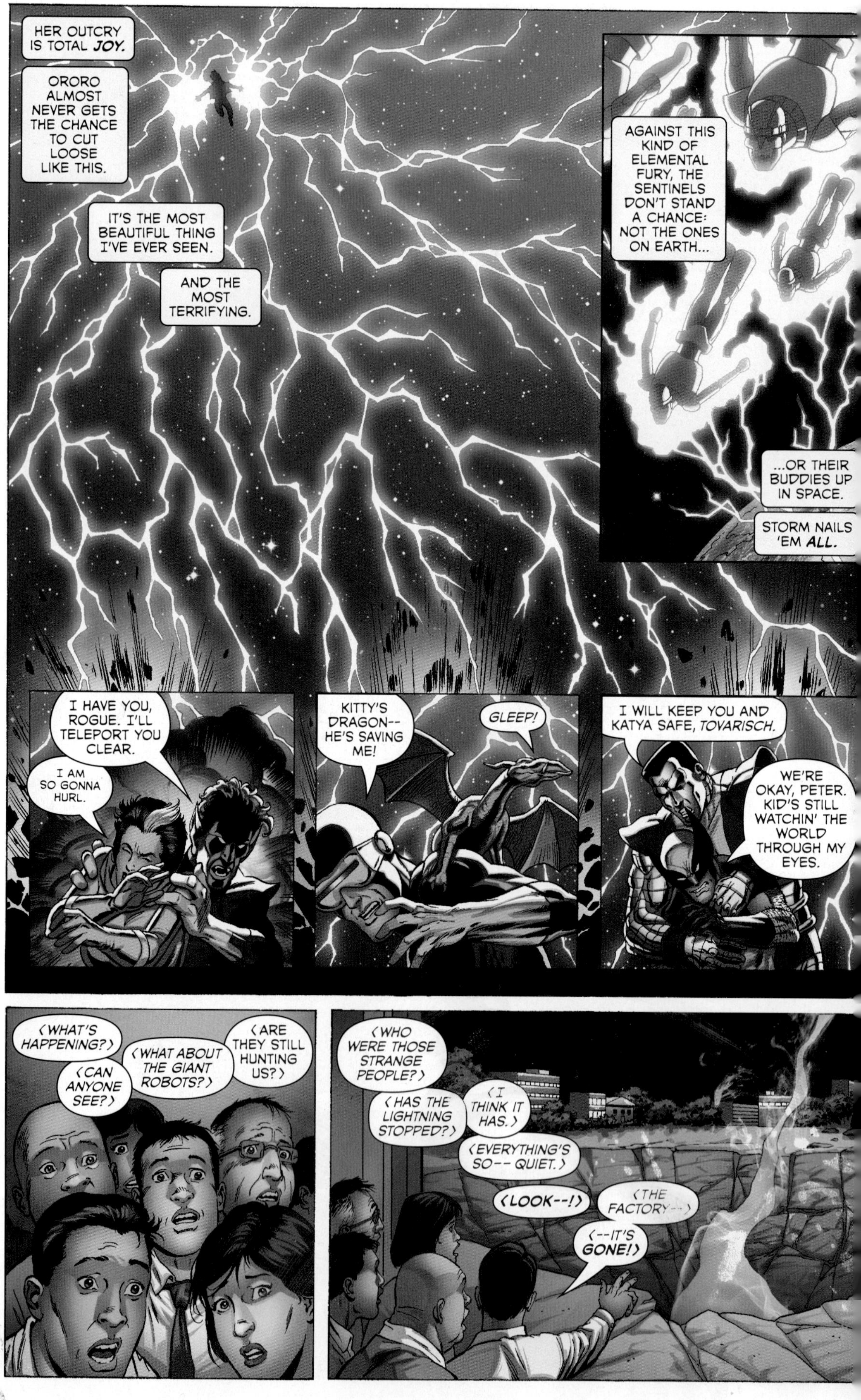

HER OUTCRY IS TOTAL JOY.
ORORO ALMOST NEVER GETS THE CHANCE TO CUT LOOSE LIKE THIS.
IT'S THE MOST BEAUTIFUL THING I'VE EVER SEEN.
AND THE MOST TERRIFYING.
AGAINST THIS KIND OF ELEMENTAL FURY, THE SENTINELS DON'T STAND A CHANCE: NOT THE ONES ON EARTH...
...OR THEIR BUDDIES UP IN SPACE.
STORM NAILS 'EM ALL.
I HAVE YOU, ROGUE. I'LL TELEPORT YOU CLEAR.
I AM SO GONNA HURL.
KITTY'S DRAGON-- HE'S SAVING ME!
GLEEP!
I WILL KEEP YOU AND KATYA SAFE, TOVARISCH.
WE'RE OKAY, PETER. KID'S STILL WATCHIN' THE WORLD THROUGH MY EYES.
‹WHAT'S HAPPENING?›
‹WHAT ABOUT THE GIANT ROBOTS?›
‹ARE THEY STILL HUNTING US?›
‹CAN ANYONE SEE?›
‹WHO WERE THOSE STRANGE PEOPLE?›
‹HAS THE LIGHTNING STOPPED?›
‹I THINK IT HAS.›
‹EVERYTHING'S SO-- QUIET.›
‹LOOK--!›
‹THE FACTORY--›
‹--IT'S GONE!›

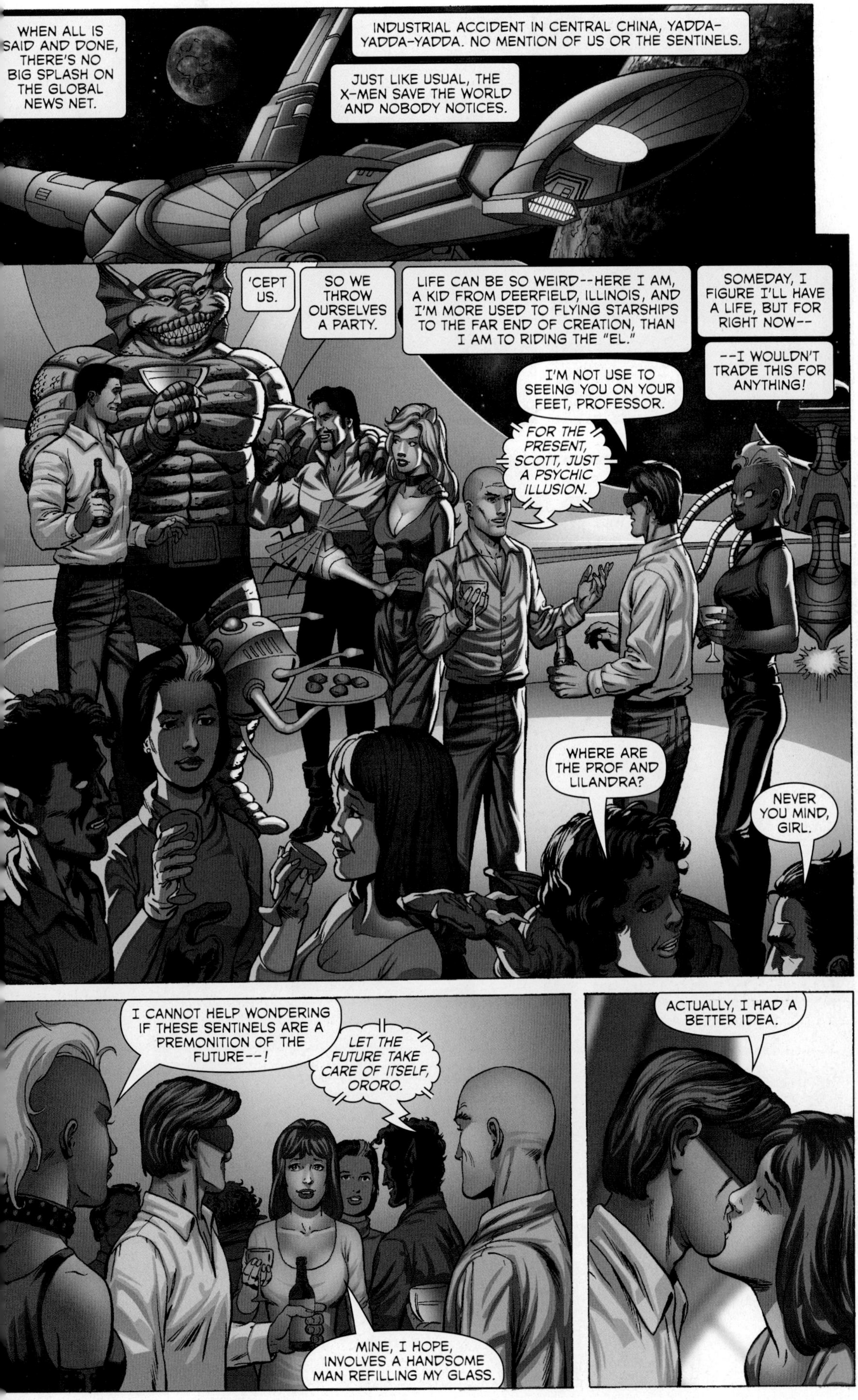

WHEN ALL IS SAID AND DONE, THERE'S NO BIG SPLASH ON THE GLOBAL NEWS NET.
INDUSTRIAL ACCIDENT IN CENTRAL CHINA, YADDA-YADDA-YADDA. NO MENTION OF US OR THE SENTINELS.
JUST LIKE USUAL, THE X-MEN SAVE THE WORLD AND NOBODY NOTICES.
'CEPT US.
SO WE THROW OURSELVES A PARTY.
LIFE CAN BE SO WEIRD--HERE I AM, A KID FROM DEERFIELD, ILLINOIS, AND I'M MORE USED TO FLYING STARSHIPS TO THE FAR END OF CREATION, THAN I AM TO RIDING THE "EL."
SOMEDAY, I FIGURE I'LL HAVE A LIFE, BUT FOR RIGHT NOW--
--I WOULDN'T TRADE THIS FOR ANYTHING!
I'M NOT USE TO SEEING YOU ON YOUR FEET, PROFESSOR.
FOR THE PRESENT, SCOTT, JUST A PSYCHIC ILLUSION.
WHERE ARE THE PROF AND LILANDRA?
NEVER YOU MIND, GIRL.
I CANNOT HELP WONDERING IF THESE SENTINELS ARE A PREMONITION OF THE FUTURE--!
LET THE FUTURE TAKE CARE OF ITSELF, ORORO.
MINE, I HOPE, INVOLVES A HANDSOME MAN REFILLING MY GLASS.
ACTUALLY, I HAD A BETTER IDEA.

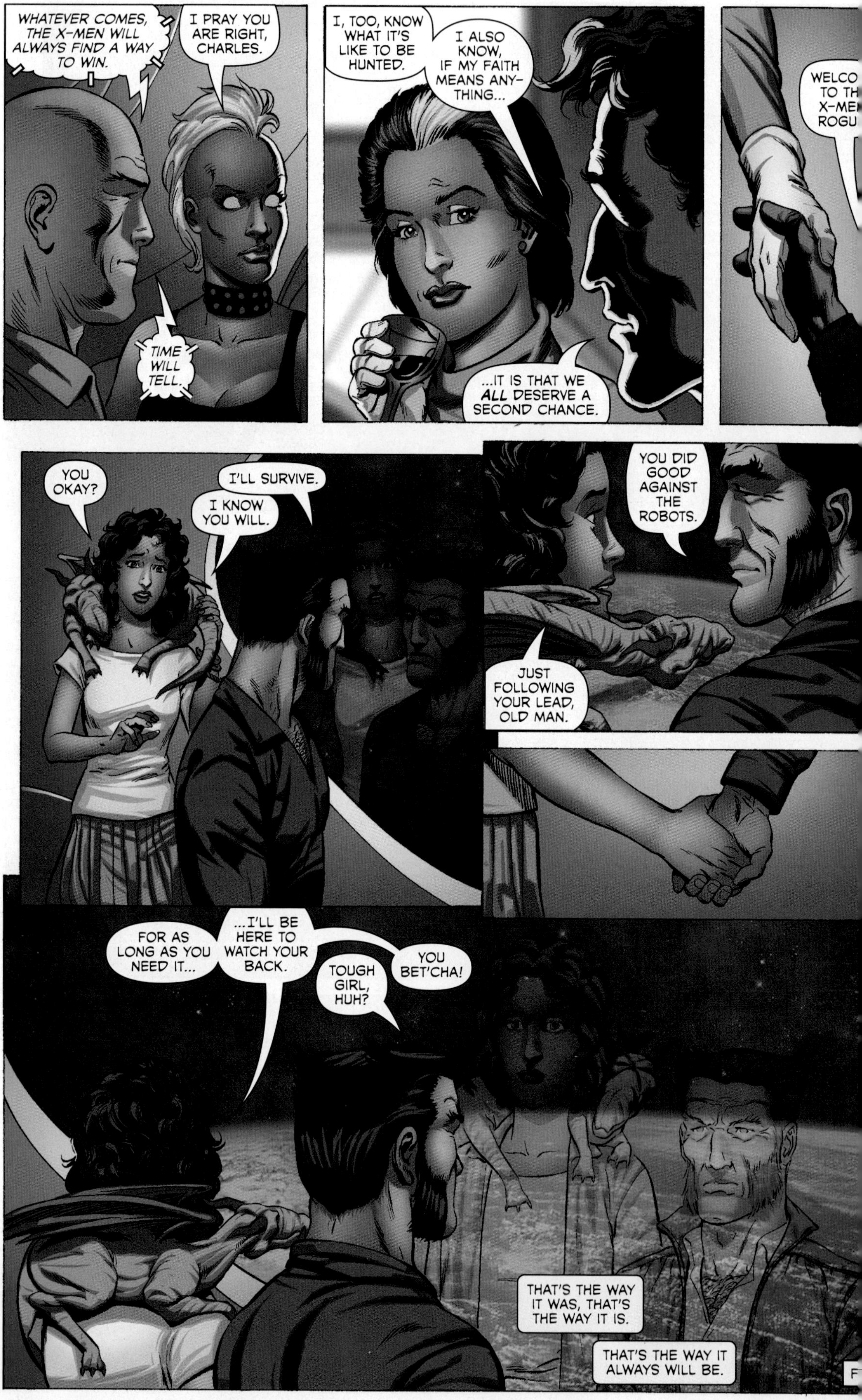

WHATEVER COMES, THE X-MEN WILL ALWAYS FIND A WAY TO WIN.
I PRAY YOU ARE RIGHT, CHARLES.
TIME WILL TELL.
I, TOO, KNOW WHAT IT'S LIKE TO BE HUNTED.
I ALSO KNOW, IF MY FAITH MEANS ANY-THING...
...IT IS THAT WE ALL DESERVE A SECOND CHANCE.
WELCO TO TH X-ME ROGU
YOU OKAY?
I'LL SURVIVE.
I KNOW YOU WILL.
YOU DID GOOD AGAINST THE ROBOTS.
JUST FOLLOWING YOUR LEAD, OLD MAN.
FOR AS LONG AS YOU NEED IT...
...I'LL BE HERE TO WATCH YOUR BACK.
YOU BET'CHA!
TOUGH GIRL, HUH?
THAT'S THE WAY IT WAS, THAT'S THE WAY IT IS.
THAT'S THE WAY IT ALWAYS WILL BE.
F

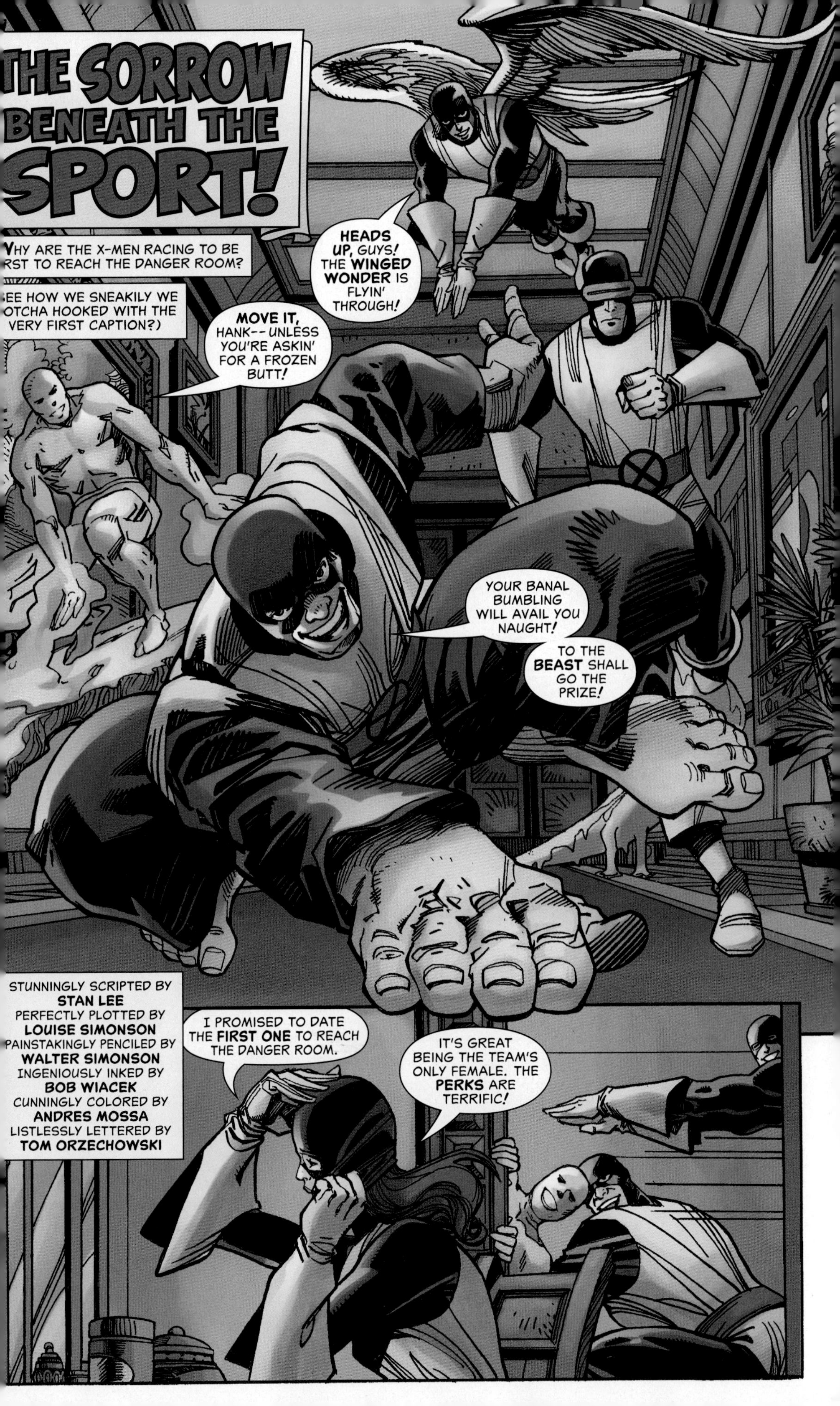

THE SORROW BENEATH THE SPORT!
VHY ARE THE X-MEN RACING TO BE RST TO REACH THE DANGER ROOM?
EE HOW WE SNEAKILY WE OTCHA HOOKED WITH THE VERY FIRST CAPTION?)
HEADS UP, GUYS! THE WINGED WONDER IS FLYIN' THROUGH!
MOVE IT, HANK-- UNLESS YOU'RE ASKIN' FOR A FROZEN BUTT!
YOUR BANAL BUMBLING WILL AVAIL YOU NAUGHT!
TO THE BEAST SHALL GO THE PRIZE!
STUNNINGLY SCRIPTED BY STAN LEE PERFECTLY PLOTTED BY LOUISE SIMONSON PAINSTAKINGLY PENCILED BY WALTER SIMONSON INGENIOUSLY INKED BY BOB WIACEK CUNNINGLY COLORED BY ANDRES MOSSA LISTLESSLY LETTERED BY TOM ORZECHOWSKI
I PROMISED TO DATE THE FIRST ONE TO REACH THE DANGER ROOM.
IT'S GREAT BEING THE TEAM'S ONLY FEMALE. THE PERKS ARE TERRIFIC!

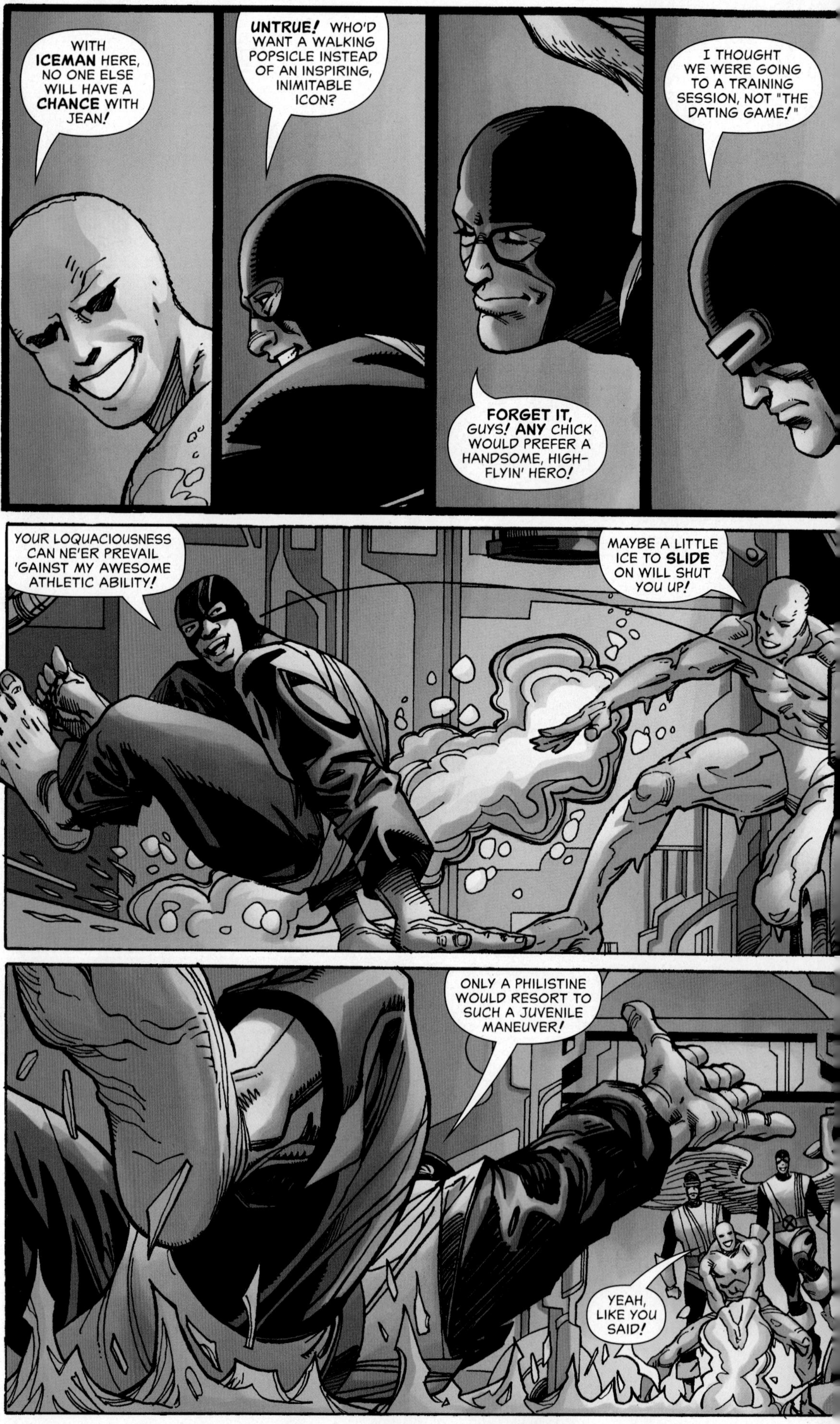

WITH ICEMAN HERE, NO ONE ELSE WILL HAVE A CHANCE WITH JEAN!
UNTRUE! WHO'D WANT A WALKING POPSICLE INSTEAD OF AN INSPIRING, INIMITABLE ICON?
FORGET IT, GUYS! ANY CHICK WOULD PREFER A HANDSOME, HIGH-FLYIN' HERO!
I THOUGHT WE WERE GOING TO A TRAINING SESSION, NOT "THE DATING GAME!"
YOUR LOQUACIOUSNESS CAN NE'ER PREVAIL 'GAINST MY AWESOME ATHLETIC ABILITY!
MAYBE A LITTLE ICE TO SLIDE ON WILL SHUT YOU UP!
ONLY A PHILISTINE WOULD RESORT TO SUCH A JUVENILE MANEUVER!
YEAH, LIKE YOU SAID!

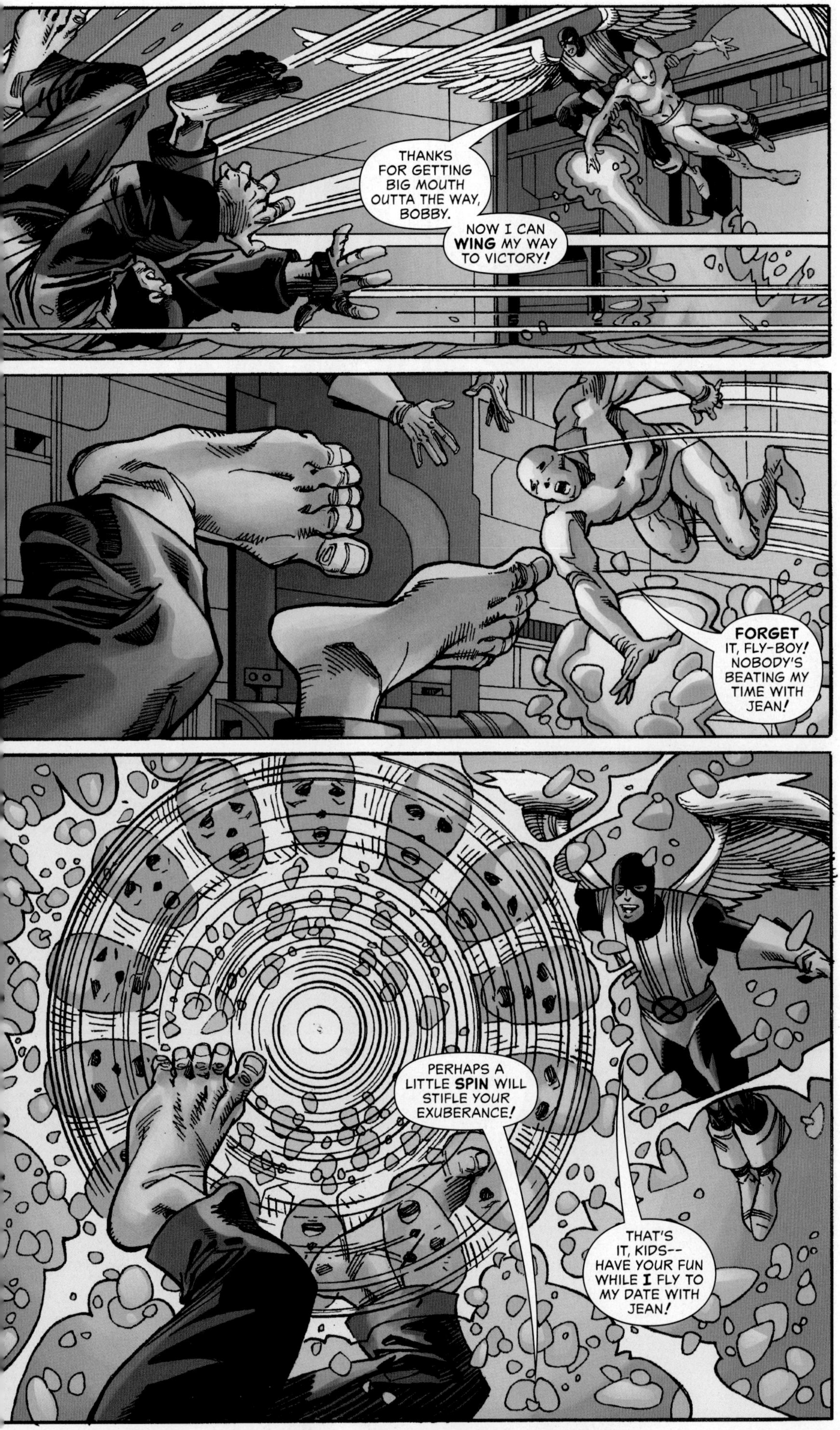
THANKS FOR GETTING BIG MOUTH OUTTA THE WAY, BOBBY.
NOW I CAN WING MY WAY TO VICTORY!
FORGET IT, FLY-BOY! NOBODY'S BEATING MY TIME WITH JEAN!
PERHAPS A LITTLE SPIN WILL STIFLE YOUR EXUBERANCE!
THAT'S IT, KIDS-- HAVE YOUR FUN WHILE I FLY TO MY DATE WITH JEAN!

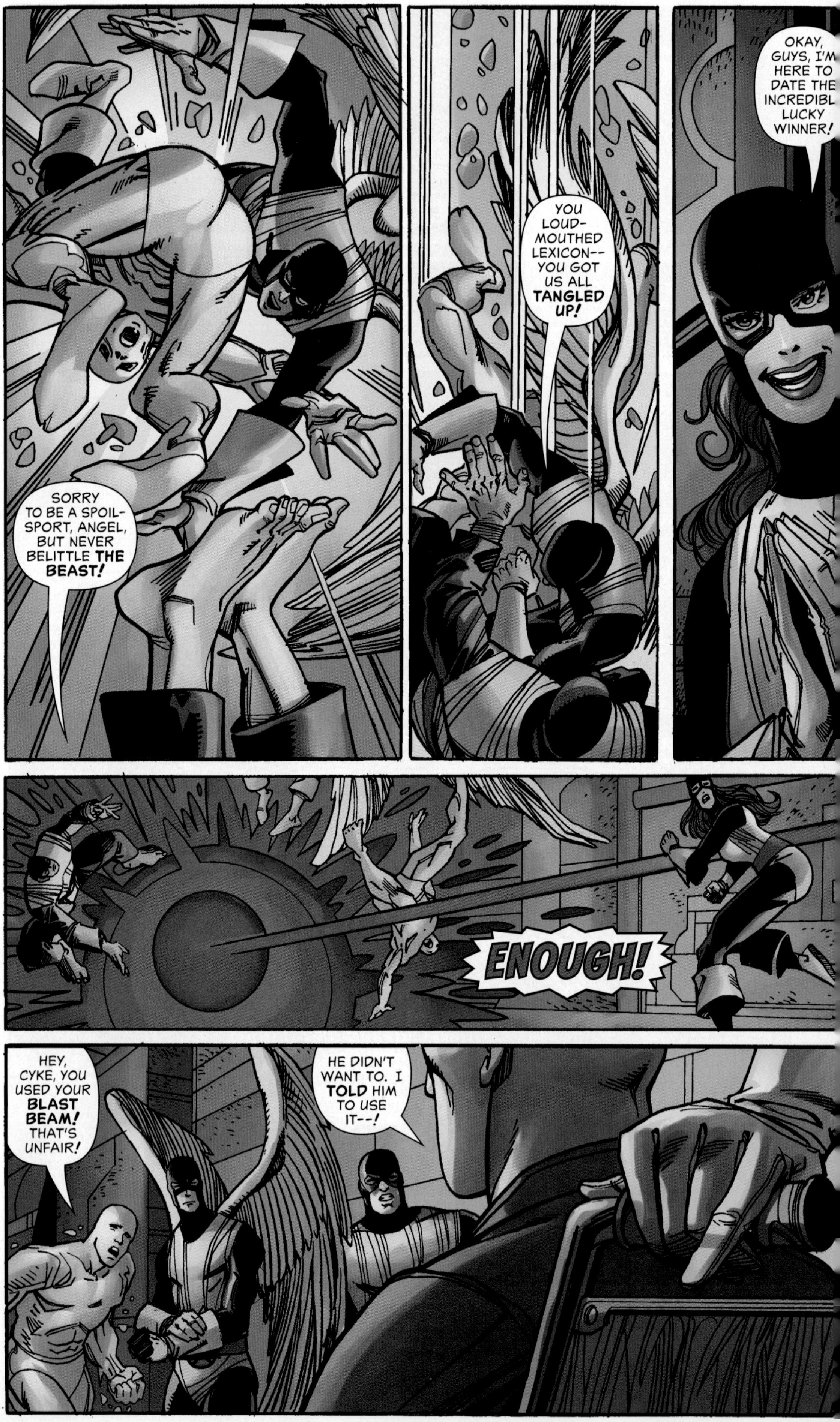
SORRY TO BE A SPOIL-SPORT, ANGEL, BUT NEVER BELITTLE THE BEAST!
YOU LOUD-MOUTHED LEXICON--YOU GOT US ALL TANGLED UP!
OKAY, GUYS, I'M HERE TO DATE THE INCREDIBL LUCKY WINNER!
ENOUGH!
HEY, CYKE, YOU USED YOUR BLAST BEAM! THAT'S UNFAIR!
HE DIDN'T WANT TO. I TOLD HIM TO USE IT--!

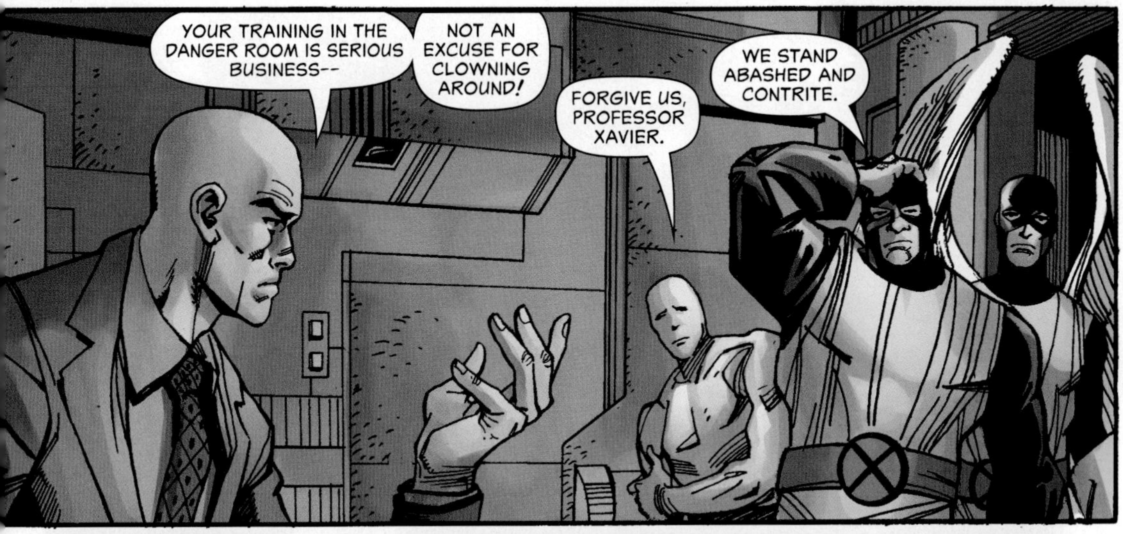
YOUR TRAINING IN THE DANGER ROOM IS SERIOUS BUSINESS--
NOT AN EXCUSE FOR CLOWNING AROUND!
FORGIVE US, PROFESSOR XAVIER.
WE STAND ABASHED AND CONTRITE.

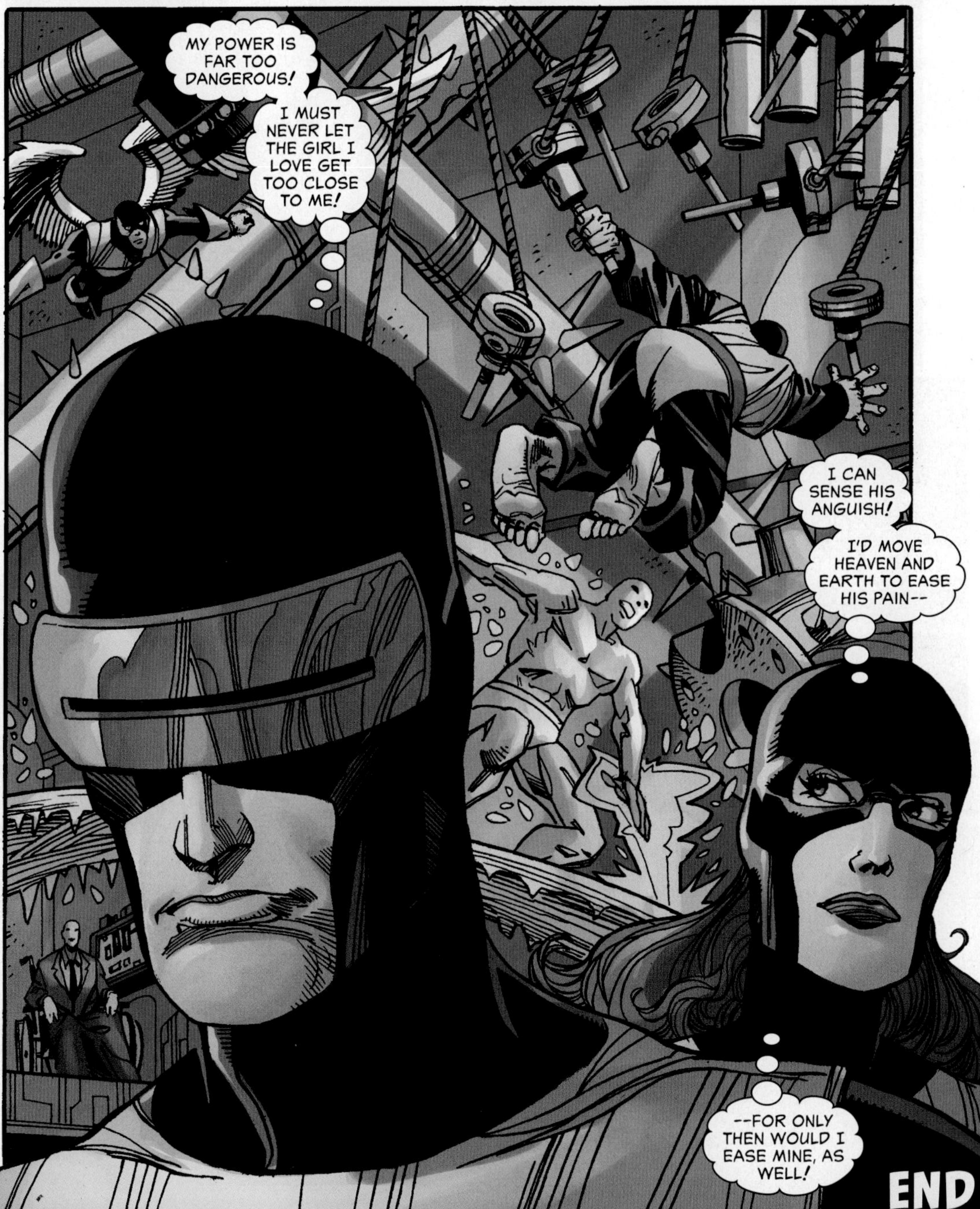
MY POWER IS FAR TOO DANGEROUS!
I MUST NEVER LET THE GIRL I LOVE GET TOO CLOSE TO ME!
I CAN SENSE HIS ANGUISH!
I'D MOVE HEAVEN AND EARTH TO EASE HIS PAIN--
--FOR ONLY THEN WOULD I EASE MINE, AS WELL!
END

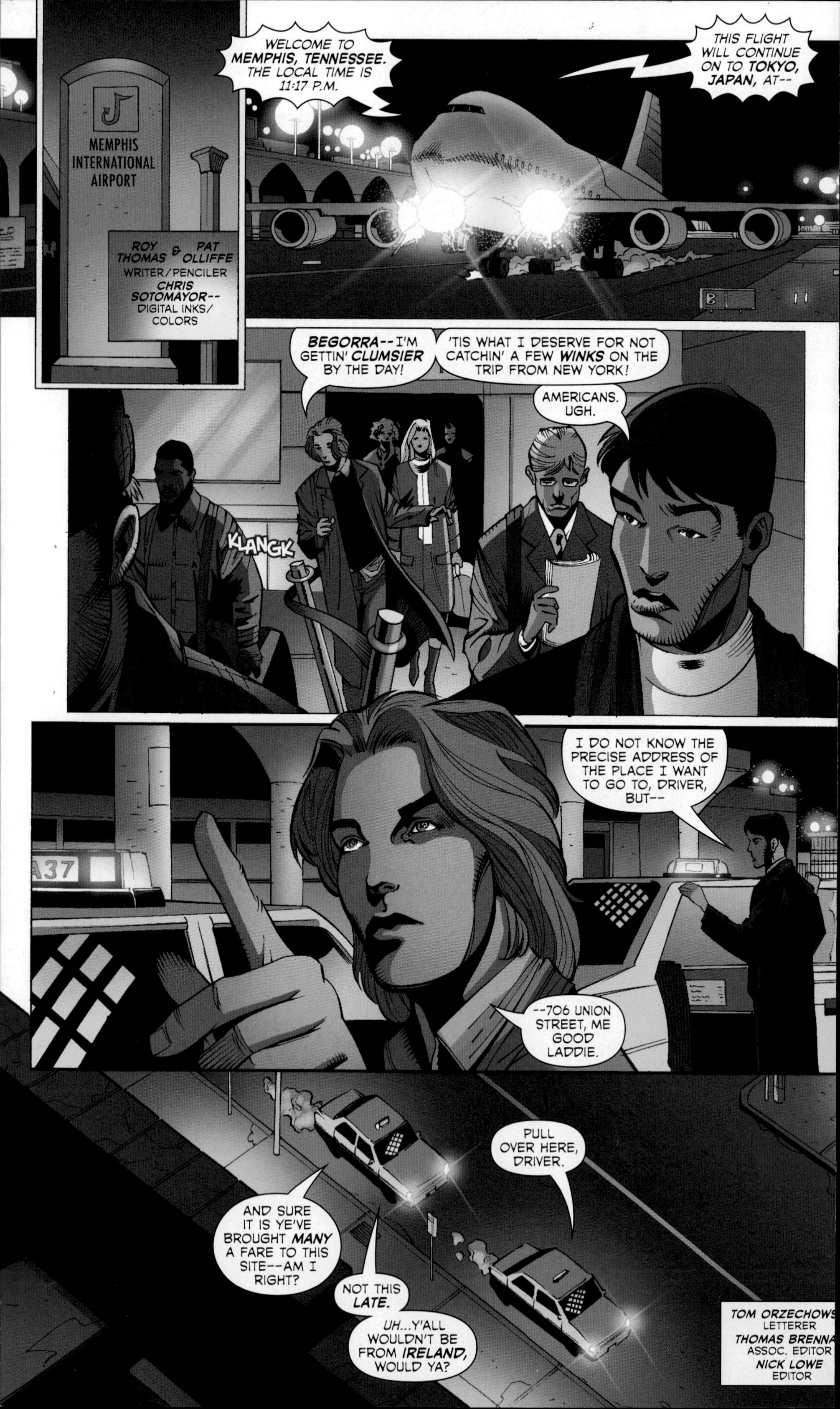
MEMPHIS INTERNATIONAL AIRPORT
ROY THOMAS & PAT OLLIFFE
WRITER/PENCILER
CHRIS SOTOMAYOR--
DIGITAL INKS/COLORS
WELCOME TO MEMPHIS, TENNESSEE. THE LOCAL TIME IS 11:17 P.M.
THIS FLIGHT WILL CONTINUE ON TO TOKYO, JAPAN, AT--
BEGORRA--I'M GETTIN' CLUMSIER BY THE DAY!
'TIS WHAT I DESERVE FOR NOT CATCHIN' A FEW WINKS ON THE TRIP FROM NEW YORK!
AMERICANS. UGH.
KLANGK
I DO NOT KNOW THE PRECISE ADDRESS OF THE PLACE I WANT TO GO TO, DRIVER, BUT--
--706 UNION STREET, ME GOOD LADDIE.
PULL OVER HERE, DRIVER.
AND SURE IT IS YE'VE BROUGHT MANY A FARE TO THIS SITE--AM I RIGHT?
NOT THIS LATE.
UH...Y'ALL WOULDN'T BE FROM IRELAND, WOULD YA?
TOM ORZECHOWS
LETTERER
THOMAS BRENNA
ASSOC. EDITOR
NICK LOWE
EDITOR

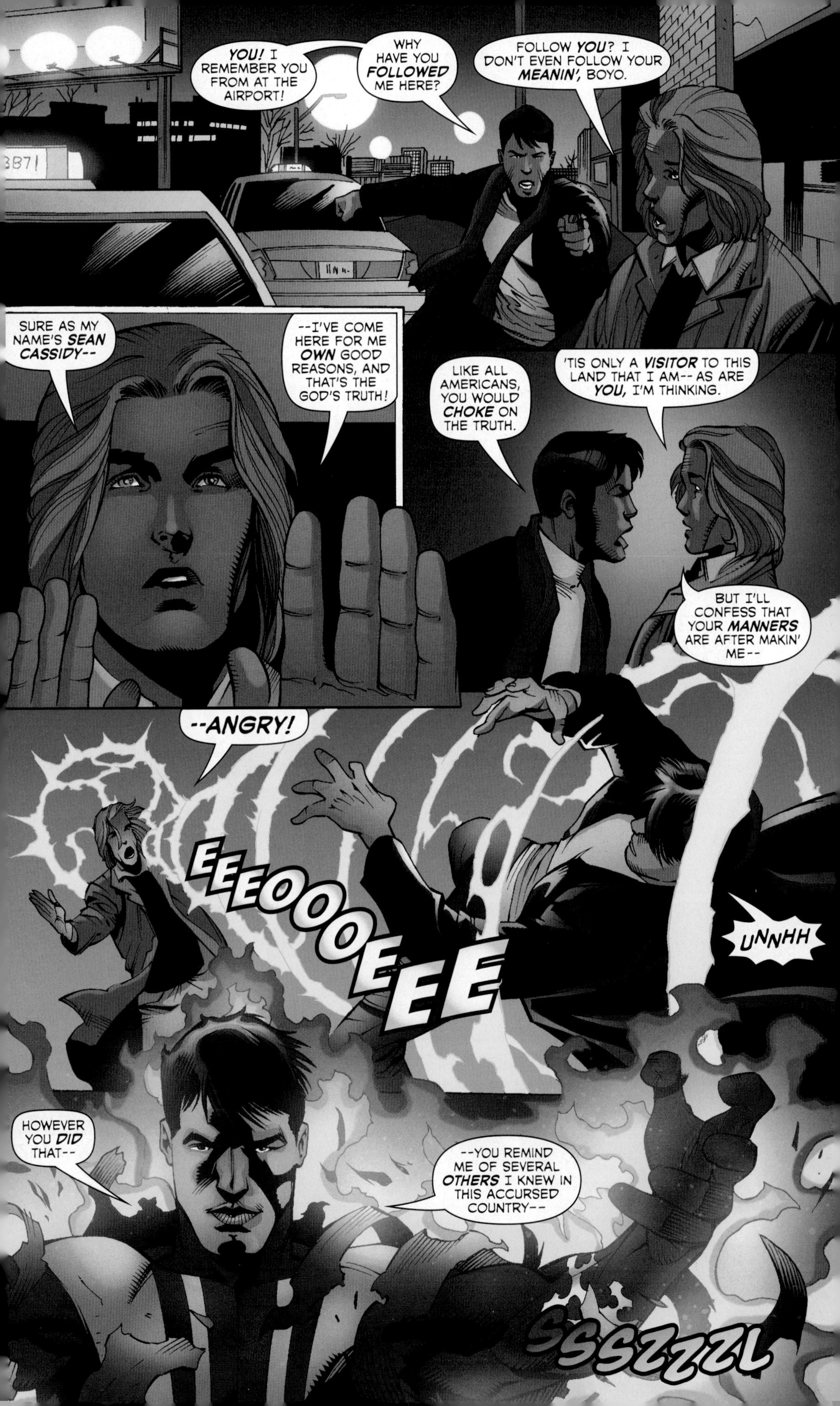
YOU! I REMEMBER YOU FROM AT THE AIRPORT!
WHY HAVE YOU FOLLOWED ME HERE?
FOLLOW YOU? I DON'T EVEN FOLLOW YOUR MEANIN', BOYO.
SURE AS MY NAME'S SEAN CASSIDY--
--I'VE COME HERE FOR ME OWN GOOD REASONS, AND THAT'S THE GOD'S TRUTH!
LIKE ALL AMERICANS, YOU WOULD CHOKE ON THE TRUTH.
'TIS ONLY A VISITOR TO THIS LAND THAT I AM-- AS ARE YOU, I'M THINKING.
BUT I'LL CONFESS THAT YOUR MANNERS ARE AFTER MAKIN' ME--
--ANGRY!
EEEOOOEEE
UNNHH
HOWEVER YOU DID THAT--
--YOU REMIND ME OF SEVERAL OTHERS I KNEW IN THIS ACCURSED COUNTRY--
SSSZZZZL

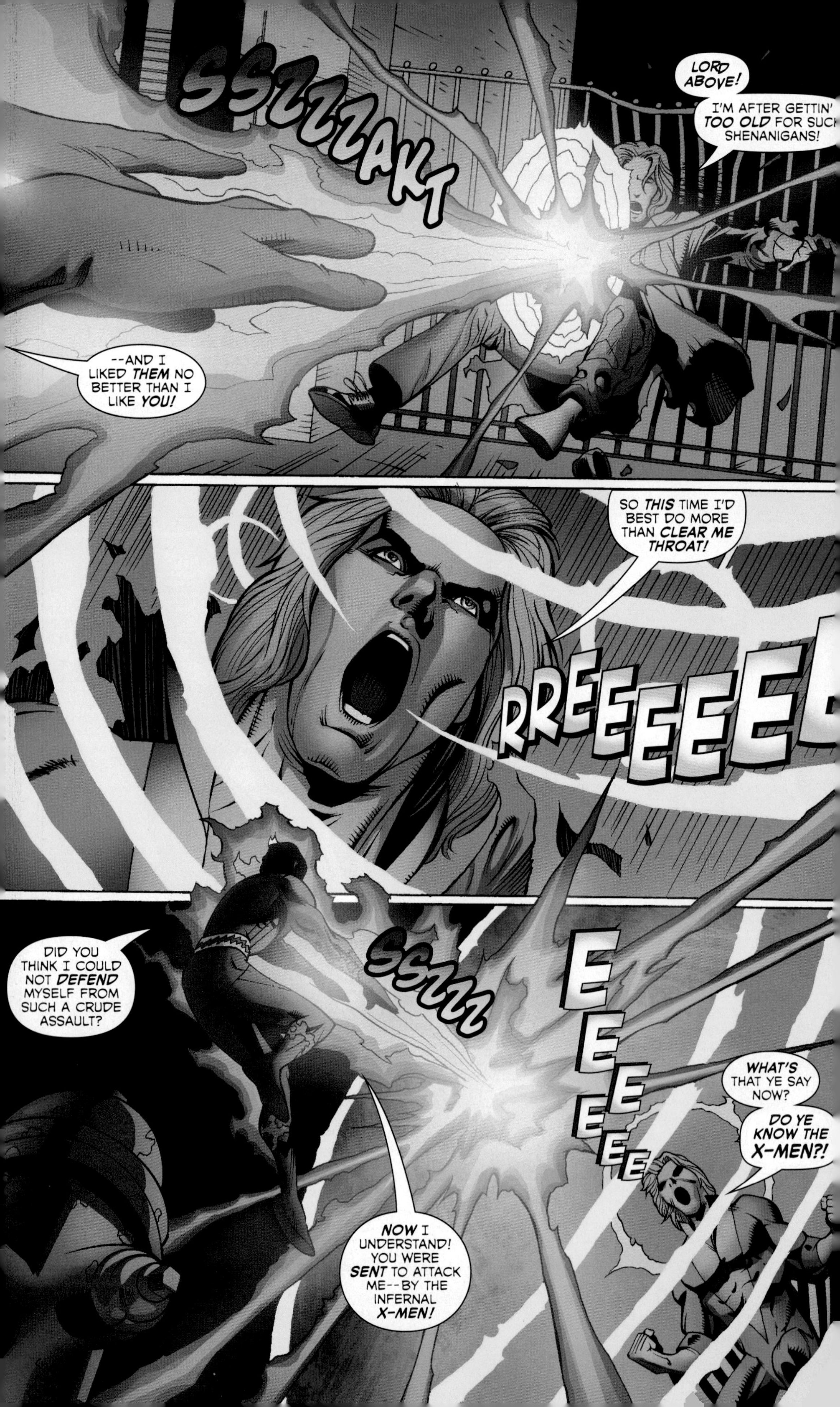
SSSZZZAKT
LORD ABOVE!
I'M AFTER GETTIN' TOO OLD FOR SUCH SHENANIGANS!
--AND I LIKED THEM NO BETTER THAN I LIKE YOU!
SO THIS TIME I'D BEST DO MORE THAN CLEAR ME THROAT!
RREEEEEEE
DID YOU THINK I COULD NOT DEFEND MYSELF FROM SUCH A CRUDE ASSAULT?
SSZZZ
EEEEEEE
WHAT'S THAT YE SAY NOW?
DO YE KNOW THE X-MEN?!
NOW I UNDERSTAND! YOU WERE SENT TO ATTACK ME--BY THE INFERNAL X-MEN!

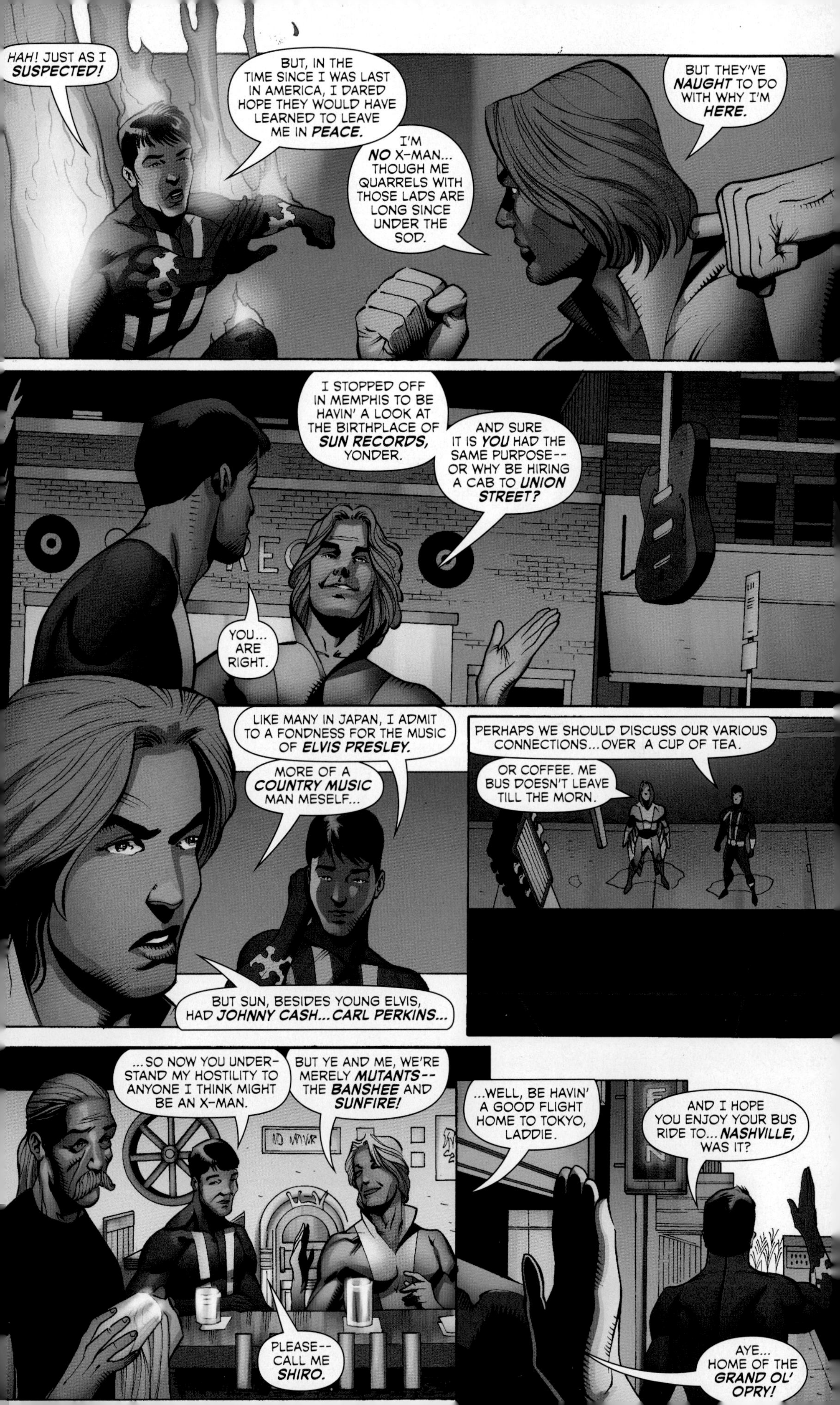

HAH! JUST AS I SUSPECTED!
BUT, IN THE TIME SINCE I WAS LAST IN AMERICA, I DARED HOPE THEY WOULD HAVE LEARNED TO LEAVE ME IN PEACE.
I'M NO X-MAN... THOUGH ME QUARRELS WITH THOSE LADS ARE LONG SINCE UNDER THE SOD.
BUT THEY'VE NAUGHT TO DO WITH WHY I'M HERE.
I STOPPED OFF IN MEMPHIS TO BE HAVIN' A LOOK AT THE BIRTHPLACE OF SUN RECORDS, YONDER.
AND SURE IT IS YOU HAD THE SAME PURPOSE-- OR WHY BE HIRING A CAB TO UNION STREET?
YOU... ARE RIGHT.
LIKE MANY IN JAPAN, I ADMIT TO A FONDNESS FOR THE MUSIC OF ELVIS PRESLEY.
MORE OF A COUNTRY MUSIC MAN MESELF...
BUT SUN, BESIDES YOUNG ELVIS, HAD JOHNNY CASH...CARL PERKINS...
PERHAPS WE SHOULD DISCUSS OUR VARIOUS CONNECTIONS...OVER A CUP OF TEA.
OR COFFEE. ME BUS DOESN'T LEAVE TILL THE MORN.
...SO NOW YOU UNDERSTAND MY HOSTILITY TO ANYONE I THINK MIGHT BE AN X-MAN.
BUT YE AND ME, WE'RE MERELY MUTANTS-- THE BANSHEE AND SUNFIRE!
PLEASE-- CALL ME SHIRO.
...WELL, BE HAVIN' A GOOD FLIGHT HOME TO TOKYO, LADDIE.
AND I HOPE YOU ENJOY YOUR BUS RIDE TO... NASHVILLE, WAS IT?
AYE... HOME OF THE GRAND OL' OPRY!

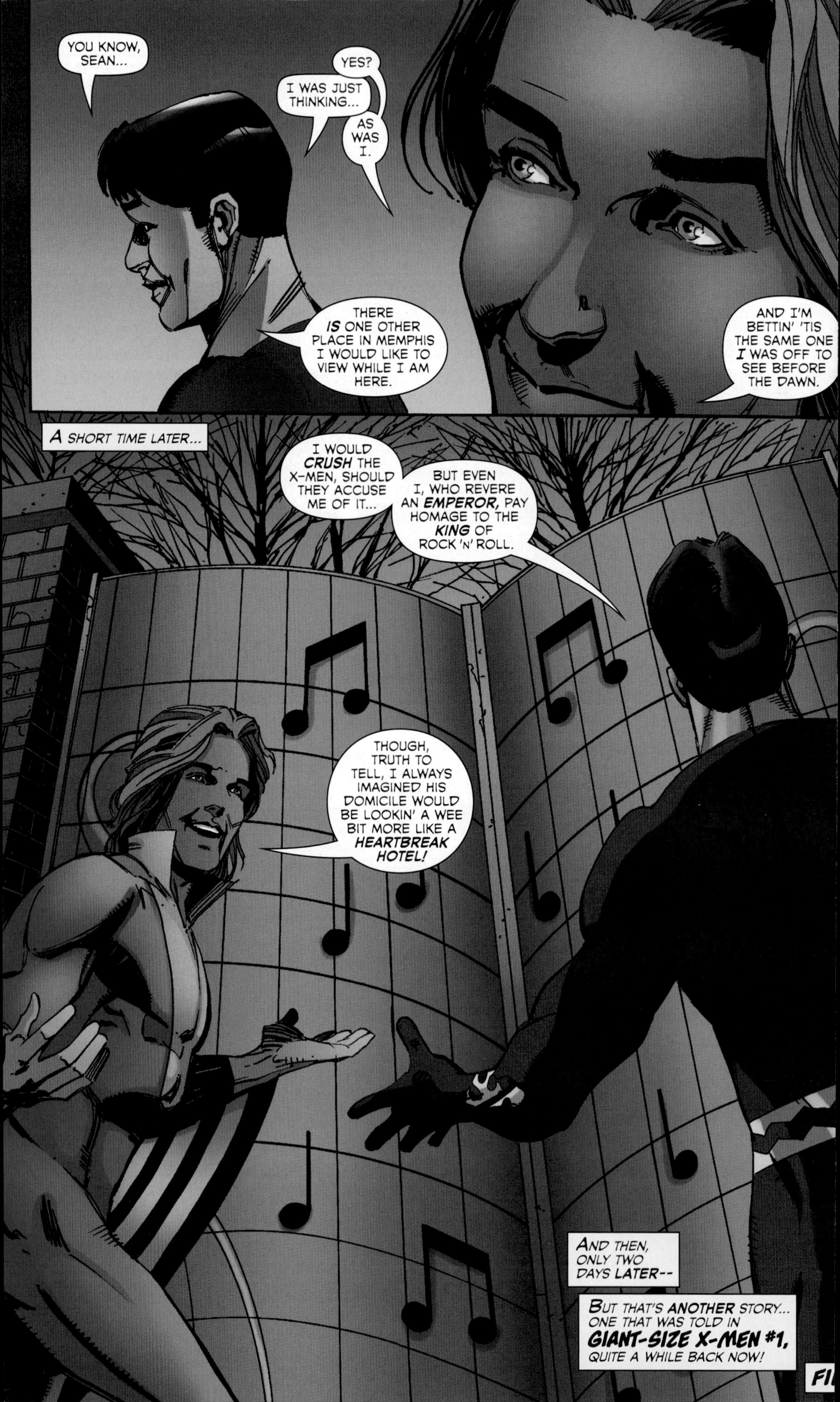
YOU KNOW, SEAN...
YES?
I WAS JUST THINKING...
AS WAS I.
THERE IS ONE OTHER PLACE IN MEMPHIS I WOULD LIKE TO VIEW WHILE I AM HERE.
AND I'M BETTIN' 'TIS THE SAME ONE I WAS OFF TO SEE BEFORE THE DAWN.
A SHORT TIME LATER...
I WOULD CRUSH THE X-MEN, SHOULD THEY ACCUSE ME OF IT...
BUT EVEN I, WHO REVERE AN EMPEROR, PAY HOMAGE TO THE KING OF ROCK 'N' ROLL.
THOUGH, TRUTH TO TELL, I ALWAYS IMAGINED HIS DOMICILE WOULD BE LOOKIN' A WEE BIT MORE LIKE A HEARTBREAK HOTEL!
AND THEN, ONLY TWO DAYS LATER--
BUT THAT'S ANOTHER STORY... ONE THAT WAS TOLD IN GIANT-SIZE X-MEN #1, QUITE A WHILE BACK NOW!
FI

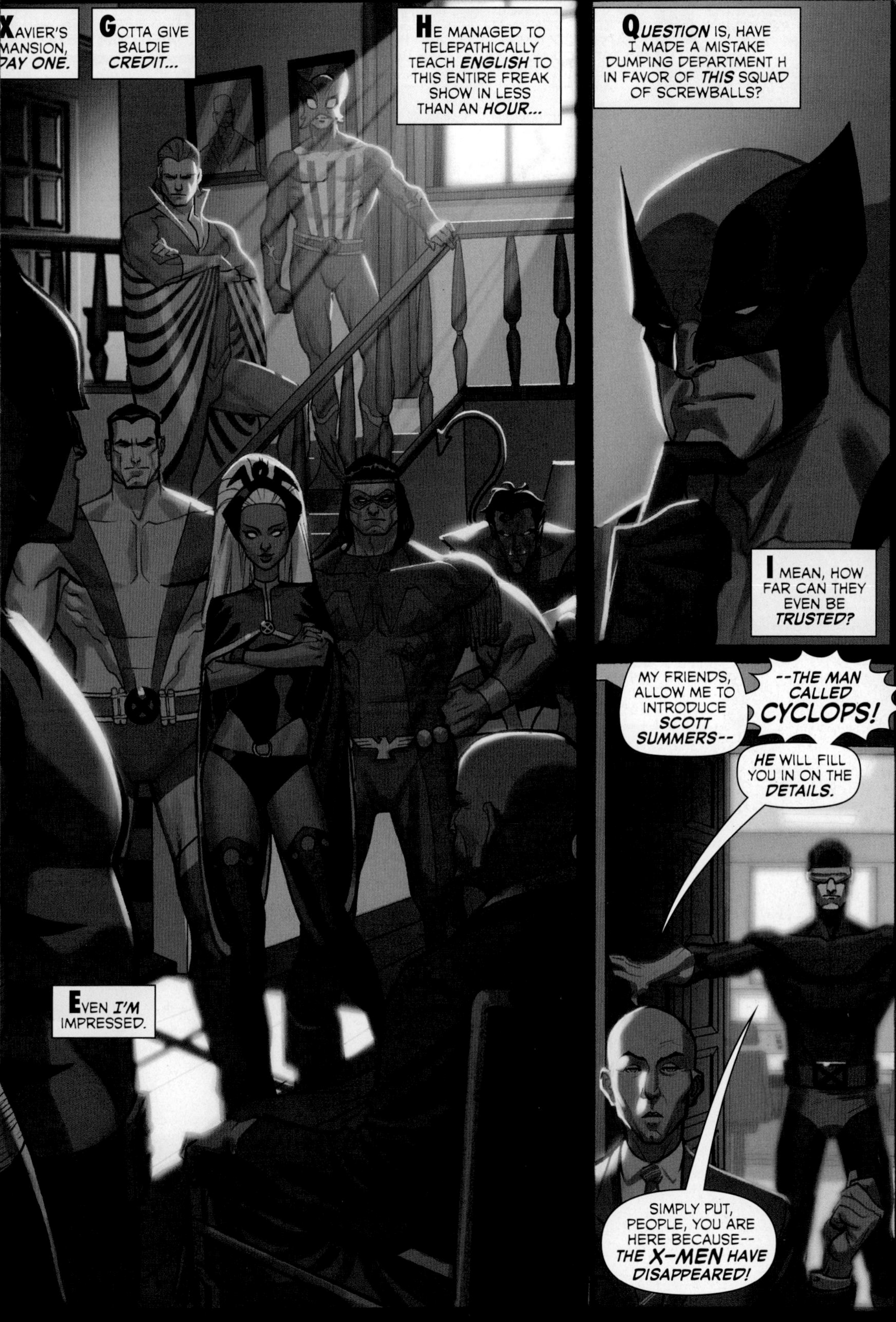
XAVIER'S MANSION, DAY ONE.
GOTTA GIVE BALDIE CREDIT...
HE MANAGED TO TELEPATHICALLY TEACH ENGLISH TO THIS ENTIRE FREAK SHOW IN LESS THAN AN HOUR...
EVEN I'M IMPRESSED.
QUESTION IS, HAVE I MADE A MISTAKE DUMPING DEPARTMENT H IN FAVOR OF THIS SQUAD OF SCREWBALLS?
I MEAN, HOW FAR CAN THEY EVEN BE TRUSTED?
MY FRIENDS, ALLOW ME TO INTRODUCE SCOTT SUMMERS--
--THE MAN CALLED CYCLOPS!
HE WILL FILL YOU IN ON THE DETAILS.
SIMPLY PUT, PEOPLE, YOU ARE HERE BECAUSE-- THE X-MEN HAVE DISAPPEARED!

OPTIONS!

LEN WEIN
WRITER
JORGE MOLINA
ARTIST
TOM ORZECHOWSKI
LETTERER

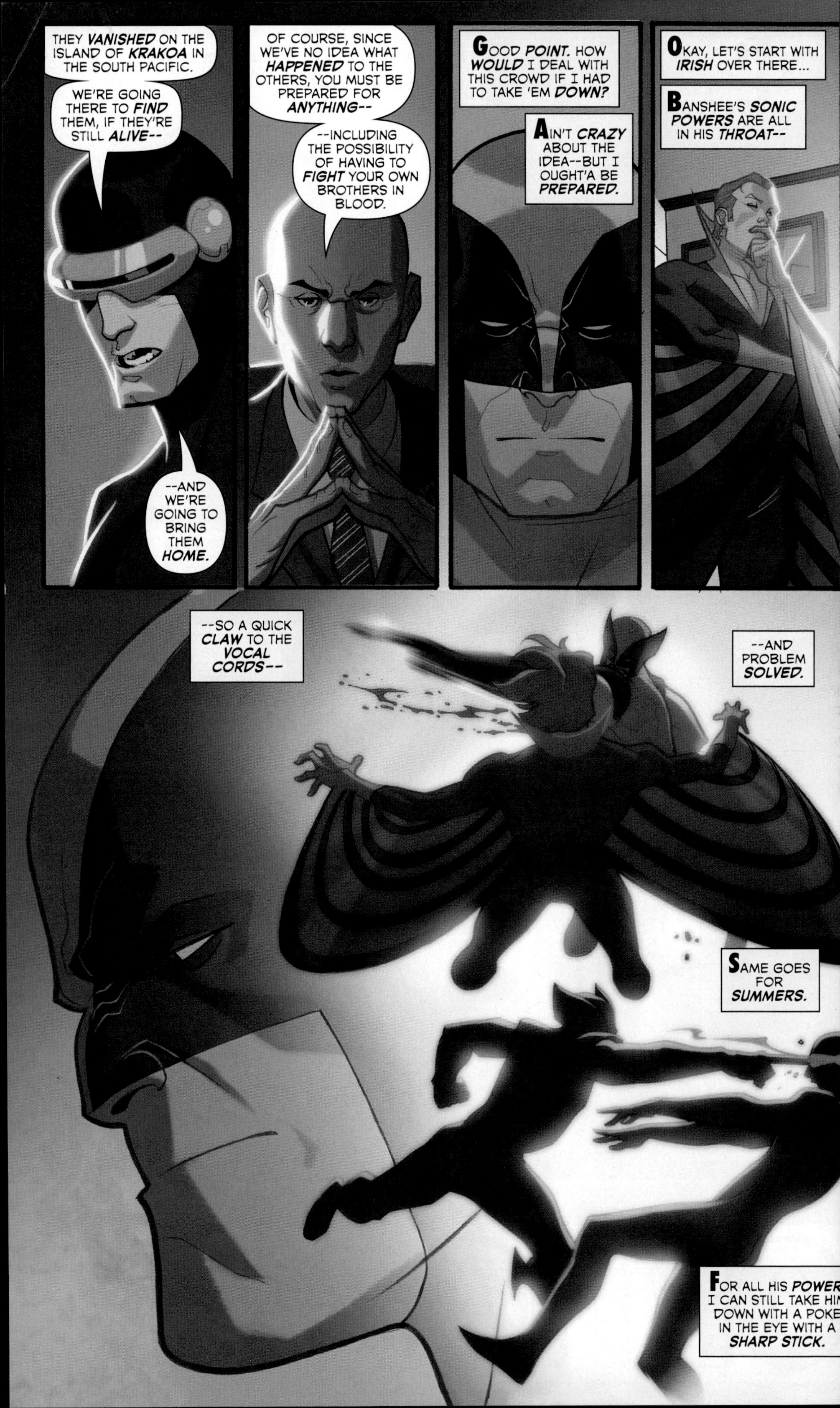

THEY VANISHED ON THE ISLAND OF KRAKOA IN THE SOUTH PACIFIC.
WE'RE GOING THERE TO FIND THEM, IF THEY'RE STILL ALIVE--
--AND WE'RE GOING TO BRING THEM HOME.
OF COURSE, SINCE WE'VE NO IDEA WHAT HAPPENED TO THE OTHERS, YOU MUST BE PREPARED FOR ANYTHING--
--INCLUDING THE POSSIBILITY OF HAVING TO FIGHT YOUR OWN BROTHERS IN BLOOD.
GOOD POINT. HOW WOULD I DEAL WITH THIS CROWD IF I HAD TO TAKE 'EM DOWN?
AIN'T CRAZY ABOUT THE IDEA--BUT I OUGHT'A BE PREPARED.
OKAY, LET'S START WITH IRISH OVER THERE...
BANSHEE'S SONIC POWERS ARE ALL IN HIS THROAT--
--SO A QUICK CLAW TO THE VOCAL CORDS--
--AND PROBLEM SOLVED.
SAME GOES FOR SUMMERS.
FOR ALL HIS POWER
I CAN STILL TAKE HI
DOWN WITH A POKE
IN THE EYE WITH A
SHARP STICK.

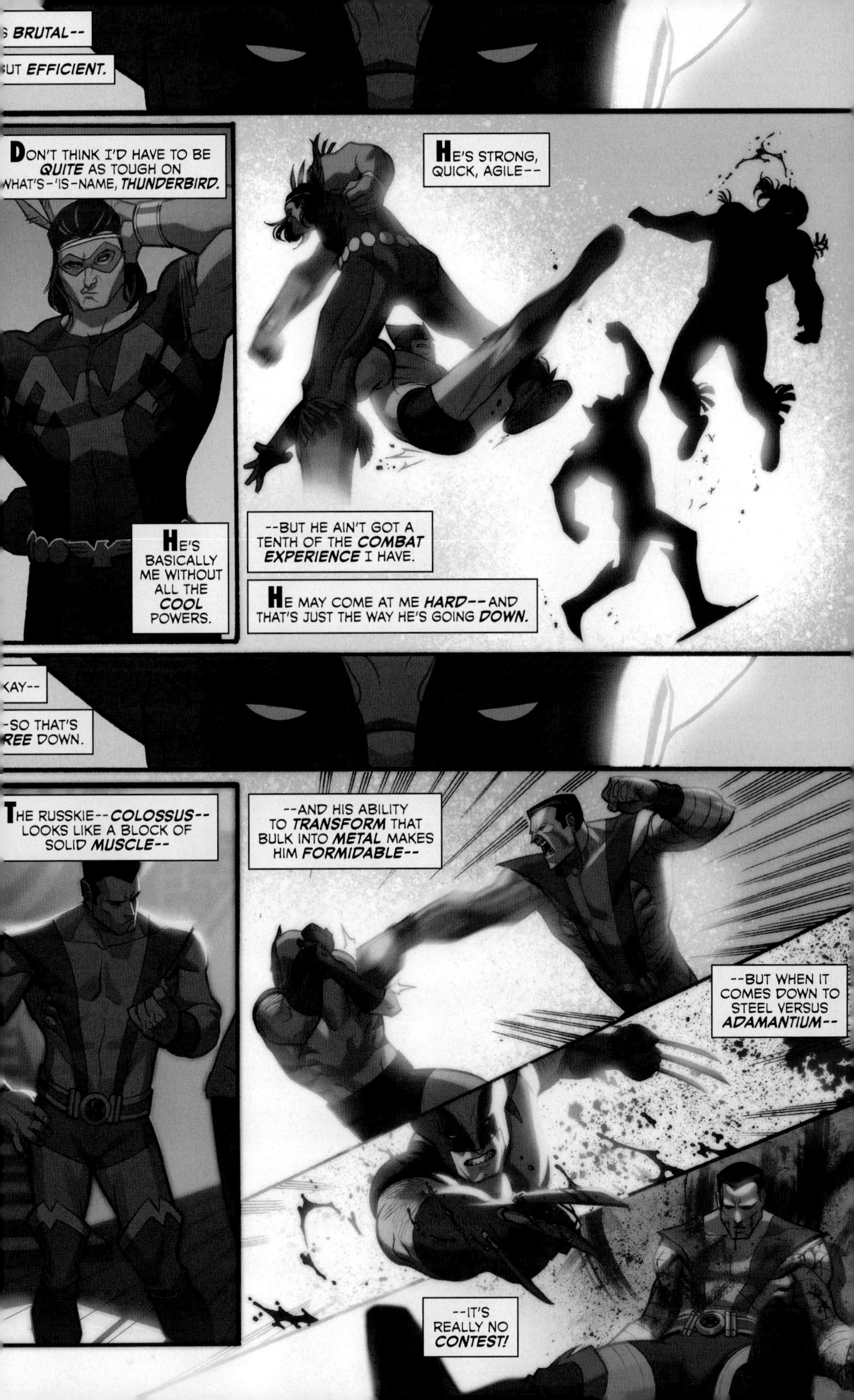

S BRUTAL--
UT EFFICIENT.
DON'T THINK I'D HAVE TO BE QUITE AS TOUGH ON WHAT'S-'IS-NAME, THUNDERBIRD.
HE'S STRONG, QUICK, AGILE--
--BUT HE AIN'T GOT A TENTH OF THE COMBAT EXPERIENCE I HAVE.
HE'S BASICALLY ME WITHOUT ALL THE COOL POWERS.
HE MAY COME AT ME HARD--AND THAT'S JUST THE WAY HE'S GOING DOWN.
KAY--
-SO THAT'S REE DOWN.
THE RUSSKIE--COLOSSUS--LOOKS LIKE A BLOCK OF SOLID MUSCLE--
--AND HIS ABILITY TO TRANSFORM THAT BULK INTO METAL MAKES HIM FORMIDABLE--
--BUT WHEN IT COMES DOWN TO STEEL VERSUS ADAMANTIUM--
--IT'S REALLY NO CONTEST!

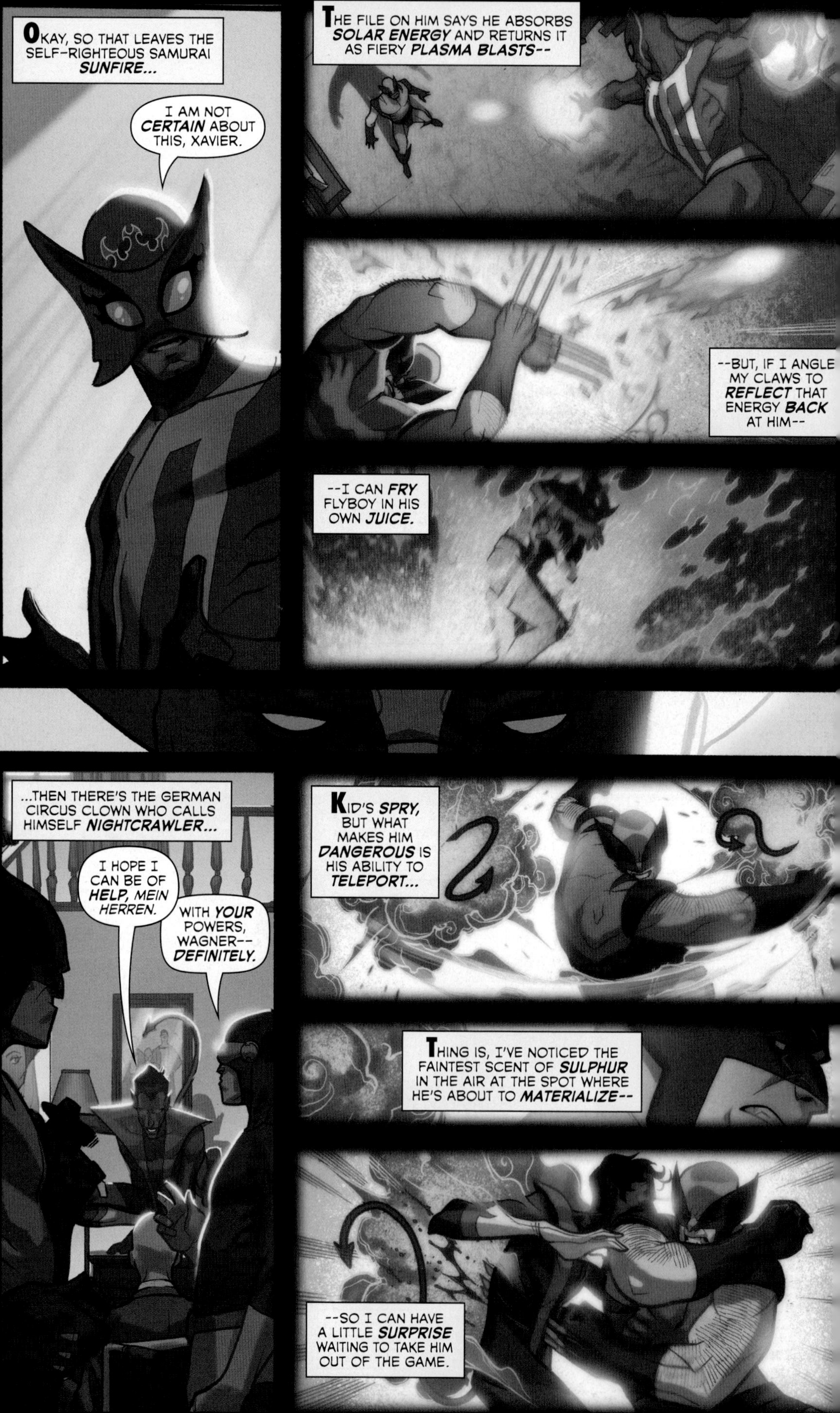
OKAY, SO THAT LEAVES THE SELF-RIGHTEOUS SAMURAI SUNFIRE...
I AM NOT CERTAIN ABOUT THIS, XAVIER.
THE FILE ON HIM SAYS HE ABSORBS SOLAR ENERGY AND RETURNS IT AS FIERY PLASMA BLASTS--
--BUT, IF I ANGLE MY CLAWS TO REFLECT THAT ENERGY BACK AT HIM--
--I CAN FRY FLYBOY IN HIS OWN JUICE.
...THEN THERE'S THE GERMAN CIRCUS CLOWN WHO CALLS HIMSELF NIGHTCRAWLER...
I HOPE I CAN BE OF HELP, MEIN HERREN.
WITH YOUR POWERS, WAGNER-- DEFINITELY.
KID'S SPRY, BUT WHAT MAKES HIM DANGEROUS IS HIS ABILITY TO TELEPORT...
THING IS, I'VE NOTICED THE FAINTEST SCENT OF SULPHUR IN THE AIR AT THE SPOT WHERE HE'S ABOUT TO MATERIALIZE--
--SO I CAN HAVE A LITTLE SURPRISE WAITING TO TAKE HIM OUT OF THE GAME.

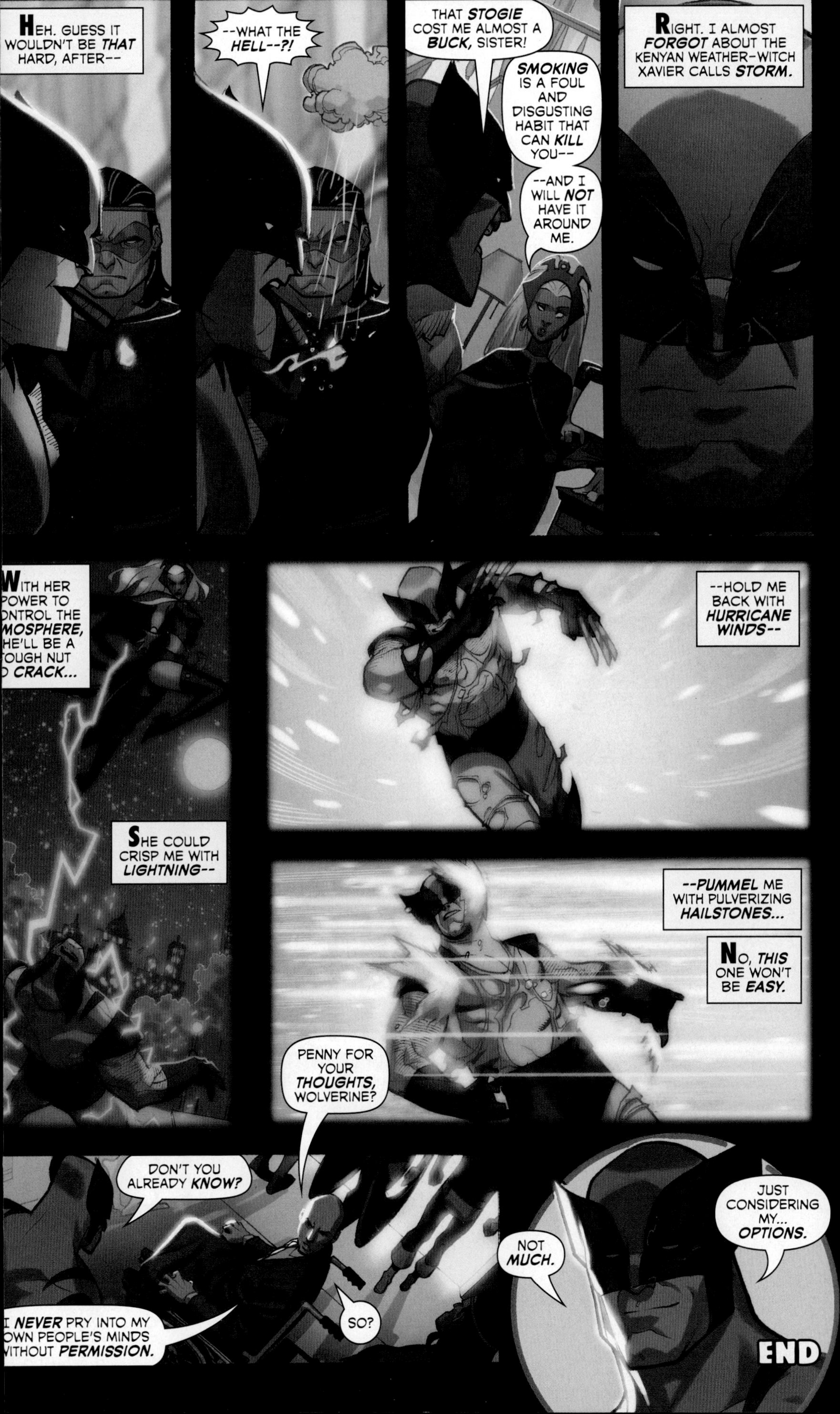
HEH. GUESS IT WOULDN'T BE THAT HARD, AFTER--
--WHAT THE HELL--?!
THAT STOGIE COST ME ALMOST A BUCK, SISTER!
SMOKING IS A FOUL AND DISGUSTING HABIT THAT CAN KILL YOU--
--AND I WILL NOT HAVE IT AROUND ME.
RIGHT. I ALMOST FORGOT ABOUT THE KENYAN WEATHER-WITCH XAVIER CALLS STORM.
ITH HER POWER TO ONTROL THE MOSPHERE, HE'LL BE A OUGH NUT CRACK...
--HOLD ME BACK WITH HURRICANE WINDS--
SHE COULD CRISP ME WITH LIGHTNING--
--PUMMEL ME WITH PULVERIZING HAILSTONES...
NO, THIS ONE WON'T BE EASY.
PENNY FOR YOUR THOUGHTS, WOLVERINE?
DON'T YOU ALREADY KNOW?
I NEVER PRY INTO MY OWN PEOPLE'S MINDS WITHOUT PERMISSION.
SO?
NOT MUCH.
JUST CONSIDERING MY... OPTIONS.
END

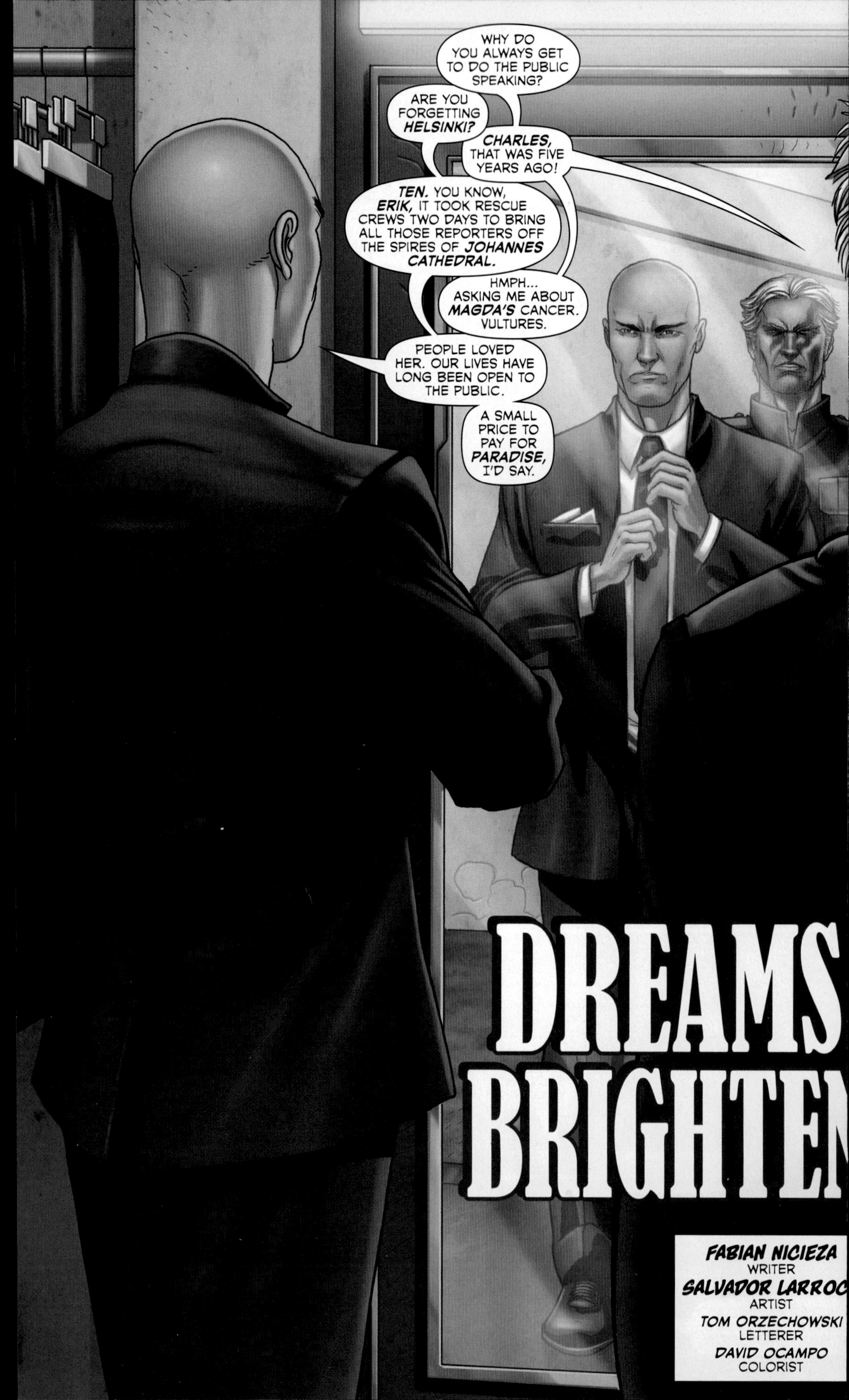
WHY DO YOU ALWAYS GET TO DO THE PUBLIC SPEAKING?
ARE YOU FORGETTING HELSINKI?
CHARLES, THAT WAS FIVE YEARS AGO!
TEN. YOU KNOW, ERIK, IT TOOK RESCUE CREWS TWO DAYS TO BRING ALL THOSE REPORTERS OFF THE SPIRES OF JOHANNES CATHEDRAL.
HMPH... ASKING ME ABOUT MAGDA'S CANCER. VULTURES.
PEOPLE LOVED HER. OUR LIVES HAVE LONG BEEN OPEN TO THE PUBLIC.
A SMALL PRICE TO PAY FOR PARADISE, I'D SAY.
DREAMS
BRIGHTEN
FABIAN NICIEZA
WRITER
SALVADOR LARROC
ARTIST
TOM ORZECHOWSKI
LETTERER
DAVID OCAMPO
COLORIST

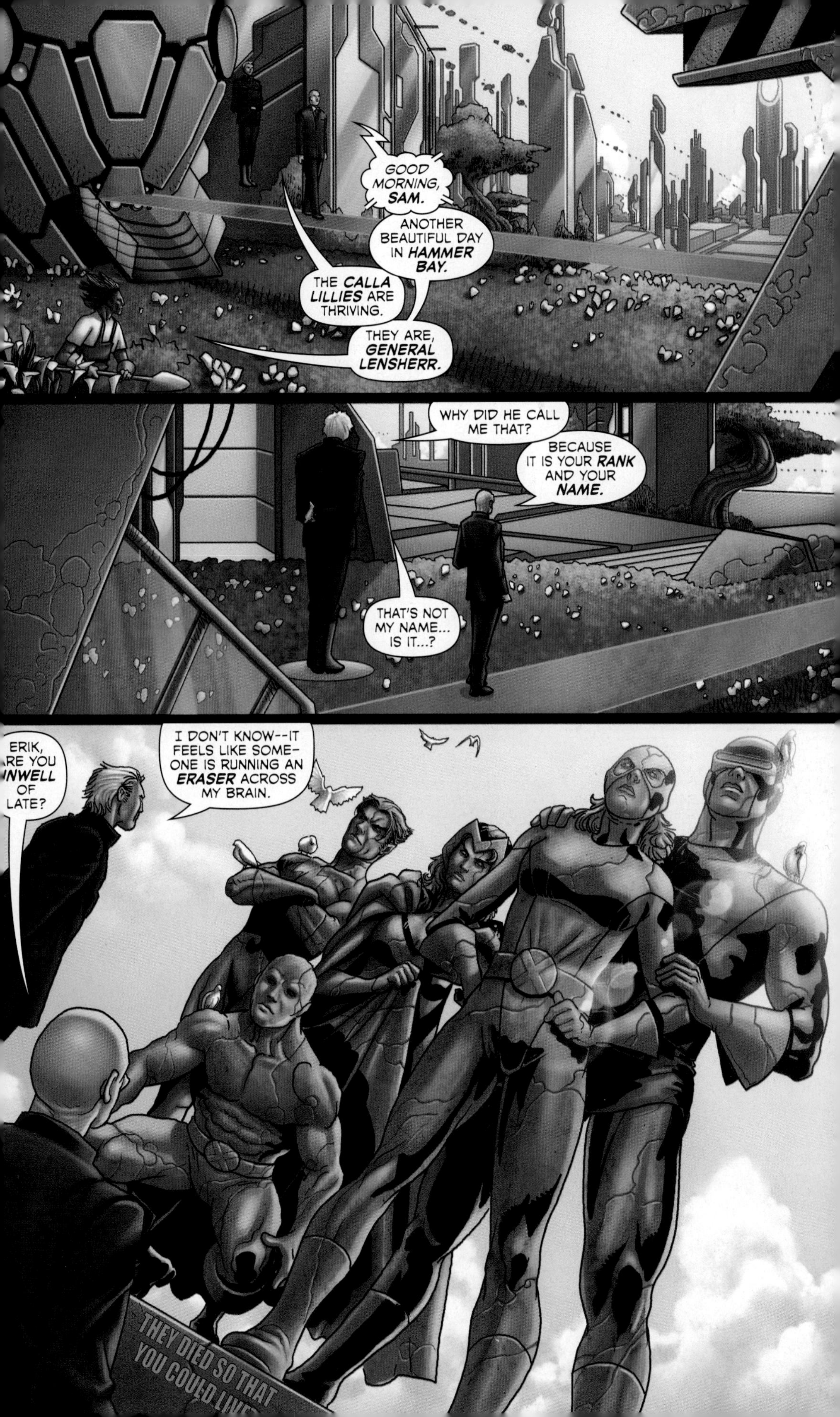
GOOD MORNING, SAM.
ANOTHER BEAUTIFUL DAY IN HAMMER BAY.
THE CALLA LILLIES ARE THRIVING.
THEY ARE, GENERAL LENSHERR.
WHY DID HE CALL ME THAT?
BECAUSE IT IS YOUR RANK AND YOUR NAME.
THAT'S NOT MY NAME... IS IT...?
ERIK, ARE YOU UNWELL OF LATE?
I DON'T KNOW--IT FEELS LIKE SOME-ONE IS RUNNING AN ERASER ACROSS MY BRAIN.
THEY DIED SO THAT YOU COULD LIVE

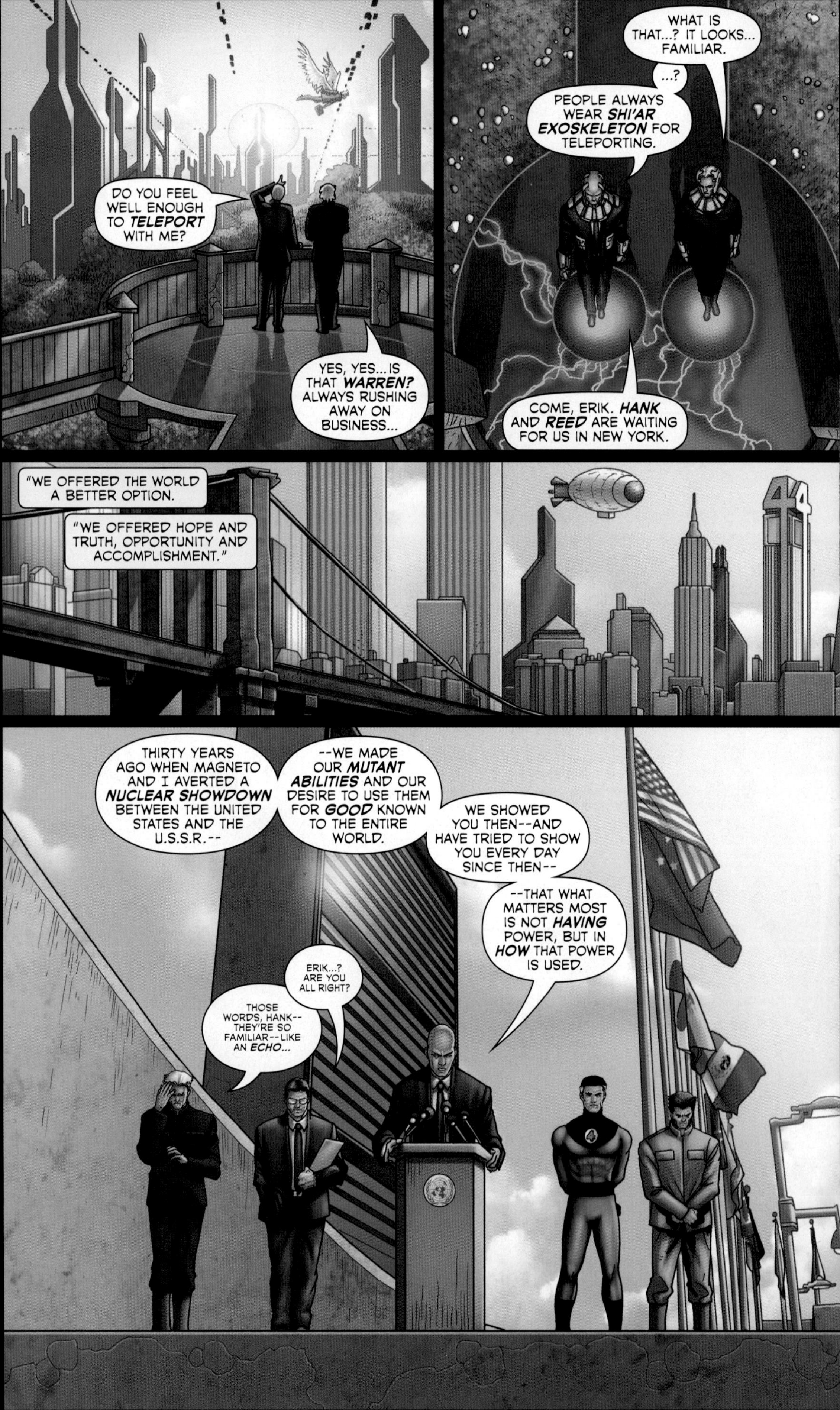
DO YOU FEEL WELL ENOUGH TO TELEPORT WITH ME?
YES, YES... IS THAT WARREN? ALWAYS RUSHING AWAY ON BUSINESS...
WHAT IS THAT...? IT LOOKS... FAMILIAR.
...?
PEOPLE ALWAYS WEAR SHI'AR EXOSKELETON FOR TELEPORTING.
COME, ERIK. HANK AND REED ARE WAITING FOR US IN NEW YORK.
"WE OFFERED THE WORLD A BETTER OPTION.
"WE OFFERED HOPE AND TRUTH, OPPORTUNITY AND ACCOMPLISHMENT."
THIRTY YEARS AGO WHEN MAGNETO AND I AVERTED A NUCLEAR SHOWDOWN BETWEEN THE UNITED STATES AND THE U.S.S.R.--
--WE MADE OUR MUTANT ABILITIES AND OUR DESIRE TO USE THEM FOR GOOD KNOWN TO THE ENTIRE WORLD.
WE SHOWED YOU THEN--AND HAVE TRIED TO SHOW YOU EVERY DAY SINCE THEN--
--THAT WHAT MATTERS MOST IS NOT HAVING POWER, BUT IN HOW THAT POWER IS USED.
ERIK...? ARE YOU ALL RIGHT?
THOSE WORDS, HANK--THEY'RE SO FAMILIAR--LIKE AN ECHO...

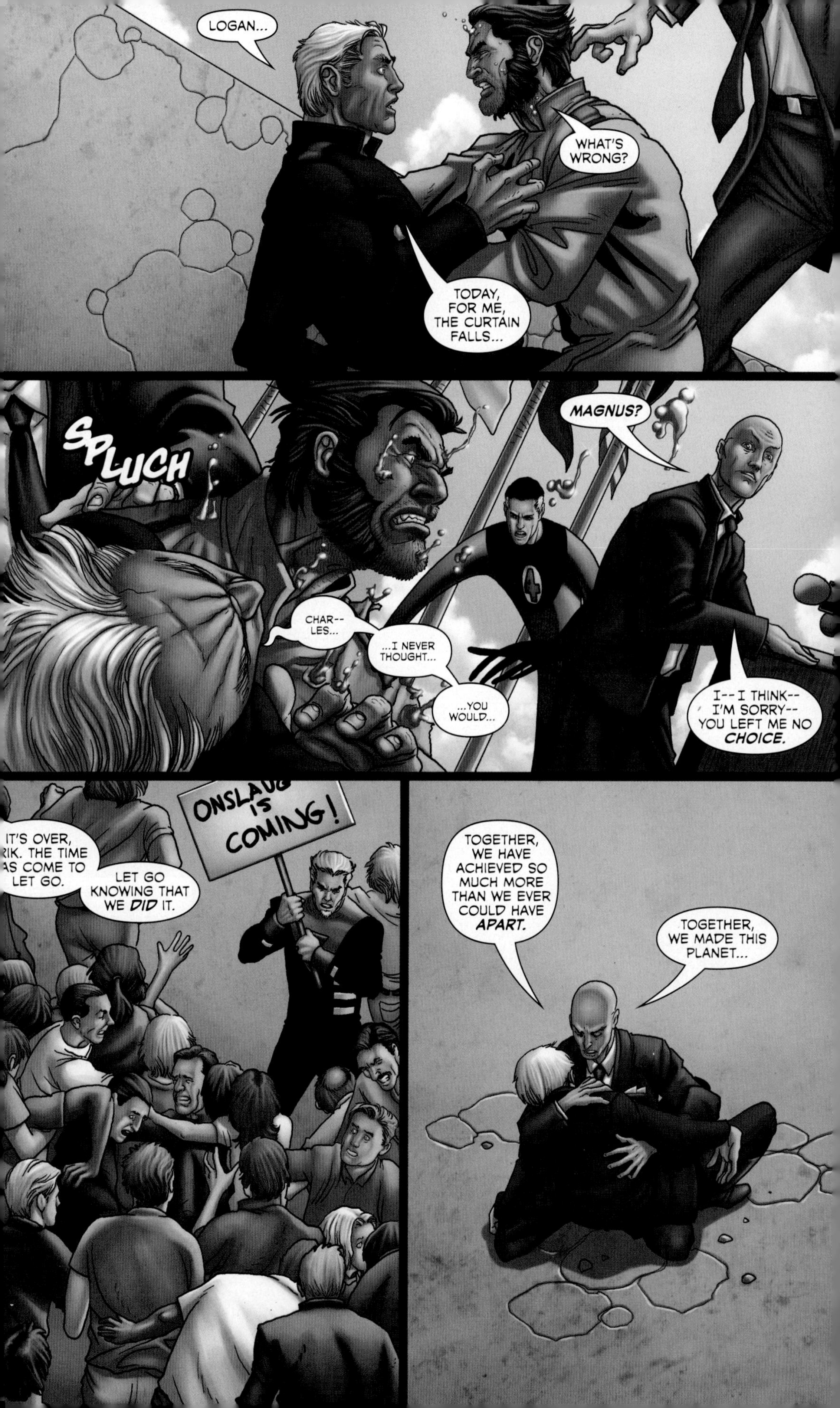
LOGAN...
WHAT'S WRONG?
TODAY, FOR ME, THE CURTAIN FALLS...
SPLUCH
MAGNUS?
CHAR-- LES...
...I NEVER THOUGHT...
...YOU WOULD...
I-- I THINK-- I'M SORRY-- YOU LEFT ME NO CHOICE.
ONSLAUG IS COMING!
IT'S OVER, RIK. THE TIME AS COME TO LET GO.
LET GO KNOWING THAT WE DID IT.
TOGETHER, WE HAVE ACHIEVED SO MUCH MORE THAN WE EVER COULD HAVE APART.
TOGETHER, WE MADE THIS PLANET...

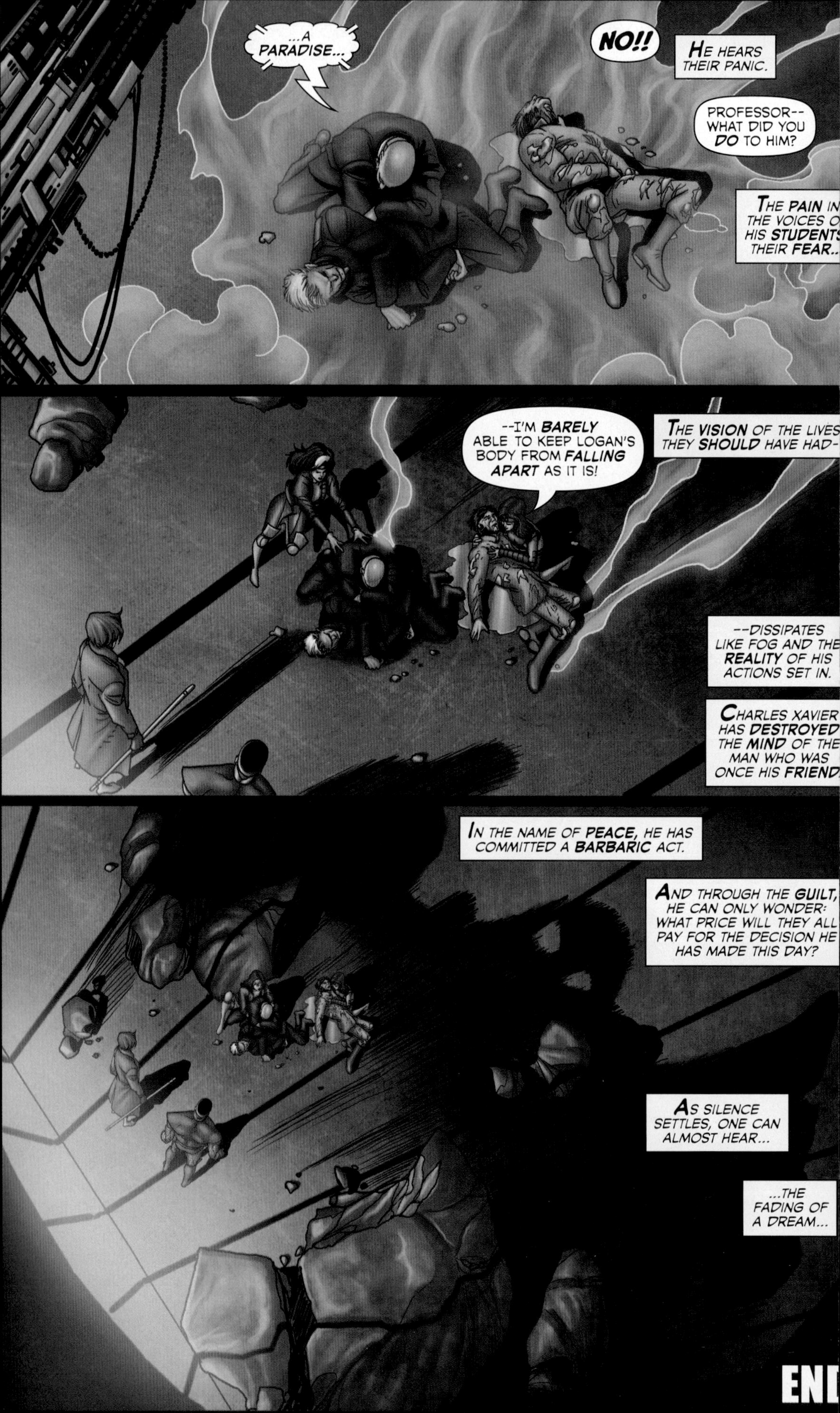

...A PARADISE...
NO!!
HE HEARS THEIR PANIC.
PROFESSOR-- WHAT DID YOU DO TO HIM?
THE PAIN IN THE VOICES OF HIS STUDENTS THEIR FEAR...
--I'M BARELY ABLE TO KEEP LOGAN'S BODY FROM FALLING APART AS IT IS!
THE VISION OF THE LIVES THEY SHOULD HAVE HAD--
--DISSIPATES LIKE FOG AND THE REALITY OF HIS ACTIONS SET IN.
CHARLES XAVIER HAS DESTROYED THE MIND OF THE MAN WHO WAS ONCE HIS FRIEND.
IN THE NAME OF PEACE, HE HAS COMMITTED A BARBARIC ACT.
AND THROUGH THE GUILT, HE CAN ONLY WONDER: WHAT PRICE WILL THEY ALL PAY FOR THE DECISION HE HAS MADE THIS DAY?
AS SILENCE SETTLES, ONE CAN ALMOST HEAR...
...THE FADING OF A DREAM...

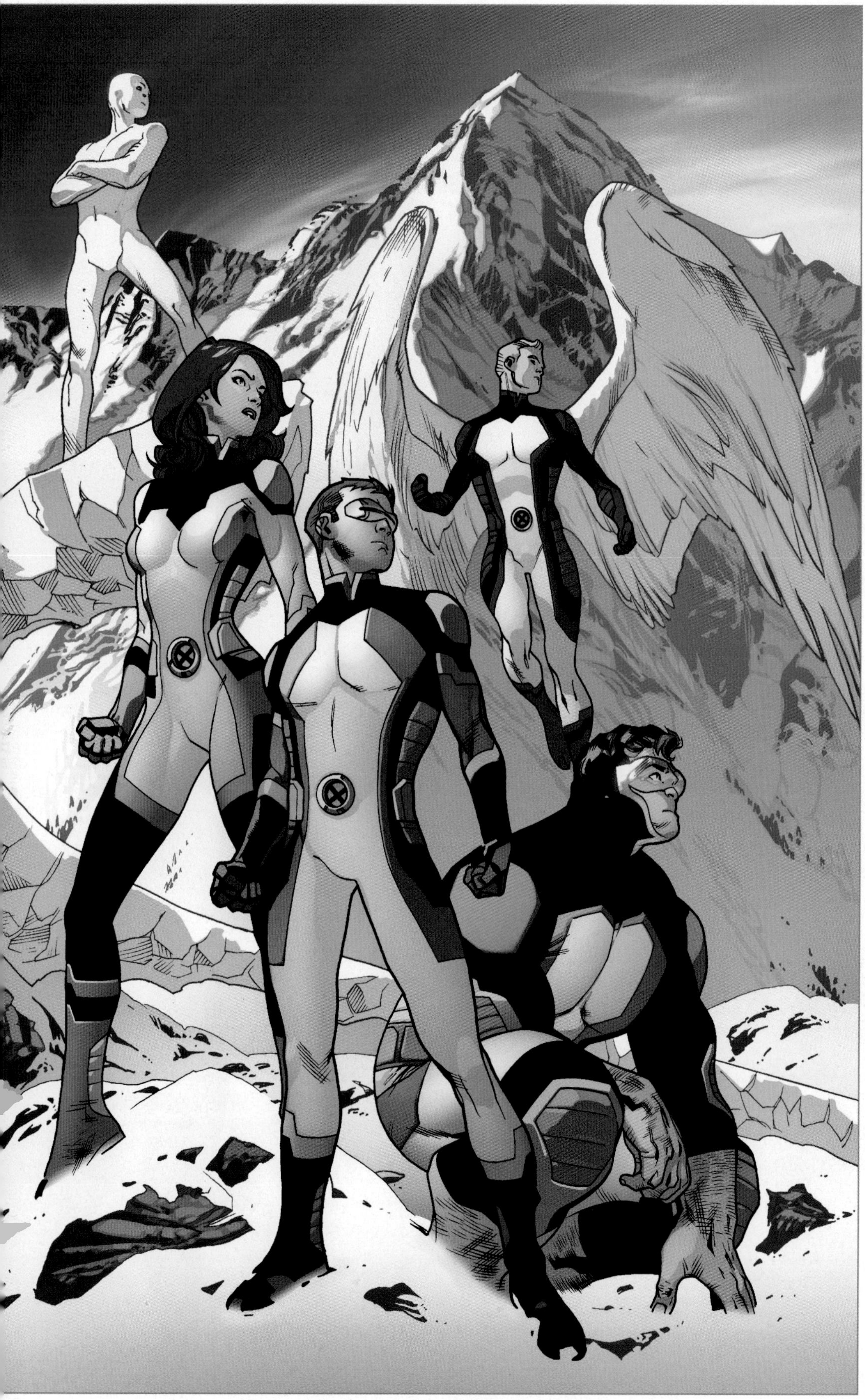

ALL-NEW X-MEN #18 VARIANT

BY STUART IMMONEN, WADE VON GRAWBADGER & MARTE GRACIA

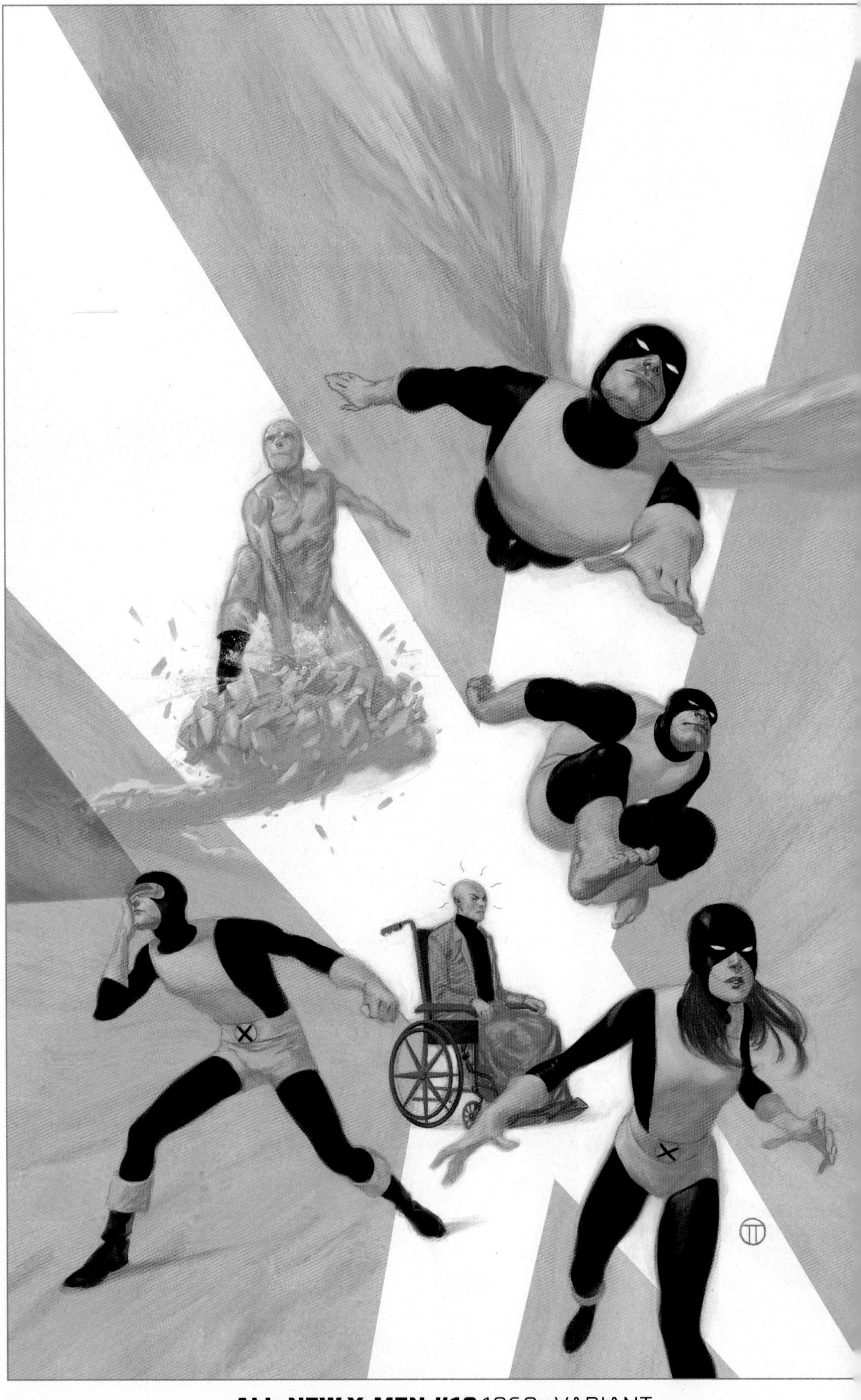

ALL-NEW X-MEN #18 1960s VARIANT
BY JULIAN TOTINO TEDESCO

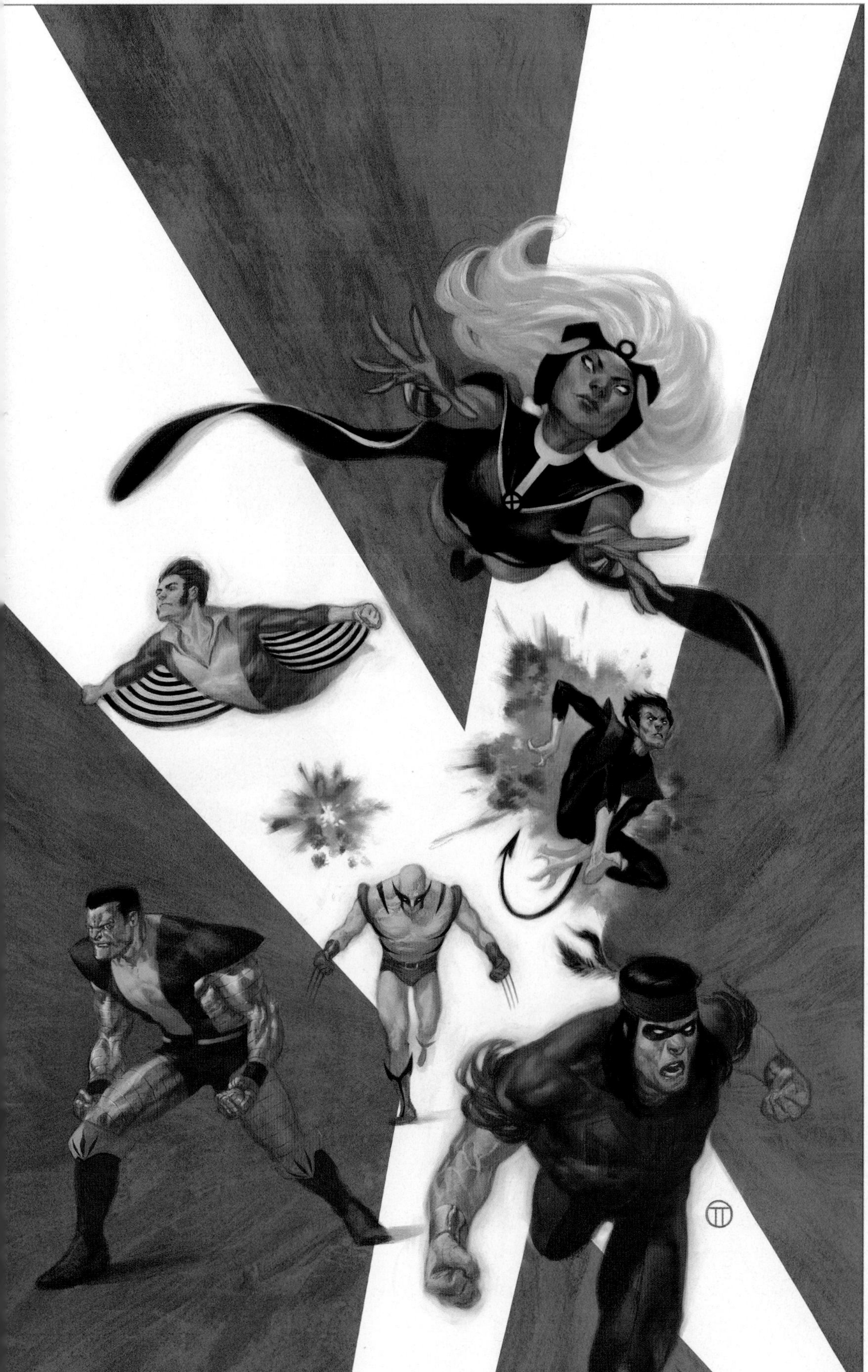

ALL-NEW X-MEN #18 1970s VARIANT
BY JULIAN TOTINO TEDESCO

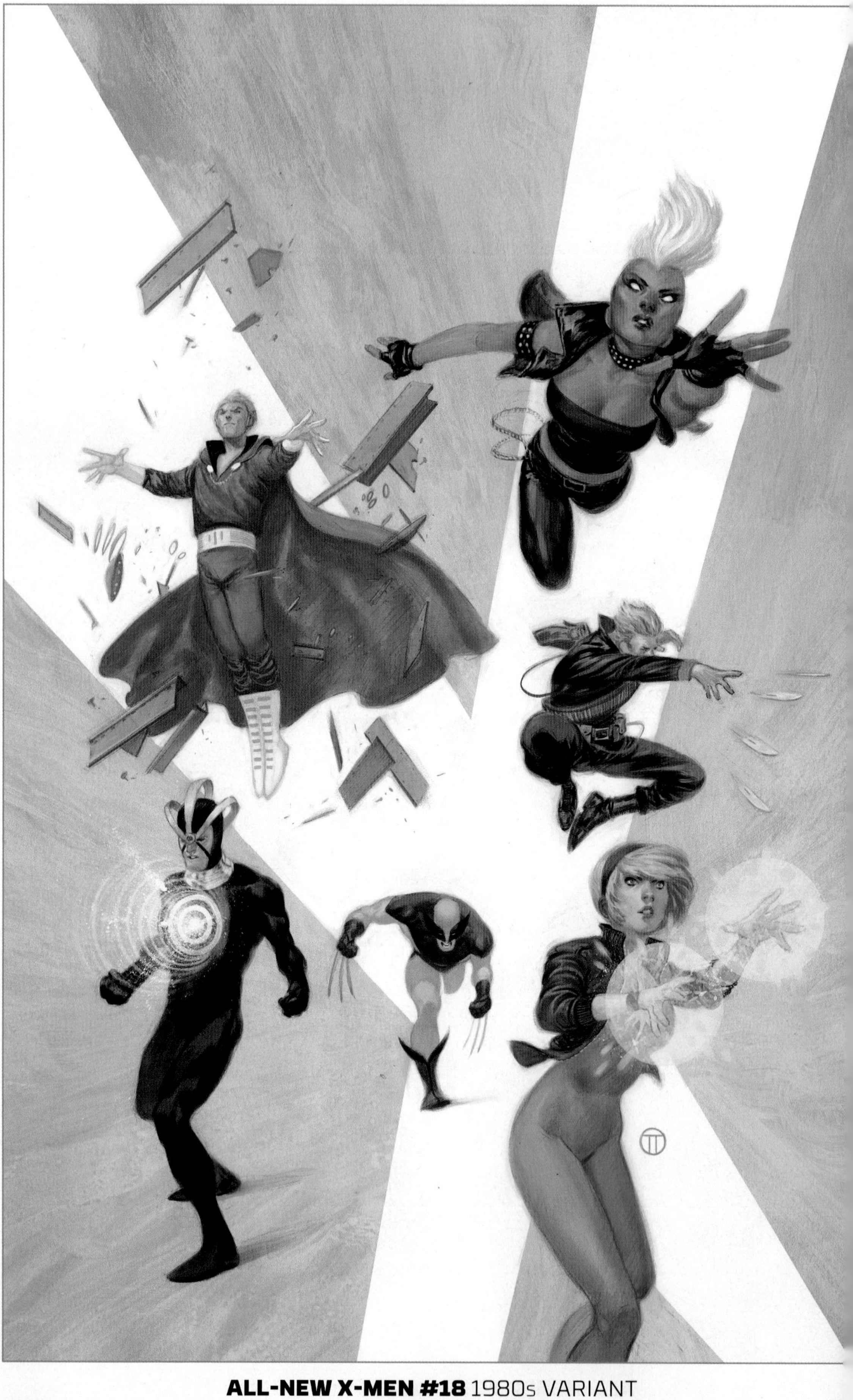

ALL-NEW X-MEN #18 1980s VARIANT
BY JULIAN TOTINO TEDESCO

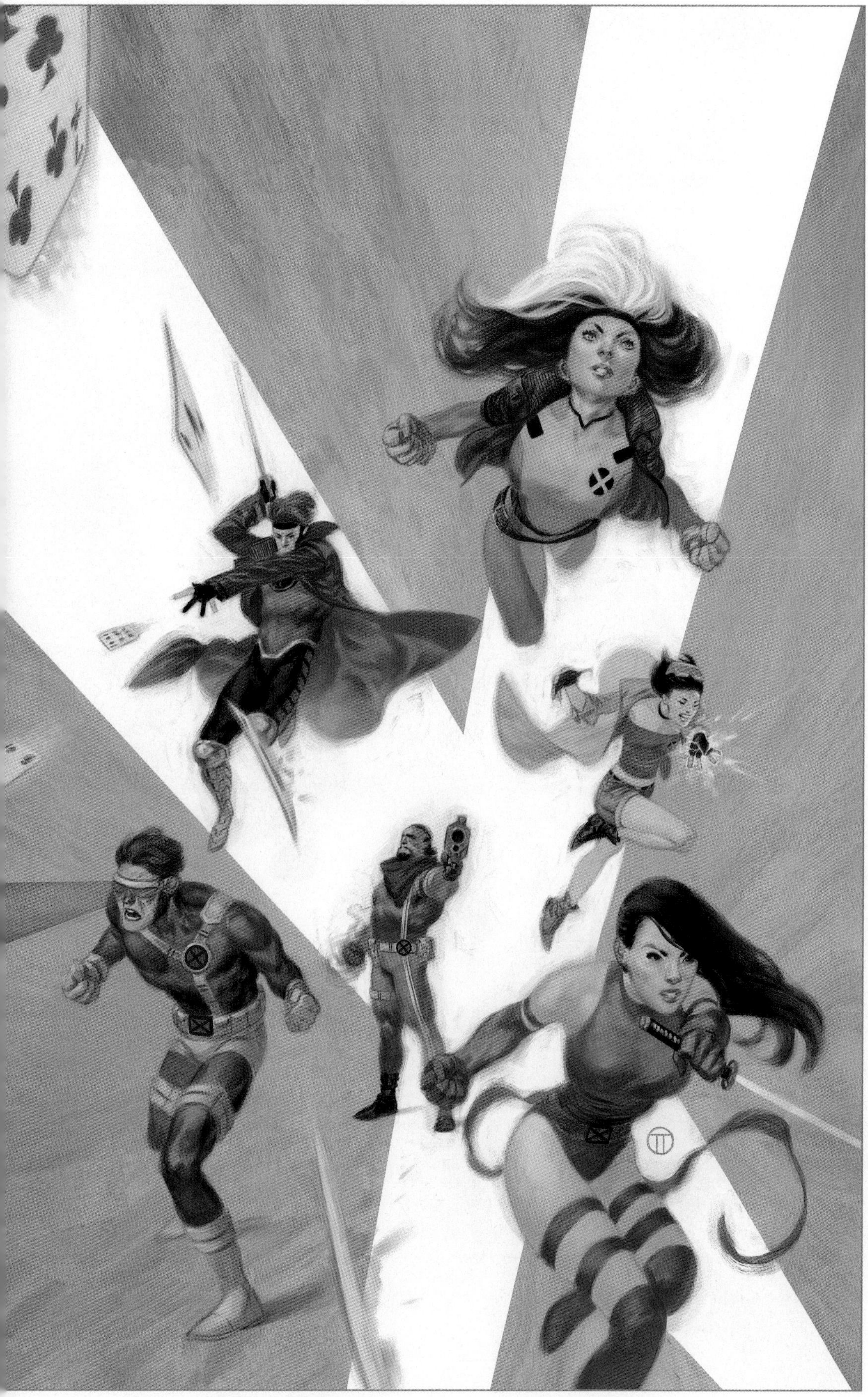

ALL-NEW X-MEN #18 1990s VARIANT
BY JULIAN TOTINO TEDESCO

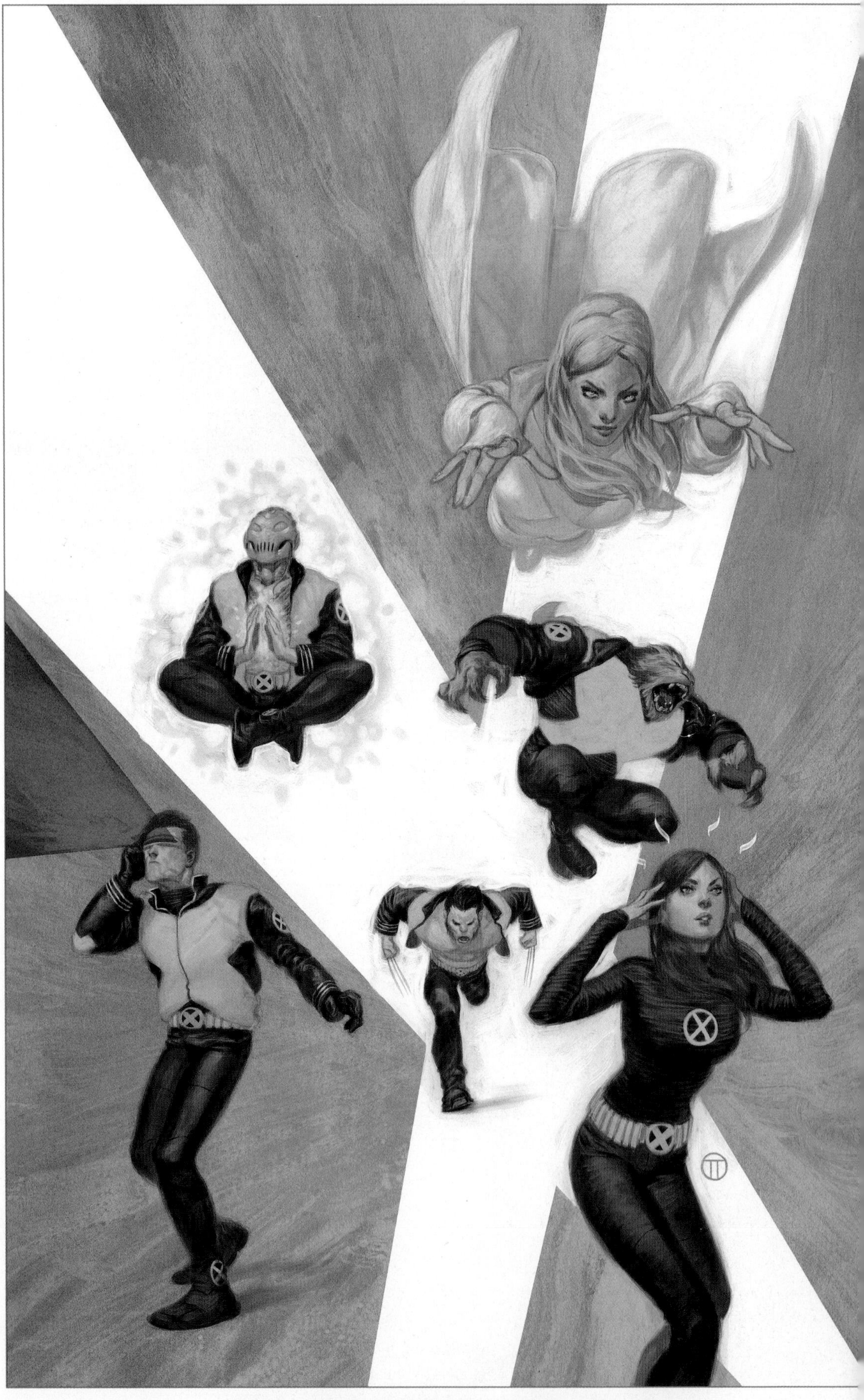

ALL-NEW X-MEN #18 2000s VARIANT
BY JULIAN TOTINO TEDESCO

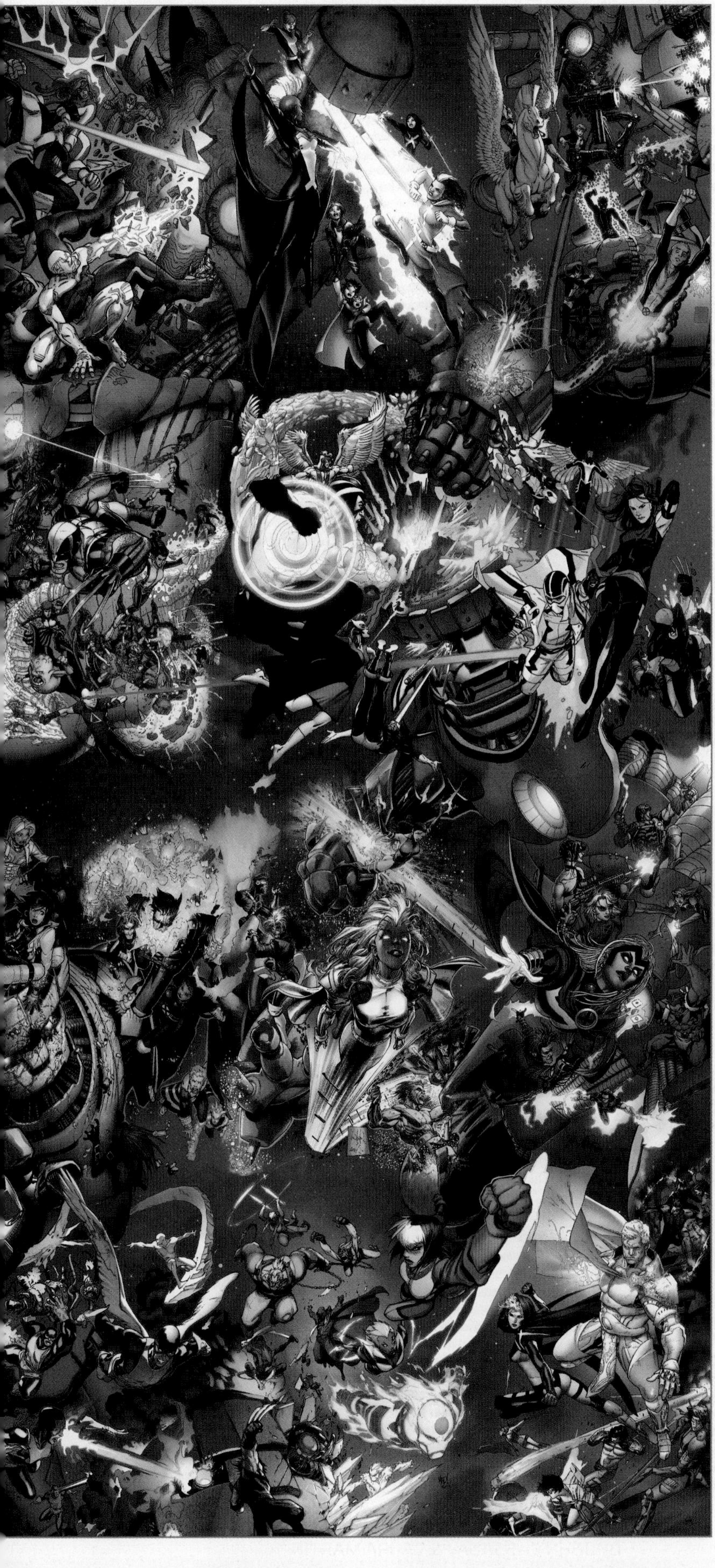

THE TWELVE X-MEN 50TH ANNIVERSARY VARIANT COVERS INTERLOCK TO FORM A GIANT POSTER.

LEFT TO RIGHT,
TOP TO BOTTOM:

SAVAGE WOLVERINE #6
BY WALTER SIMONSON
& JASON KEITH

WOLVERINE #11
BY DAVID LÓPEZ &
MORRY HOLLOWELL

ALL-NEW X-MEN #20
BY ARTHUR ADAMS
& JASON KEITH

ALL-NEW X-MEN #7
BY NICK BRADSHAW
& JASON KEITH

UNCANNY X-MEN #10
BY NEAL ADAMS &
DAVID CURIEL

UNCANNY X-FORCE #12
BY PHIL NOTO

ALL-NEW X-MEN #6
BY CHRIS BACHALO
& TIM TOWNSEND

CABLE AND X-FORCE #8
BY WHILCE PORTACIO,
CAM SMITH &
ANDRES MOSSA

UNCANNY X-FORCE #11
BY SALVADOR LARROCA
& FRANK D'ARMATA

ALL-NEW X-MEN #8
BY STUART IMMONEN,
WADE VON GRAWBADGER
& MARTE GRACIA

X-MEN #1
BY JOE MADUREIRA
& JASON KEITH

WOLVERINE & THE X-MEN #33
BY CLAY MANN
& DAVID CURIEL

POSTER TOUCH-UP
COLORING BY
JASON KEITH

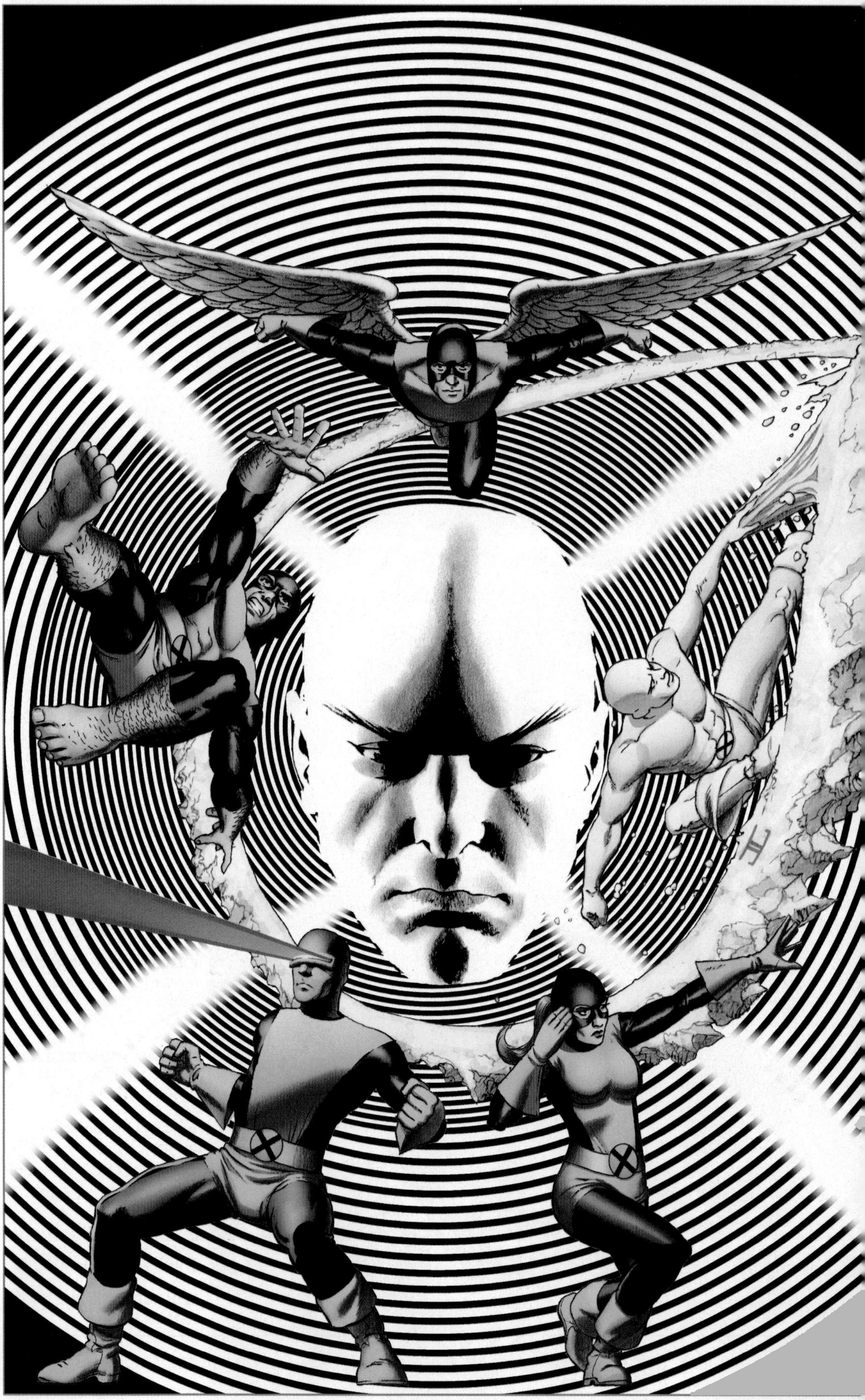

X-MEN: GOLD #1 VARIANT
BY JOHN CASSADAY & LAURA MARTIN

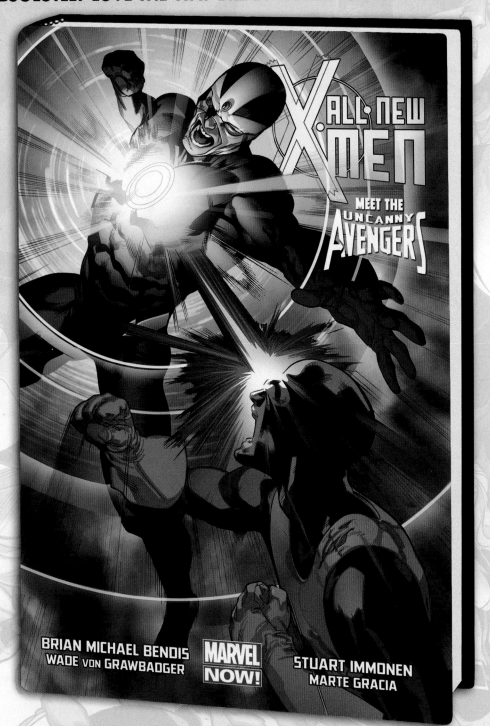

TO ACCESS THE FREE *MARVEL AUGMENTED REALITY APP*
THAT ENHANCES AND CHANGES THE WAY YOU EXPERIENCE COMICS

1. **Download the app for free via**
   marvel.com/ARapp

2. **Launch the app on your camera-enabled**
   Apple iOS® or Android™ device*

3. **Hold your mobile device's camera over**
   any cover or panel with the AR **graph**

4. **Sit back and see the future of comics**
   in action!

*Available on most camera-enabled Apple iOS® and Android™ devices. Content subject to
change and availability.

ALL·NEW X·MEN AR INDEX

Issue #18
As the Page Turns episode 2 .... Pages 7-8, Panel 1
Cyclops talks to Kitty and Magik .... Pages 11-12, Panel 2

Issue #19
As the Page Turns episode 4 .... Pages 1-2, Panel 1
Scapie on X-23 .... Page 20, Panel 1

Issue #20
Cyclops and X-23 talk .... Page 10, Panel 5

Issue #21
Lowedown on *Avengers Arena* .... Page 8, Panel 4
As the Page Turns episode 9 .... Pages 13-14, Panel 7

TO REDEEM YOUR CODE
FOR A FREE DIGITAL COPY:

1. **GO TO MARVEL.COM/REDEEM.**
   OFFER EXPIRES ON 4/30/16.

2. **FOLLOW THE ON-SCREEN INSTRUCTIONS**
   TO REDEEM YOUR DIGITAL COPY.

3. **LAUNCH THE MARVEL COMICS APP TO**
   READ YOUR COMIC NOW!

4. **YOUR DIGITAL COPY WILL BE FOUND**
   UNDER THE *MY COMICS* TAB.

5. **READ & ENJOY!**

TMAZARFPMA0Y

YOUR FREE DIGITAL COPY WILL BE AVAILABLE C

| MARVEL COMICS APP | MARVEL COMICS APP |
| FOR APPLE® iOS DEVICES | FOR ANDROID™ DEVICES |